# THE Single Mother's BOOK

A Practical Guide

to Managing

Your Children,

Career, Home,

Finances, and

Everything Else

## 2ND EDITION

### Joan Anderson

PEACHTREE
ATLANTA

*To Laura, Jonathan, Andrea, and Michael, with the hope that you will always say yes to life, reaching outside yourselves to embrace others because, in the end, we are all one family*

Published by
PEACHTREE PUBLISHERS
1700 Chattahoochee Avenue
Atlanta, Georgia 30318-2112

*www.peachtree-online.com*

Book and cover design by Regina Dalton-Fischel
Composition by Robin Sherman

10 9 8 7 6 5 4 3 2 1

Manufactured in the United States of America

**Library of Congress Cataloging-in-Publication Data**

Anderson, Joan, 1947-
  The single mother's book : a practical guide to managing your children, career, home, finances, and everything else / Joan Anderson.-- 2nd ed.
     p. cm.
  Includes bibliographical references and index.
  ISBN 1-56145-327-7
  1. Single mothers--United States--Life skills guides.  I. Title.

HQ759.915.A54 2004
306.85'6'0973--dc22                                    2004029912

All verses used in the text are the original work of Joan Anderson, unless otherwise cited.

# SOC

# CONTENTS

■■■ ■ ■■■

# Chapter 7: Child Care 117

Choosing a preschool or
  child-care center
Evaluating the facility
Health care provisions
Sniffles day-care program
Babysitters

When is a child old enough
  to stay alone?
When your child begins staying
  home alone
Summers: beyond day care

# Chapter 8: Life with Dad 133

Life without Dad
Talking about your ex-partner
Your relatives and your
  ex-partner
Love game

Tales of two houses
When your child doesn't want to
  visit Dad
Maintaining communication when
  the children are away

# Chapter 9: Taking Care of Yourself 143

"No wonder I'm frazzled!"
Support group
Self-esteem
A sense of self
Euphoria
Grief
Loss and depression
Turning around a blue day
Anger
Assertiveness
Stress
Action/reflection cycle
Fear
Defining your needs and goals
Learning to say "No"

Asking for and accepting help
Crisis times
Journal writing
Counselors
Spirituality
Ritual
Exercise
Nutrition
Alcohol and drug abuse
AIDS
Other sexually transmitted diseases
  (STDs)
Breast exams
Pap smears
Healthy body/healthy mind

# ACKNOWLEDGMENTS

■ ■ ■

Writing a book can bolster your faith in people. Perfect strangers—individuals and representatives of organizations and agencies—will go out of their way to help you find information and offer their ideas for the project. And like ingredients for a good stew, each person's offering makes the finished product a little better.

As I reflect on writing this book, I would like to offer personal thanks to the following generous contributors: the women who participated in the original Vanderbilt University Single Mothers Group, especially Diane Sword and Ellen Jewel; my parents, Maxine and Ralph Anderson; the Margaret Cuninggim Women's Center staff, especially Nancy Ransom, Kathy Thornton, Susan Seay, and Judy Helfer; consultants Marguerite Anderson, Moses Dillard, Glenda Lingo, Margaret Meggs, Carol Wedekind, Jim Cheek, Jean Strecker, Mary Frances Lyle, Pam Bergman, John H. Cobbs, Nancy Evins, Penny TeSelle, Joe Driscoll, Melanie Allen Cail, Eddie Settles, Joyce Beisswenger, Margaret Behm, Annell St. Charles, and James Cooper; writer John Egerton, who generously offered to make the phone call to Peachtree Publishers; my editor, Susan Thurman, who pulled and pushed when I needed it; Melinda Boyer, and all the other Peachtree folks; my friend and neighbor Frank Ritter, who says the first rule of good writing is "keep your ass in the chair"; Hogan Yancey, who has been a steady source of faith for this and all my endeavors; and my two resident children, Laura and Jonathan, who chose to make some sacrifices so that their mom could write the book.

# INTRODUCTION

■ ■ ■

One night in October 1986, four women—strangers to each other—gathered in the Vanderbilt University Child Care Center for the first meeting of the Single Mothers Group. Organized by the Margaret Cuninggim Women's Center of Vanderbilt, the group was the first of its kind in Nashville. That was not important to the women who had come to talk about their lives as single mothers with others who, they hoped, would understand. All four women soon learned that they shared the same problems: difficulties with ex-partners, overwhelming responsibilities, too little money, and uncertain futures.

The Vanderbilt group grew in number and in a sense of community. In coming together, the mostly middle-class women aired problems with both practical life skills and human relations, and they found solutions to those problems. Members of the group discovered effective ways to reduce their feelings of isolation, frustration, anger, desperation, low self-esteem, and on occasion, hopelessness, and they replaced them with a sense of empowerment.

Ellen Jewell and I co-facilitated the meetings. I had been a single mother for four years, and I identified strongly with the concerns expressed by the group; they had been or still were my own as well. Because other local women wanted to attend meetings but were unable to do so, it soon became apparent that one way to share the information generated by the group would be to write a book. The tremendous work of the Single Mothers Group members in identifying their problems and finding solutions became the foundation of this book. With the help of many people, the idea has become real.

## Who is a single mother?

Anyone who considers herself a single mother is a single mother. She may be divorced, married but separated, never married, caring for a family member's child, a widow, a separated stepmother, or in some circumstances, a married woman. Proximity to a man —or lack thereof—does not make a woman a single mother; the presence of a child in her home does. (Some women are married or live with men who abdicate their responsibility to their children or even may be dangerous to them. Some women are married to men who for whatever reason are absent from the home for long periods, such as military duty in another location.) The single mother shoulders heavy responsibilities, including the financial, physical, emotional, social, and spiritual well being of the children who live with her.

▪ ▪ ▪ ▪ ▪ ▪ ▪

The single mother shoulders heavy responsibilities, including the financial, physical, emotional, social, and spiritual well being of the children who live with her.

## What's in a name?

Two terms are used in this book when referring to fathers: ex-partner and ex-husband. An ex-husband has specific legal rights, which requires the term "ex-husband." In more general circumstances, the term "ex-partner" is used. As you read, adapt the "ex" terms to fit your own circumstances.

## A game plan

This book identifies options, information, and advice that have worked for other single mothers. You will find a resource section at the end of the book for more sources of information.

The stories of single mothers who have met their own challenges and prevailed are meant to be instructional and inspirational.

It is as if the women you will read about are on the other side of a ravine, holding out their hands to single mothers following behind them. The book shows paths taken by others who have gone before. It includes personal challenges, strategies, triumphs, and wisdom.

Single motherhood can have some advantages:

- control of your time and resources
- doing things your way
- not having to be accountable or subservient to a partner.

Still, single motherhood is never an easy road, especially in the early stages when economic and emotional crises often overwhelm a woman. But crisis does not mean doom. It is often said that the Chinese character for crisis is a combination of the symbols for "danger" and "opportunity." If you can overcome your fear, maneuver through danger, and take advantage of opportunities for positive change, you will grow stronger.

When a woman first becomes a single mother, her problems may seem insurmountable. Some women collapse under the weight of responsibilities. Many problems are due, in part, to a faulty societal structure that pays women too little for their work, does not legally mandate paid leave for working mothers to stay home with their newborn children, undervalues the importance of good quality and affordable child care, and too readily excuses fathers from their caretaking responsibilities.

If you are a single mother, it is up to you to carve out your own success. While the possibility of disappointment is real, so is the possibility of success. With careful planning and the passage of time, your life can and probably will settle down to a secure and comfortable pattern, and you will see that you have done a fine job for your child—and for yourself.

I hope this book serves as a useful tool in that process.

■ ■ ■

# CHAPTER 1

# Redefining the Family

*I, a tomato born,*
*Budded from flower,*
*Fleshed red from green vine,*
*Ripened in the sun,*
*Grew heavy with life,*
*Fell to ground,*
*Rolled away to blank soil,*
*Relaxed, and*
*Seeded new life from the old.*

## What happened?

Some time after you have become a single mother you may wake up in bed one morning and ask yourself, "What happened? The kids are tucked in their beds, and I'm in mine. But there is supposed to be a man in this bed too." Maybe your hand glides slowly over the empty sheets next to you. You remember well a man, the father of your children. Gone.

If you were married to him, you probably had a traditional biological family—Mom, Dad, and the kids. But many families no longer fit that model. As of 2002,

- 68.7 percent of families with dependent children in the United States had a father and mother living together (either married or blended)
- 22.7 percent were headed by single mothers
- 4.5 percent were headed by single fathers
- 4 percent were made up of other combinations, mostly grandparents.

(*U.S. Census Bureau Population Division, Table C2, March 2002*)

It is important to know the great numbers of families that now fall outside the traditional pattern. Since World War II in the 1940s, the family has changed dramatically. Television is one media indication of change. The series "One Day at a Time," which premiered in 1975, was the first to feature a divorced mother and her children. Now, people are well aware, and often accepting, of the single mother with children as an established family pattern in society. Children are raised in families that may be traditional, single parent, or blended. Families with two same-sex parents (gay/lesbian) are gaining legal acceptance. Today's young parents may have grown up in non-traditional families.

In the twenty-first century, people accept a wide range of living circumstances before, during, after, and instead of marriage. The rapid change that defines U.S. culture in this century makes the family less like the rock of Gibraltar and more like elastic.

When a father no longer lives in his children's home, the family structure in the home changes, but the family continues, redefining itself as members die, are born, marry, or divorce. The essence of family remains regardless of whether there are two parents or only one parent in residence. With or without Dad, the family nurtures, protects, promotes, worries about, nudges, celebrates with, and otherwise interacts with its members. When there is a commitment to living and loving together, there is family. Nonrelatives may be accepted into the residential family unit. Young children are often quick to adapt. They seem to think operatively, so that their Dad's new live-in partner, for example, may soon become an emotionally adopted member of their family. When they say, for example, "I wish my parents would take us to see that new movie," they may define "parents" as Mom in one house and Dad and his partner in another house.

When a biological family breaks apart, it is not shattered like glass but rather knocked horizontal for a while, like fallen building blocks. Usually, by the time a judge pronounces a husband and wife divorced, the family has already begun to rebuild in a different form. Later, either parent may add other people, like building blocks, to alter its form again.

If a man leaves his wife, people may say, "He broke up the family." And they could be right. But the woman needs to remember that she has the power to redefine her family and rebuild it into a structure that suits her as much or more than the original family. It will not be an intact biological family, but it need not be inferior, either.

A lot of guilt may accompany single motherhood, whether the woman leaves the man or vice versa. Because society emphasizes the importance of the biological family, the break up of that family generates strong feelings, a collective grieving for the loss of the ideal. Even to say that the family has "broken up" connotes failure. How refreshing to read Owen Edwards's article "There Are No Failed Marriages" in *Working Woman* magazine. He wrote, "Even when a marriage doesn't last, it often can be viewed as a success rich with the rewards—children, knowledge, growth—that do last... a life-time." He talked not about his own "divorce," but about his "completed marriage." While that phrase may seem to sugarcoat the wrenching feelings and the complicated and sometimes expensive process that accompany divorce, the idea has merit. When you think about your marriage as completed, you allow for the good times, the meaningful intimacies, the rituals, the explorations, and the struggles together—the closeness which was also a part of your life with the person who is the father of your child.

It is useful to see and accept your marriage or relationship as part of a continuum of your life history. If your partner had died, you would not burn all the evidence of your lives together just because the leaving was painful. Nor do you have to deny the value of your completed marriage—the good part *and* the bad—just because it is over. To deny it would be to bury part of yourself. The more open you can be about your completed relationship, the easier it will be for you to learn from it and accept your involvement in it with assurance.

If you are open about the subject, that will help your child talk with you about what happened, rather than dwell privately on his muddled thoughts. One twelve-year-old boy, for example, overheard his mother complain that the children did not keep their rooms clean; then she left the family without an explanation. The boy went to his bedroom, cleaned it up, and announced, "She didn't leave because of my room." But it was clear that he did think that, and throughout his teenage years, his room was always oddly immaculate. Since his mother never explained why she went away, he was left with a sense of guilt and a groundless, self-imposed penance. Talking openly with your child about your completed relationship will absolve his perceived guilt, should he have such feelings, and help him through a difficult period, allowing him to feel good about his family history and claim it for his own. (Chapters four and eight go into detail on this topic.)

From the time you and your child's father choose to live apart, your "family" and your child's "family" are different. Your family is you and your child; it doesn't include his father. Your child's family, on the other hand, includes you, his father, and any stepparents and relatives on either side of his family. The original biological family has become two overlapping circles with your child in the middle, so that when you talk about "our" family, your child thinks, "Mom's side of my family." And it is natural for you to speak to your child about "your dad's family," or "your other house."

## The Wall of History

A certain woman married for the second time and moved into the home of her new husband. She found pictures throughout the house of his female friends and his former wife—all of which caused a slow burn somewhere in the core of her insecurities. She wanted those pictures gone, especially those of his ex-wife. He refused. "That's my history," he would say. "Do you think I was a virgin when I met you? And what about my kids? They need to be reminded of their mother. She's part of their life." He had a point, but the new wife had a lousy feeling that she needed to address.

First, she found a photo of her ex-family that featured her children, her "ex," and herself. She went through photo albums and found several other pictures to frame. Then she gathered up all her new husband's photos from around the house and, along with her photos, nailed them onto what she called "The Wall of History" —his on the left, hers on the right. Fortunately, everyone loved the wall. It localized the new husband's history, maximizing it as a statement about the important people in his life, but minimizing its negative impact on her as she walked through the house. As the years went by, this couple added to the Wall of History, so that now it represents "Yours, Mine, and Ours" in a kind of chronological family review.

The wife says that she often looks at the photo of her "first-husband family." In it the children are young. She is young. Together with her ex-husband, they were a unit; they had good times, and he was a part of those times. In a way, the picture represented the best of their lives together. Putting it up on the wall has enabled her to claim that part of her life with some pride. Six years after the divorce, her ex-husband could still push her buttons to make her furious or depressed, though he did so much less frequently. But the photo expressed the better part of their relationship; it was a gift that allowed her to think and feel posi-tively about her ex-partner family. Somehow, that reflected positively on her self-image. It also made a positive statement to her children about their biological family. It made them feel more secure.

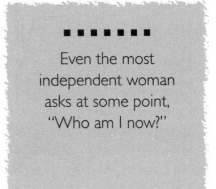

■ ■ ■ ■ ■ ■ ■

Even the most independent woman asks at some point, "Who am I now?"

## "Who am I now?"

When a woman first becomes a single mother, she likely will be confused about her identity. Previ-ously she was defined, at least in part, in relation to her husband, as in, "This is Sarah, John's wife." The more independent Sarah's life was from John's, the more she has to lean on while rebuilding her family structure and personal identity. Still, she was John's wife and now she is not. It takes time to separate herself emotionally from her ex-husband. On former Saturday nights when she might have been at home with her ex-husband thinking, "We never go out on Saturday night anymore," now she is at home by herself, not being able to think "we" thoughts; instead, she feels a void.

Even the most independent woman asks at some point, "Who am I now?" The answer, first of all, is that you are a provider and protector for yourself and your child, since food and shelter come first in the natural order of life. Second, you are a nurturer in the traditional sense of mothering. The traditional roles of provider and nurturer are no longer divided between two partners, the father and the mother, but reside within the same person—you. Even if you and your ex-partner share joint custody, when your child is with you, you are responsible for fulfilling both roles.

Your salary may be less than your ex-partner's. You may not be able to support yourself and your child as well as your ex-partner could. Few women receive enough child support and alimony to allow them to stay at home and care for their children. Even when they do, that money may come after a bitter court battle that is destructive to the adults and the children. And while men often complain about the financial burden of child support, the average man's standard of living goes up after his divorce, while the average woman and children's standard of living goes down, often dramatically and especially during the first years after the divorce. Society may view the man as the provider for his family, but the reality is that over 27 percent of families are headed by single parents—most of them women—with custody of their children. Those women are the major providers for their families.

The societal view of the ideal family remains Mom, Dad, and the kids. But that biological family is having a hard time surviving intact, according to contemporary divorce statistics, which predict that 50 percent of first marriages will end in divorce. Eighty-five percent of those who divorce will remarry and form blended families that include children from previous marriages. But blended marriages fare even worse; 60 percent end in divorce, according to Census figures. The third family structure, single-parent families, has its own set of challenges, which this book addresses. Calling any of these three family structures ideal is misleading.

In the best scenario, the biological family in which Mom and Dad live together and are best friends and nurturing parents is the least complicated family structure. Sadly, regardless of high hopes and good intentions, traditional biological families can break apart. Partners forget to nurture each other. Dual careers and a fast-paced society place pressure on the family. The temptation to wander from one partner to another in a society that emphasizes the thrills of new sexual encounters destroys some families. So this best scenario of Mom, Dad, and the kids living happily ever after faces heavy odds against its survival.

The other two family structures—the single-parent family and the blended family—face challenges as well. First of all, they are more complicated than the biological family. But the problems are solvable, the compensations bring their own rewards, and these family structures, while also vulnerable to dangers within and without the family, can be nurturing to each family member. And they may be an improvement over the biological families that preceded them.

Important elements in the success of any family are:

- economic stability
- trust
- commitment among family members
- unconditional love.

Each of these elements involves a daily recommitment to the family. Through thick and thin, you stick together, work out your problems, and share the good times and the bad. That's it. And whether that happens in the biological family, the single-parent family, or the blended family, it is possible in all three.

The answer to the question, "Who am I?" for you as a single mother begins with the roles of provider, protector, and nurturer for your child. Beyond that, how you choose to define yourself (work, community, and social involvements) and to structure your family is up to you.

## Blood, paper, and heart

Relatives come in all sizes and shapes, but you may define them to fit your special circumstances. One woman divides her relatives into close family and extended family. Not all relatives are biological. Families have often included people outside the family. These people may even have all the rights and privileges of family —voice, vote, and inheritance—depending on the choices everyone makes.

It is helpful for a single mother to have a vocabulary that gives voice to the important relationships in her life, those that may be different from the ones she would have if she were in a traditional biological family with the father of her children. Here are some words that may help express meaningful relationships:

▪ *blood*—relatives who are connected to you biologically, such as a grandmother

▪ *paper*—relatives who are connected by marriage, such as a brother-in-law

▪ *heart*—relatives who are not blood or paper, but who are like family, such as a close friend who is like a sister, or a next-door-neighbor's child for whom you are a second mother. You choose them. If your father is dead or otherwise out of the picture, find a substitute father of the heart. For chosen relatives of the heart, your home is their home. You share time, experiences, joys, and sorrows.

> ▪ ▪ ▪ ▪ ▪ ▪ ▪
>
> Relatives come in all sizes and shapes, but you may define them to fit your special circumstances.

The last category of relatives offers a new way of thinking about family and an opportunity to develop a family that is mutually supportive. Ideally, blood and paper relatives are also relatives of the heart. But if not, you can create your own family, including relatives of the heart who meet your needs and those of your child.

## Transformation

Single parenthood brings freedom: Friday night relaxing with just your child, a video, and a bowl of popcorn; sleeping till noon one day a week when your child is with her father; and doing things your way. With freedom comes responsibility. But you must understand and believe that as the years pass, you will become stronger emotionally and financially. You will have more time for yourself as your child grows. And watching her flower into a healthy, caring adult will bring you great joy.

The choices that you make will define you. The rhythm of the days will become a new, familiar hum in your life. Your child—needing to be fed, needing to be bathed, needing to be hugged—may keep you frazzled for a while, but she will also keep you grounded in reality and will draw out of you a strength you did not know you had. And your family and friends—some old and some new; blood, paper, or heart relatives—will walk with you while you figure out a new game plan for your life.

As a single mother, you may feel you are alone in your struggle to answer the question "Who am I?" and to build your new family structure. But you are not alone. Over 9 million single mothers in the United States are living through the same process. A few of them may become some of your new friends. As with much of the rest of your life, the choice is yours.

# CHAPTER 2

## Your Ex-partner and His Relatives

Till death do us part

"I'm gonna wash that man right out of my hair"

Second thoughts

When your ex-partner gets married

Your child's ally

Maybe my child would be better off with him

Getting along with him

It's OK to be friends

Communication breakdown

Parents' time out for self-control

Training your ex-partner

Negotiating

When your ex-partner threatens you

Raising children the "wrong" way

When your ex-partner flounders

Protecting your child

When your ex-partner is in prison

The weekly phone call

Your ex-partner's relatives

Fearing your ex-partner's relatives

"Hello!" he said
blindly into the receiver.
I heard the call
in the bell forest of colored wires
vibrating anticipation.

It could have been anyone,
a friend from work,
or someone who might become a friend, or
a lover...
It even could have been
a light bulb seller.

I said, "Hi," and heard
his flat response.
The wind of his voice,
Even the jagged wind,
was gone.

It wasn't anyone.
It was a function calling.
Yes,
His ex-wife.

## Till death do us part

Strange things happened to me when I went through my divorce. I remember sitting in the lawyer's office with my soon-to-be ex-husband and crying as we divided our assets. Doing business and crying. It was to become a pattern.

I remember the judge pronouncing us divorced some months later. My whole body tensed and then I felt—nothing. I had expected both to feel different myself and to feel differently about my now ex-husband. Instead, I felt just the same. I certainly didn't feel divorced—whatever that was supposed to feel like.

I learned that when you divorce or separate, you do not erase your ex-partner like you erase a pencil mark. All the time you spent together has made a profound impact on your life. A few years of sharing meals and bills and seasons with a man melds the two of you together, even if you weren't having a good time. That togetherness does not go away with brief words spoken in a courtroom.

And while appearing before a judge can end your marriage, it simultaneously begins your divorce. Divorce is an active thing, a living thing. Even when you remarry you remain divorced from your first husband forever.

## "I'm gonna wash that man right out of my hair"

The good news is that time heals all wounds (yes, and wounds all heels). But it takes years to wean yourself emotionally from your ex-partner. You think about him. You get angry with him. You spend emotional time with him even though he's not around. But the longer he's gone, the less of an emotional factor he will be in your life.

## Second thoughts

If you left your partner, or if you and your partner agreed that divorce was the only way to settle things, then you actively chose to end your relationship. Still, it is normal to ask, at some point, "Were we right?"

It may come up when you are financially stretched and you see your child doing without. It may come up when you see your ex-partner drive up in his car, which is nicer than yours, and get out wearing a suit—or jeans and a sweater—and looking good. It may come up on a Saturday night when you are without a man, even just a male friend with whom to watch TV.

"Were we right?" There is no simple answer to that question. But when you're at a low point in your life, it's not the time to evaluate the worth of a relationship. When that question comes up, the best thing to do is to sleep on it. In the morning, when the sun is shining, the question will probably have vanished. If it has not, you should take a cool, unemotional look at the pluses and minuses of the relationship and weigh them. You can take out a piece of paper and make two lists: Good Things and Bad Things. Add up the totals. If you feel either of you were too hasty in ending the relationship, there may be time to give it another try.

■ ■ ■ ■ ■ ■ ■

"Were we right?" There is no simple answer to that question.

Lark was divorced when I met her. Her husband had withdrawn emotionally from their relationship, and Lark wanted him to go to counseling with her. He refused. She got a divorce and custody of their two boys. They sold their house. About two years after the divorce, her ex-husband asked her out to dinner. She went, and that began the trip back to a renewed life together. They remarried and had a third child, their first girl, and the delight of the family. One day, Lark said to me, "You know, the bad times count too." All the time they were quarreling and living apart bound them together, just as the good times did. They had a common history; they had both suffered through the time that they were divorced, and they could share that with each other.

Such happy endings don't always happen. Belinda had a daughter with her live-in companion. They separated and Belinda got custody of their child. Later, they began living together again and, finally, after a few cancellations, got married. Belinda got pregnant with their second child. Things soured again, and her husband moved out, leaving Belinda pregnant, jobless, and facing a couple of rough years ahead.

Other couples almost throw away their marriages. Rachael, for example, was happily married. Her husband came home one day and said, "I'm leaving you. I've fallen in love with Diane [a good friend of theirs], and we are going to live together and get married." Rachael was very bitter. One day, several years later, Rachael's ex-husband—who was now helping to support his new wife's children and paying child support to Rachael—said to her, "You know, looking back on it, there was nothing wrong with our marriage. I just got carried away."

"Were we right?" is an unanswerable question. The concept of right or wrong is not the issue. Commitment is the issue. The more compatible you are with a man, the easier it is to keep your commitment. But he has to keep his commitment to you too. If the two of you want to carry through, you will. If one of you does not, you probably won't. The daily decision to stay married is a matter of choice, just like the decision to marry.

I look at first-marriage couples who have been together for years. Pictures of their children and grandchildren grace their homes. They have a settled quality, a certain ease with each other, brought about by years of working through things. They may argue, but they defined and set acceptable boundaries for arguing long ago. They were young together, middle-aged together, and old together. That's a long road, and it makes me remember Lark's words—the bad times count too.

Sometimes people cut and run too soon. If you feel there's a way back, I suggest you explore it. If there's not, then don't look back.

## When your ex-partner gets married

When you and your partner split up, you probably had some negative feelings about each other: anger, resentment, repulsion, fear. But even if you said to yourself, "I wish I never had to see that man again in my life! I can't stand to look at him. He turns my stomach," you may go through a difficult time when you learn that "that man" is going to marry another woman.

You may well feel a renewed sense of loss. At one time, "that man" was your man. Even after you no longer lived together, you lived in the shadow of the relationship. But when your ex-partner marries another woman, you know, "This is really the end. Now he's gone forever." It can be a big letdown.

▪ ▪ ▪ ▪ ▪ ▪

If you know what lies ahead, you can prepare for it.

You may doubt your femininity. After all, another woman is replacing you. She may be younger or prettier or smarter or wealthier. Whatever her qualities, she will probably best you at something, and that can make you feel less than adequate, less worthy as a woman.

Your child may go through a tough time too. His feelings may be complicated—wanting Daddy to be happy, wanting the new stepmother to like him, and wanting to be loyal to you at the same time. It's a kind of push-pull way of looking at his father's new marriage.

If you know what lies ahead, you can prepare for it. You can recognize the symptoms of distress when they happen and see them as normal. You can realize that while the new woman in your ex-partner's life may be better than you at some things, you are better than her at others. It's probably a trade-off. In the end, he doesn't want a perfect woman—neither of you is—but a romantic partner.

You were OK. She is OK. He is out of your life, as far as commitment goes, so let him try for that golden ring of happiness. If he gets it, he will feel better about himself and have good feelings left over for your child—and maybe even for you.

Have a talk with your child. Ask him how he feels about his father remarrying. Listen to what he has to say. Tell him how you feel too. Avoid all temptations to say negative things like, "I hope they rot in hell together," or, "She's probably a sleaze bag," or, "Stepmothers can be hard on kids that aren't their own. If you have any trouble over there, you let me know." You can—and should—be absolutely honest with your child, as in, "Frankly, I feel a little funny about your daddy marrying this woman. I hope they are happy together, and that they love you very much, but I want you to remember that I am your one-and-only biological mother. I will always love you." Your child will probably respond with love, and be glad for the chance to clear the air.

Some women have parties when their ex-partners remarry. They invite friends who love them and are there to have a good time. Others go out for a quiet evening, perhaps dinner and a movie with a friend. An Atlanta woman flew to San Francisco for the weekend when her ex-husband remarried. Planning a special event can be a most supportive experience, a far better one than dwelling on your ex's wedding while you are at home alone. It's times like this that friends are solid gold.

## Your child's ally

When you share a child with a man, he may well be part of your life in many ways, at least until your child is grown. Emotionally, you don't want him on the scene. But if he wants to be involved in the life of his child, you have to interact with him in innumerable ways to make arrangements and even to help you out when you need it.

Each child comes into this world with two biological parents. In cultures in which extended families—grandparents, aunts, uncles, and cousins—live in the same house or neighborhood, the family can better absorb the loss of one parent. But in the United States, families are often far-flung geographically and children may not know their extended families well. They live in other cities and cannot provide much support on a daily basis to children or their parents. After a divorce, both parents have to work hard to maintain that daily support for the children.

Your ex-partner, the father of your child, need not be your enemy. He can be your best ally in the care for and support of your child. He can provide a male role model, which children need, and numerous other things as well. Diane's ex-partner provides a substantial amount of money for child care, though he lives in another state. Lynn's ex-partner has a farm where her son can play with the cows and catch crawdads in the creek. Jane's husband shares custody, which gives her time to herself that she can count on to break up the strain of twenty-four-hour child care; he also pays for music lessons. Carol's husband keeps the children when she travels on business—or for pleasure.

> ▪ ▪ ▪ ▪ ▪ ▪ ▪
> Your ex-partner,
> the father
> of your child,
> need not be
> your enemy.

None of these fathers are especially revered by the mothers of their children, but they all provide something that adds to their children's quality of life. It makes good sense to be supportive of your ex-partner to your child, so that he will be proud of him, look up to him, feel more stable about who he is, have a better self-image, and be better able to cope with life as an adult. And when you look ahead to such big-ticket expenses as a college education, it makes sense to promote a solid relationship between your child and his father so that he will be more willing to share his resources with your child when the court order ends.

## Maybe my child would be better off with him

Single mothers often fear that their children might be better off living with their fathers. A single woman's standard of living is often lower, sometimes dramatically so, than a single man's; there may be good economic reasons for that fear. Working women make an average of 80 cents for every dollar that men make. Sheila is an example. She lives in a small house with her two children and a dog and not much discretionary money coming in each month for things like movies, eating out, and new clothes. Bills are an ever-present concern. Her ex-husband and his second wife live in "the big house on the hill," which has large, nicely decorated bedrooms for the children, a playroom with a computer, a whirlpool bath, and more. They have lots of money to eat out, buy clothes, and travel. One day when Sheila was feeling down about finances, she asked her daughter if she would prefer to live with her father. "Oh, no!" the daughter cried, "I want to live with you. I love my bedroom in the other house, but I would miss you, and Mindy [the dog], and the fires in winter. And here it's... it's more relaxed. We can mess things up, and it's OK. It's freer here. And you just understand me better than Daddy does." Sheila was surprised at how strong her daughter's reaction was.

Of course, every case should be judged on its own merits. Some children would be better off living primarily with their fathers. But financial status is not the only determining factor. If your child receives unconditional love from you, her time with you is beneficial. She needs her mother as well as her father, and the price or amenities of her house or apartment have nothing to do with her feelings. Love is its own gift—and the best one.

## Getting along with him

Pride, hurt, anger, and revenge are big obstacles standing in the way of a positive relationship with your ex-partner. When they dominate your interactions with each other, look out.

Louise had just had her fourth child when she left her husband and moved west with the children. They divorced and the court awarded joint custody to the parents. But living in different cities has made it difficult to shuttle them back and forth; now they live with Louise most of the time. Jim pays hefty child support for his children. He resents not being able to participate in their lives more. He resents the child support payments, and he resents Louise for leaving him in the first place. He sometimes gives Louise only twenty-four hours notice when he wants to pick up the children for a trip to his house. He takes Louise to court regularly to try to reduce his child support. He sends her registered letters about the children, which she must go to the post office to sign for and pick up.

Louise fights him all the way. In court. Through the mail. With the children. She calls him immature and irresponsible and a rat. He calls her unreasonable, a neglectful mother, and an ass. They talk to each other through the children on the phone. "Tell your mother. . ." "Tell your father. . ." One day as Jim was driving into town to claim the children for a visit that Louise had not approved, he happened to spot her van. The children were with her. The van was stopped at a red light and Jim pulled up alongside. She saw him, and when the light changed she took off like a bullet. They raced through the city streets until Louise saw a police officer. She screeched to a stop and told the officer that her ex-husband was trying to take the children illegally. The officer directed Jim to leave town without the children, and told them both to solve their problems in court. Can you imagine how the children reacted to all this?

All too often—certainly in the case of Louise and Jim—court solves nothing. You have to work together with your ex-partner for the sake of your child. Building an unemotional relationship can bring peace and freedom to your lives. It's almost a business relationship. Some couples are fortunate never to go through a nasty period following the end of their relationship. But most do. Some never get over the nastiness. If you can, you are so much better off.

In that bruised period immediately following divorce, it's hard to forgive. But it's necessary in order to wipe the slate clean of miscommunication, imbalance, thoughtlessness, and other negative feelings. You need to give your ex-partner clemency. We're all prone to error. People need to try to learn from their mistakes and to move on.

So one of your toughest jobs is to forgive your ex-partner for whatever he did during your relationship that caused you pain. If he was alcoholic or a drug abuser, look at it as an illness. If he wouldn't do his share of the housework, let that go. If he was negative or emotionally absent with you and your child, try to understand why. Otherwise it will eat at you and affect all of your dealings with him. That kind of emotional acid is too destructive to allow it to continue unchecked.

The more businesslike your relationship is, the easier arrangements will be—vacations, babysitting, and fuller lives for your child through contact with his father, whom he needs.

If your ex-partner is sick or dangerous, it makes sense that you limit your child's contact with him. But if he is within the range of normal—chock full of strengths as well as weaknesses—then you can probably build a business relationship with him. (See page 87, "Child Abuse and Neglect.")

But you will have to compromise. If you want your child to take guitar lessons and your ex-partner prefers violin, you might go with violin. He will still have music lessons. Later he can switch to guitar if he chooses. If you want your child to go to a camp three states away and your ex-partner wants him to go to a day camp in town, you might consider the day camp this year and the sleep-away camp next year. If your ex-partner wants child care reduced by fifty dollars per month, think about whether or not you can swing that, if you know that he has a good reason for it and genuinely has your child's interest at heart.

This does not mean that you let your ex-partner do what he will with his time and resources, demonstrating little responsibility to your child or regard for your wishes. But you are different people; you are going to have different views on things. That can work to a child's advantage when his parents are together. But when they live independently and each wants to be in control, that can be a problem. Each of you needs to prevail some of the time. Even though you are no longer together, you still need to compromise on occasion.

Former partners often have a difficult time listening to each other. Rae's ex, Steve, had a short memory and a hot temper. Shortly after separating, they were dividing their property. The house, a fixer-upper that never got fixed up, was a big issue. Steve was a carpenter, but he had no interest in repairing his own home. He wanted to give the house—in poor repair and with a heavy mortgage—to Rae. She didn't want it either, but she also didn't want to sell the house in its sad condition and lose the money that they had put into it. She knew that someone needed to take the house, and she knew that it would be her, Ms. Responsible. Steve had been critical of Rae throughout their short marriage; he didn't think she was cooperative—a view with which Rae did not agree. She knew that later Steve might forget important details in the separation of their property, so she wrote Steve a letter that went something like this:

> You wanted to buy a house, so we bought one. You wanted a fixer-upper, so ours is. You wanted to buy a car for Jody [Steve's daughter], so we bought one. You wanted a trial separation, so we separated. You wanted a divorce, so we are getting a divorce. You wanted to give me the debts and the house, so I will take the debts and the house. I am writing these things down because I want a record of the facts so that in the future, and if anyone needs to know, we will have one.

The letter was unemotional, but it painted quite a story—who had called the financial shots during their marriage and how they had gotten where they were at the time of their divorce. Steve read the letter and was surprised to remember how compliant Rae had been through all the decisions—his decisions. He actually apologized for perhaps being overly critical of her at times.

It is good that you and your ex-partner are two very different people; he can provide your child with a worldview different from your own. This gives your child a fuller view, more to think about, a broader range of choices. But it can be frustrating when you tackle issues related to values and lifestyle. Charese felt comfortable letting her teenage son roam around the city with friends. He could go exploring, she told him, as long as he returned by twilight. Her ex-husband felt that Charese should know where their son was at all times, and that he should stay within limited boundaries in their neighborhood. He accused Charese of being dangerously loose with their son. She accused him of being unrealistically conservative. They also disagreed on religion. She had the two children on Sundays; sometimes she took them to a charismatic church and sometimes she didn't. He felt that the children should have regular and rigorous religious instruction in a traditional, non-charismatic church. They did not compromise on these issues, though they did on others. The two houses were very different, but the children operated well in each. Each house offered things that they did not like and things that they did. Fortunately, both Charese and her ex-husband came to view the different lifestyle options as a plus in the lives of their children.

## It's OK to be friends

One day you might be by yourself after your ex-partner has picked up your child. He came, he got the kid, he left. You find yourself thinking, "He's not such a bad guy." Is this heresy? You might even say to yourself, "But he's my ex; he's not supposed to be a good guy." What you're probably wondering is, if he's such a nice guy, why did you split up?

Two people split up because they want to. That's all. And they can *both* be decent people who simply chose not to live together.

No one will strike you dead because you have positive feelings about your ex-partner. Good feelings will help you express support for him to your child. They help you make it through the frustrations that are bound to come up in your relationship with each other. Good feelings mean that you have put some distance between yourself and your ex-partner. You are relaxing; you have done some good work, maybe at first for the benefit of your child, then on your own behalf and, you now realize, for your ex's benefit too. Some former couples even see each other socially, with new partners, especially on family occasions like Thanksgiving and birthdays. Do whatever works. Feeling good about your ex-partner—*and* his new partner, if he has one—and becoming friends again is healing.

At first, however, people outside the family may be uncomfortable with that friendship. A woman was registering voters at a grocery store prior to a presidential election. She asked the site director who would relieve her when her shift was over.

He read a woman's name off a list.

"Oh, that's my ex-husband's new wife!" the woman said.

He looked disturbed.

"I know her well," the woman continued, "I checked her out when I found out she was going to be my children's stepmother. She's really a great person."

The site director looked at another man standing nearby and said, "I'm not even going to touch that comment."

What other people do not understand is not your problem. There are few rules when it comes to your relationship with your ex-partner. *Whatever works* is the main rule. Be as comfortable as you can in your relationship with your ex-partner and don't worry about what others think.

## Communication breakdown

No one can push Camille's buttons like her ex-partner. He can send her out of control faster than Halley's comet. He can drive her up one wall and down another. If she's up, he can knock her down. If she's down, he can knock her out. The truth is, both Camille and her ex-husband try to get along because of the children. Sometimes they succeed. Sometimes they don't.

It usually happens on the telephone. A subject comes up, like paying the children money for good grades, and they disagree. They both feel strongly about the issue, and they can't compromise. She raises her voice. He matches hers and raises the volume. She says he has never understood the value of... He says she is just as blind as she always was. This can go on until one of them (usually Camille) hangs up on the other. They are both left with unresolved business and a ton of anger.

When a communication breakdown happens, there is always a way back. Options include:

■ *Cool off.* Give yourself time to stop, deflate, cool down, and *think*. Maybe that means a walk around the block. (Walking works off depression and anger in a physically beneficial way.) Maybe it means trying to forget about it until tomorrow. Maybe it means screaming into a pillow and cussing out your ex's photo until you have spent your anger.

■ *Ask yourself some questions. How can we resolve this for the benefit of our child, short-term? And long-term? How can I provide him with more information, so that he will understand what I am trying to say? What if we did what he wants to do? What is the worst-case scenario? Would our child suffer? Would I? What might the benefits of compromise be? Do they outweigh the liabilities?* Keep on asking questions. Work it one way and then another until you think it through. Then...

■ *Telephone him.* Begin the next conversation with a safe remark like, "I would like for us to try to talk about grades again. Is this a good time?" Words like "us" and "we" are non-confrontational and work to promote unity. Or you can...

▪ **Write him.** If you think you can't control yourself over the phone, write him a letter or an e-mail. This gives you the opportunity to do all the "talking" without interruption. Make your case. It also lets him read your letter without feeling that you are looking for his weak spots; as a result, it may be easier for him to "listen" to what you have to say. Try to keep your emotional reaction out of the letter. Keep cool.

▪ **Go through a third party.** If you have a friend, relative, counselor, or clergy member that your ex-partner respects, you can ask that person to help you talk with your ex. The third person can literally make a phone call for you, or you and your ex-partner can meet and talk in his or her presence.

▪ **Use "I" statements.** When you feel confused, upset, or frustrated, tell your ex-partner in a non-threatening and non-judgmental way. Follow this pattern: "*I feel _____ (emotion) whenever you _____ (action) because _____.*" For example, "*I feel* **threatened** *whenever you* **mention paying the children for grades because I am afraid they will grow up thinking that they don't have to do anything unless they get paid for it.**"

When you use an "I" statement, you are not judging your ex-partner or his logic, you are just telling him how you feel. He may counter with, "Well, that's just not going to happen." You can repeat, "But I feel threatened because . . ." That may encourage your ex-partner to join you in a fuller discussion of the issue, this time without emotional overcharge.

▪ **Never use your child as an intermediary.** It puts her smack in the middle of a conflict between two people she loves. It's not fair, and it's destructive. She may feel anxious, insecure, and helpless. It imposes too much responsibility on her, responsibility she would probably not have if her parents were together.

It is OK to tell your child that you and her father are having some communication difficulties. In fact, if she is around when it happens, it will probably help your child to hear it from you. You might add that all people have trouble communicating from time to time, and that you and her father intend to work through this problem to a satisfactory conclusion. That lets her know that you respect and trust her; you are willing to share your concerns with her, but you are responsible for the solution, not her. It also tells her that you are confident that there will be a resolution, and that underneath the current communication problem, all is well. Or at least OK.

> ▪ ▪ ▪ ▪ ▪ ▪ ▪
>
> It is OK
> to tell your child
> that you and her father
> are having
> some communication
> difficulties.

## Parents' time out for self-control

When you are talking on the phone with your ex-partner, and things are obviously heading toward a major clash, you can say, "I feel frustrated/angry/embarrassed and I can't talk about this anymore right now. I need to go. I'll get back to you later." And hang up. *Do not pick up the phone if it rings.* If your child answers it and tells you, "Daddy wants to talk to you," tell her, "I can't talk on the phone right now." Don't allow your ex-partner to use your child to give you messages and don't do it yourself either. Go to a room where you can shut the door. Put out a "Do not disturb" sign and cool off. Whenever you feel out of control, cut off a telephone conversation with as much tact as possible and say, "I'll get back to you later."

## Training your ex-partner

Try to get your ex-partner to stick to whatever commitments he makes to you. If he is *always* 30 to 90 minutes late, for example, take your child with you and do a small errand so that no one is home when he comes to pick him up, late again. Give him a 15-minute grace period—and tell him you're doing so—and then take off. When you return, if he is there, waiting, explain that you thought he had been held up, so you decided to run an errand. If he still has not arrived, well, at least you accomplished the errand. But if he does have to wait for your return a few times, he may become more prompt.

Men sometimes believe that their job is more important than yours—their time, their money, their involvements. If you allow your ex-partner to inconvenience you by not honoring his commitments, you are reinforcing that mindset. You will pay in lost time, frustration, and maybe even money. But if you hold your ex-partner to the agreements you two set, you need to abide by them as well.

## Negotiating

Negotiating with your ex-partner will ideally be an ongoing process. As long as he is involved with your child, even if only financially, you have to deal with him. In most circumstances, your child will benefit. (A few exceptions are mentioned below.) Since you and your ex-partner will often not see completely eye-to-eye on things, your goal should be peaceful negotiation toward solutions that are acceptable to both parties.

There is an almost universal pattern of moving from hostility (which is not unusual during separation) toward a more workable relationship as the years go by. Time does heal wounds. At the time of separation it's natural to think, "At last I'll be able to do things my way," followed by, "And if he doesn't like it, he can go soak his head. I'm through with his trying to control what I do."

An ex-partner might think, "She got my kid, she got my money, and I'll be damned if she's going to get anything else out of me."

So we have two people who are predisposed to face off with armored tanks pointed straight at each other. In a situation like this, there is little trust, little give-and-take. It's a setup wired for difficult communication, one easily short-circuited by short tempers.

Let's say your ex-partner wants to have custody of your child for half of Christmas Day. He normally has her on weekends, but this year Christmas Day is on a Wednesday. You suggest he move his celebration to Saturday to comply with the normal visitation pattern. He says you are being unfair, that as the father, he should have a right to see his child on Christmas Day. You say you understand how he feels, but you feel that the stress of the holiday season on your child will be lessened if she doesn't hop back and forth more than usual during Christmas week.

One option is to refuse his request. There is nothing wrong with that, but you run the risk of angering your ex-partner; he may try to take it out on you directly (verbal battering or even taking you back to court) or indirectly (by talking bad about you to your child), or by pulling away from your child.

There is, however, something wrong with refusing all requests. If you are doing this, you might take a look at whether you're making decisions with your head or your heart. Some of your ex-partner's suggestions are likely to be logical and productive for your child.

The other option is to grant the request for the sake of your child. This is hard to do; your ego may be tied up in continuing the power play. It feels like having to "say Uncle." It may feel weak.

But there is strength in granting concessions to your ex-partner as often and as gracefully as you can. It's a pressure release. If you say, "Well, I really would like to have our child until Saturday, but I understand how you feel, and I will agree to your special request. Have it your way this time," you tell your ex-partner that you are flexible, that you are willing to give a little, that you might even be a nice person. These fragile blocks of trust and good will are so important when you are trying to build a solid working relationship with your ex-partner for the benefit of your child.

## Tips On Negotiation

▪ It's OK to have rules on which you will not negotiate with your ex-partner, such as how much notice he has to give you before he takes your child out of town.

▪ It's reasonable for you and your ex-partner to ask each other for special favors, such as "Will you take the kids for me this weekend? I'm swamped with work."

▪ Be flexible; sometimes say yes and sometimes say no to special requests. If you always say no, you are setting up a power struggle, and your child will lose.

▪ When you say yes, be sure your ex-partner knows that you have made a concession in good faith, even though you would have preferred to do otherwise. (Not "You are getting your way this time, and don't you forget it," but "This plan is not my first choice, but I understand your point of view, and I'll do it your way this time.")

▪ Give in to him whenever you can, in order to accumulate good points for when you have to stand your ground on an issue. Give so that you can take when you really need to. Keep track of your own concessions and remind him of them, but only if you really need to.

▪ Avoid seeing him as the enemy. You may feel like he is, but unless he is physically or emotionally or sexually abusive to or neglectful of your child, he is a friend.

▪ Thank your ex-partner when he agrees to your request. ("I know you want to do otherwise in this situation, but I really appreciate your helping me out in this way. Thanks.") He may be a little more likely to say yes the next time.

▪ If you cannot reach an agreement, talk it out, agree to disagree, or avoid talking about the issue until it resolves itself in one way or another.

Not all people are reasonable during separation, however. Some seem stuck in the Terrible Twos phase of behavior, like petulant toddlers screaming "No." Some people, often those who are insecure and have low self-esteem, are going to lash out at their ex-partners, no matter what. They want power and control. They are angry. If you are dealing with someone like this, you may have to do a majority of your communicating through a lawyer, a time-consuming and expensive practice.

## When your ex-partner threatens you

Sharice finally left her husband, who had physically battered her for much of their twelve-year marriage. It was worse near the end. Some time after she left him, he broke the front door of her apartment, trying to get in. For safety, she took the three children to a battered women's shelter. He began calling her at work every ten minutes. He threatened to drag her out of church on Sunday and create a scene. Sharice tried getting help from the police, which temporarily deterred him, but in the end, she moved to another town for safety.

If your ex-partner threatens you or your child, call the police immediately and ask what help is available from the police and other sources in your community. Do not live in fear. Get information and seek out help in order to protect yourself and your child from a harassing or potentially dangerous ex-partner.

## Raising children the "wrong" way

Diane got home from work one day to find a note on her door from a social worker from the Department of Human Services (DHS). Her ex-husband had accused Diane of neglect and asked the department to investigate her care of their four children. Diane had to go to DHS and defend herself. A home visit from the social worker followed. And on the day the note was left, her school-aged children had been taken out of class and interviewed by the social worker. They were frightened. Diane was enraged.

Her ex-husband lived in another town. He and Diane could barely communicate civilly with each other. Because they were unable to communicate, her ex-husband couldn't talk with Diane about his fears for their children. This fiasco was just the latest in a string of sad miscommunications and power plays.

The social worker found nothing wrong with the way Diane cared for her children. Diane's responsibilities were heavy, but the children were well fed, adequately clothed, and obviously loved. Her ex-husband's fears were unfounded.

Even when children are well cared for, how they are managed can cause great conflict between separated parents. Values, safety, sex, friends, dress, and any number of other things are fertile ground for conflict.

Take movies, for example. You may feel it is all right for your fourteen-year-old to see R-rated movies; your ex-partner may feel that PG is the limit. Your ex-partner may let your child ride around town on the back of his motorcycle; you abhor the idea. You may allow your child to cut and color her hair in any desired manner; your ex-partner says the child looks like trash.

You say, "So what? When my child is with me, I set the rules." Right. The flip side of that is that when your child is with your ex-partner, he sets the rules.

This can be amusing. For example, you let your son have long hair. He goes to your ex-partner's house and he has to get a haircut. He comes back to your house, shaves half of his hair off entirely, and spikes the rest—very popular at school. He goes back to his father's house, and your ex-partner goes into cardiac arrest.

Some issues—freedom and control, widely varying value differences—never resolve themselves. However, it's a good idea to recognize that:

▪ No two people will agree completely on how to raise their child.

▪ An older child may side with one parent over the other when they disagree.

▪ It is not up to the child to decide how he should be

raised. A child needs and wants guidance.

■ There is value in a child's experiencing two different lifestyles and parenting styles; the child will probably find some good in both.

■ As long as you can trust your ex-partner's motives, allow him to guide your child as he sees fit, giving him the same freedom you demand for yourself.

■ If your ex-partner is involved in drug abuse or behaves in ways that are abusive or neglectful toward your child, take appropriate action.

### When your ex-partner flounders

Your ex-partner may go through financial hard times at some point following the divorce. His reduced resources may well affect your child as a result of irregular or reduced child support or in other, more intangible ways. Your child may worry about her father. Support your child by explaining what you know of the situation (not "Your know-it-all father got fired," but "Things weren't working out for your father at work, so he is out of a job right now. He's looking for another one"). Keep her image of her father as untarnished as possible. Children need fathers they can look up to. Everyone makes mistakes, everyone goes through slumps. We need to support each other—even ex-partners—when that happens, in order to keep the fiber of our families strong.

Your ex-partner may experience depression, self-doubt, loneliness—heavy-duty negative feelings that he can't seem to shake for a while. This can affect his behavior toward your child. Explain the altered behavior (not "Well, your father has finally gone wacko," but "Your father is going through hard times right now. This is when you need to be sensitive to his feelings and try to be helpful and cheerful.") The idea of family, after all, is that we support each other and stick together through thick and thin. Your child's family includes her father, and this can be an opportunity for her to take on some responsibility for caring for a temporarily weak link in her family chain.

At the same time, if the emotional problem is ongoing (if it is depression brought on by alcoholism, for example), if your child is exposed to physical or emotional violence, or if you suspect that your ex-partner is an unfit parent, either temporarily or long-term, you must protect your child.

You have a few options:

■ Confront your ex-partner with your concerns in as calm and objective a manner as possible. Express your fears of how his behavior may adversely affect your child and then ask him how he feels about the situation. He won't tell you anything unless he trusts you, and even if he does, he still may tell you nothing, but he'll know you are aware of a problem. It's good for him to know you are monitoring the situation, and he may try a little harder to control himself around your child.

■ Contact one of the following sources for advice on how to handle these situations:
- *alcoholism*: Alcoholics Anonymous and Al-Anon
- *drug abuse*: Narcotics Anonymous
- *depression*—a social services counselor who can help advise you on what to do for the welfare of the children
- *suspected emotional abuse of the children*—a counselor and your lawyer, if temporary limitation of visitation seems advisable.

## Protecting your child

The following acts are illegal and can be grounds for denial of visitation rights or even imprisonment:

■ physical abuse
■ sexual abuse
■ neglect.

If you suspect that your ex-partner is mistreating your child in any of these ways, you may temporarily deny him visitation rights. See a lawyer. Do not let your child get into a situation that you feel is dangerous. Your first responsibility is to protect your child.

Every day, we hear stories about children who have been victims of abuse. Some of those children are put in foster homes. Some are put through gut-wrenching trials during which their parents battle publicly; the evidence, accusations and pain become public knowledge, and the children feel forever scarred by shame, scandal, and guilt.

If you suspect your ex-partner of abuse or neglect, take your next step with grave concern and caution. Make sure your suspicions are valid. If you tell anyone about the suspected abuse, that person is legally bound to report it to the authorities. Only lawyers, clergy, and certain mental health practitioners (psychiatrists, but not counselors) are legally allowed and professionally required to

> ▪ ▪ ▪ ▪ ▪ ▪ ▪
>
> Protecting your child should be your highest priority.

keep that kind of information confidential. Once the authorities—police, Human Services, etc.—know about the suspected abuse, their job is to investigate it and take action. If they find abuse or neglect, they may remove the child from that parent. If the abuse is severe enough, they may bring the parent to trial. When the authorities become involved, you lose control over the situation.

If you tell your lawyer about the suspected abuse, she can act confidentially as an intermediary and outline to your ex-partner his options:

- Give up visitation, at least temporarily.
- Get counseling.
- Join a child abuse prevention program.
- Face a trial on the charges.

Your ex-partner may at least listen to a lawyer, and your lawyer can report the results of the conversation to you. You can choose to proceed privately or publicly, depending on the outcome of the conversation.

Or you can contact the authorities yourself with your report of suspected abuse, and let them handle it. Protecting your child should be your highest priority.

Child abuse is such a tough, heartbreaking situation; there are always scars. Decisions surrounding child abuse are never easy, but these are the steps you should consider taking:

1. Get your child into a safe situation immediately.

2. Try to get more information about the nature of the abuse before going to the authorities; if you are going to make a formal complaint, going on the record in charging child abuse, you must be able to establish some validity in your accusation.

3. Confront your ex-partner about the abuse, either directly or through a lawyer.

4. Get information on child abuse and abusers from professional agencies like the National Association for the Prevention of Child Abuse.

5. Decide on an action plan that will do the least damage to your child and prevent the abuse from ever happening again.

When the situation is less severe than child abuse or neglect, try to encourage your ex-partner to seek help for his personal problems. You can do this either directly or through an intermediary, such as a friend or relative. If you can be supportive and work to maintain a healthy bond between your ex-partner and your child, then everyone concerned benefits. Your child needs a father, even an imperfect one.

## When your ex-partner is in prison

Robert Jr., was eighteen months old when his father went to prison for armed robbery. His father was in prison for thirteen years and then was released. For many of those years, his son cried every Christmas because his father was not with the family, not with him.

Fathers in prison want to get out of prison, want romantic partners, and want relationships with their children. Family members sometimes try to prevent prisoners from communicating with their children. But when they are old enough to express themselves, the children almost always say, "I want my daddy."

A prisoner can be a good and loving father, even though he made a mistake. Most stepfathers don't have the feelings for your child that the natural father has. There are often strong emotional bonds between prisoners and their children. If your ex-partner is an inmate and you feel he loves your child and would not emotionally, physically, or sexually abuse him, strongly consider supporting that emotional bond. Every child needs a father.

## The weekly phone call

More than one divorced family gets together to talk regularly about their children. One formerly married couple meets annually to have lunch and talk about their visions for their children in the coming year. Some ex-partners talk over business whenever it seems necessary.

In one case, both parents have remarried; they, and one of the two new spouses, talk on the telephone every Wednesday night after the children's bedtime to go over whatever has come up. Each parent has a list of items to discuss, and anything goes: finances, school, friends, health and hygiene, and growth and development. Often this is a time when the parents share stories about the children that the other parent would miss, such as the time their daughter had her first romantic conversation with a boy, or the time their son cried when his best friend left town. This weekly phone conversation creates a better understanding of the children for both parents. It is a useful time for problem solving as well as for devising action plans for the children's enrichment and growth. It is a way for all the parents to work together for a common purpose and for harmony in the family.

The weekly phone call emerged from counseling sessions that

were designed to promote better communication between two very different households. At first, both parents resisted the effort, but in time it proved to be so successful that they have continued it for many years. The children know that they are the topic of discussion every Wednesday night. They feel their parents care about them in setting aside this time. They feel important, and they feel loved.

## Your ex-partner's relatives

Jane's ex-partner had custody of their children during the summers and some holidays. He was a salesman and traveled part of the time. While he was away from town, his parents kept the children and provided them with walks to the park, cookie baking, and round-the-clock, loving care.

Megan, Lisa's children's stepmother, was from New England. Her parents, brothers and sisters, and their spouses still lived there. Megan's close and happy family held twice-yearly reunions to which Lisa's children went eagerly. In addition, Megan took her stepmother role seriously and conveyed her love of nature, her interest in politics, and her knowledge of health to the children.

Joyce's husband died of cancer leaving two young children for Joyce to raise alone. Her mother-in-law lived in the same city and continued to play an active, positive role in the lives of the children, including providing crucial help as an emergency child-care source and cooking and hosting family holiday meals.

In so many ways, your ex-partner's relatives, sometimes including those of his new wife, can contribute to your child's life. They can provide child care, a broader perspective, and love for your children. If your ex-partner's family care enough about your child to want to participate in her life, then she is lucky.

Sometimes, of course, relatives can interfere in the same way that your ex-partner may: asking for too many special visiting privileges or trying to tell you, either through your ex-partner or directly, how you should be raising your child. If you have a good relationship with your ex-partner, you can tell him how you feel about the problem and request his help. Otherwise, you have to either negotiate directly with the relatives or try to ignore the problem.

Marlene was an unwed mother of a perky little toddler. The parents of the father found out about their granddaughter and wanted to visit her regularly. Marlene refused; she wanted nothing to do with any of her child's father's relatives. The grandparents took Marlene to court. After they presented their case, the judge asked Marlene what she thought. She said, "Your Honor, I'm trying the best I can to raise my daughter. Her father does not participate in her life, and I just want us to be left alone to start over. Give me a break." The judge looked at the grandparents and said, "Give her a break." He denied all future visitation. They did not appeal. Marlene felt that her chances of finding a man who would want to marry her and adopt her daughter would be better if she and her daughter were solo. It worked out that way, but it was a risk. Her daughter might have benefited from a relationship with her father's parents.

## Fearing your ex-partner's relatives

At first, Lisa felt threatened by Megan, her children's stepmother, and her obvious gifts. But Lisa's daughter said, "I like Megan, but you're my mom," which helped ease her mother's fears. Later, Lisa observed that Megan, while gifted, was somewhat inflexible with the children. Both Lisa and Megan conveyed their gifts and frailties to the children. In the end, Lisa believed that the children were in good hands with Megan; Lisa knew her own place in the hearts of her children was secure.

It is natural to fear the emotional tie between your child and your ex-partner and his relatives. If there were only positive interactions between them and your child, and only negative ones between you and your child, your child might decide that he wants to live with his father. One house is almost never all good or bad. But children do sometimes desire a change, especially teenagers who are looking for a closer relationship with their fathers or who are looking for a more perfect parent. Sometimes you just have to let go.

Penny's son Peter had never lived with his father, a research scientist in Germany. When he was fourteen, he decided that he wanted to live with his father. Everyone agreed to let him go. After a year, he returned to his mother's home, which he ended up preferring. But sometimes it works out the other way, and you need to be prepared for this.

Don't fear your ex-partner's family because they offer more material things than you. Children need love, not fancy things.

Don't fear your ex-partner's family because they offer your child as much love and attention as you do. Children can never get too much love, and your child will not

■ ■ ■ ■ ■ ■ ■

Sometimes you just have to let go.

give up yours. The more people who love him, the better his support system is. Allow your child to have contact with his father's loving relatives; it's good mothering.

Don't fear your ex-partner's family because you feel they can offer more material things and more love to your child than you can. Take a good look at that fear. It may be unfounded; instead, you might have a problem with low self-esteem. But it may be a valid fear; maybe you don't have a positive relationship with your child. In either case, you might think about getting counseling.

Your ex-partner's relatives may be as difficult for you to deal with as he is. But your child can almost always profit from a relationship with them, and it is worth some effort on your part to make that happen. It's best not to stand in the way of those relationships and even better to encourage them with confidence and appreciation.

# CHAPTER 3

# Legal Concerns

The system
  of family law

Joint custody

Custody concerns

Spousal maintenance
  and alimony

Child support

Getting child support
  from a reluctant
  partner

Renegotiation

Mediators

Going back to court

The cost of litigation

Finding a good lawyer

What to tell
  your child

Go with a friend

Plan time for healing
  your court wounds

## The system of family law

Family law is changing rapidly, and that affects the way divorces are structured. The first no-fault divorce law in California in 1969 changed the financial structure of divorce. Palimony, joint custody, and other newer concepts have likewise had an impact as our society redefines gender roles and the range of acceptable divorce arrangements.

Family law is increasingly sophisticated. The division of property—family assets including real property, lifelong earning power, pension plans, and more—requires someone with expertise in finance; these days many attorneys specializing in family law consult with tax lawyers when drawing up the divorce plans for their clients. Child custody alternatives increasingly involve a psychologist or psychiatrist who interviews the child and testifies in court. Sometimes, two such professionals interview the participants and testify in court—one expert for each parent, each supporting opposite claims.

There never has been room for slipshod practice in divorce and post-divorce litigation. Today, the growing complexity of family law demands that, in order to best serve their clients, lawyers keep pace with the times by having financial and human relations consultants on hand to provide accurate, well-tempered advice.

## Joint custody

Today, many more fathers are asking for—and getting—custody of their children. Joint custody is now an acceptable option in every state; some states have proposed or passed laws defining joint custody as the preferred outcome.

Research has consistently shown that, for the best results, both parents need to approve of a joint custody arrangement and to communicate that approval to their children. Otherwise, children may be adversely affected by the parental disapproval; they might even be better off with one parent having custody and the other visitation.

Depending on their maturity, children aged twelve and older can participate in the decision about custody structure. A couple in Florida had two daughters, ages twelve and thirteen. When the parents divorced, they remained in the same town and the mother was awarded custody. The twelve-year-old did not adjust well and soon began making life difficult for her sister. With the children's approval, the parents agreed on a different custody arrangement: the sisters were separated, alternating weeks with each parent.

In another divorcing family, the children wanted to stay in their home, so the parents switched residences each week between the family house and an apartment.

While many fathers genuinely want to raise or help raise their own children, sometimes a father asks for primary or joint custody as a way to control or punish his ex-wife. One father asked for and got joint custody of his children. Sometimes he would show up as scheduled, and sometimes not. He was not dependable, yet he was outraged when his ex-wife complained. He made last-minute demands for changes in the custody schedule. And for the three months of summer vacation, he left the children in the care of his elderly mother and father in another town, seeing them infrequently. He did not tell the ex-wife where the children would be during this time.

> ■ ■ ■ ■ ■ ■ ■
> When joint custody
> works well,
> it can benefit
> everyone...

When joint custody works well, it can benefit everyone; neither parent carries the crushing responsibility of twenty-four-hour care, day after day. Both parents can savor their time with their child, as well as their time alone. The child grows up in two different households with different rules, different values, different economics, and different opportunities. Such differences teach children that life is a matter of choices. Your child will learn to recognize the benefits of both homes. More importantly, he will have an opportunity to live with both of his parents, not as a guest, but as a member of each household with both privileges and responsibilities. When problems occur, parent and child can struggle through them together. This is the glue that holds families together.

For satisfactory parenting and minimally complicated joint custody, certain guidelines apply. Each parent should:

- Agree to support the arrangement.
- Affirm the other parent as a good parent.
- Trust each other enough to provide a positive environment for their child.
- Be able to forgive the other.
- Carry through with their commitments to each other (being on time, sharing supplies between the two houses, etc.).
- Plan ahead to schedule family vacations, camps, and other events that require flexible custody agreements.
- Talk to each other civilly about their child and work out mutually agreeable arrangements.
- Keep each other informed about their child's activities, telling the other parent the dates of baseball games and music recitals, as well as passing along report cards, school notes, and other important documents.
- Be patient with their child when he accidentally leaves things at his other parent's house, such as coats, medicine, tomorrow's homework, etc.
- Understand the importance of keeping siblings together as they move between homes. (There are beneficial exceptions to this rule, as in the example of the two Florida sisters.)
- Live in the same community, so that their child is not separated from his friends. This is especially important as children approach their teens.

Joint custody arrangements that do not accommodate all of these suggestions may still be beneficial.

t helps to remember that joint custody is probably the most complex custody arrangement, and the more frequently (and the farther) that children move between houses, the more complicated it gets.

## Custody concerns

Once a divorce decree is granted, custody cannot change without the mutual agreement of both parents through informal discussion, mediation, or a return to court.

As your child gets older, he may have definite views about where he would like to live—views that may conflict with the divorce decree and views that you or his father may or may not honor. Often a teenager wants to live with the non-custodial parent, sometimes because he has had little interaction with that parent. Pamela's son Jim had a father who lived in another town and who saw Jim only on vacations. When Jim was sixteen, he decided he would like to live with his father and new stepmother. His mother agreed to let him move. He and his father had never been close, and Jim wanted to make a last effort, during his senior year of high school, to form a stronger relationship with his dad. It was a difficult year for Jim, his father, and his stepmother. But Jim learned a lot about family in that year; he was glad that he had gone and that he was able to move on to college.

Though reluctant, many mothers put aside their own desires and allow their children to live with their fathers. Allowing your teenager a voice in this decision will give him a sense of control over his life. It will prevent him from resenting his custodial parent and from harboring unrealistic images of his non-custodial parent. Living on a regular basis for an extended time with the (formerly) non-custodial parent allows both the child and the parent to get to know each other.

## Spousal maintenance and alimony

Alimony all but died in the 1970s. Courts began to divide property equally between former spouses, but often neglected to

make provisions for "displaced homemakers"—women
invested their lives in their husband's careers in lieu of de
their own. Following their divorces, these women found th
with no career training and no job experience. Suddenly, they were
faced with making their way in the world alone, with few resources
or options.

In the 1980s, it became commonplace for courts to award
rehabilitative alimony to women who had no job skills or recent job
experience. They would receive either a lump sum or alimony for a
limited period of time, often two to five years, so that they could
support themselves while they went to school, sought job training,
and developed careers. Some women who contributed significantly
to their husband's careers have received lifetime awards following
their divorces, as in the case of the woman who put her husband
through college and medical school, only to have him divorce her.
His future earnings were deemed by the court to be partly hers,
since he would not have been able get his medical training without
his wife's financial support.

Today, this arrangement is called spousal maintenance. Greater
consideration is given to long-term homemakers and situations
involving significant income disparity. Lifetime maintenance awards
are given to older women who enter the job market at ages that limit
their ability to build lengthy careers. Sometimes a limited spousal
maintenance, say, 40 percent of expected financial needs, is awarded
for life. Women who earn considerably less than their husbands may
receive spousal maintenance to compensate for income disparity.
Spousal awards for homemakers validates the contribution of home-
making skills in our society and provides compensation for women
who have acted in good faith only to find their circumstances
changed.

## Child support

Child support guidelines differ at federal, state, and local
court levels. Laws aim for uniformity, but the enactment of them

allows for flexibility. Guidelines aim to ensure adequate aid for the children, to prevent gross injustice to either the paying or receiving parent, and to reduce the court's time and the parents' animosity in struggling with this emotional issue.

Child support is paid by the non-custodial parent to the custodial parent. In joint custody arrangements, child support is usually not awarded, unless there is significant disparity in the parents' incomes, and both parents share costs for health insurance and other maintenance costs that benefit the children at both houses.

## Getting child support from a reluctant partner

A 1988 federal law, the Family Support Act, mandates a wage assignment directly from the employer of the delinquent parent, through the court, to the receiving parent. The court will garnish the wages of the delinquent parent, going directly to that person's employer. In effect, the court acts as bill collector. The very first time your ex-partner is late with a child support payment, file an appropriate petition with the court. Too many women wait until their ex-partner has failed to send several payments before they seek legal help. This allows the delinquent parent to take his responsibility less seriously, to the detriment of his child. The court may even forgive part of that liability if it is significant, which means that the receiving parent has to accept financial responsibility for the failure of the delinquent parent. Her resources for her child do not go as far. The child loses.

Think twice about denying your delinquent ex-partner visitation privileges; it may also result in your losing back child support. A judge may penalize you by erasing some or all of the debt from the period of time you denied visitation. Though this punishes children for the behavior of their parents, it does happen. Plus, if you deny visitation solely because your ex-partner has not paid child support, your child loses out as well—on potentially valuable time with his father that has nothing to do with money. Attempts to control your ex-partner through money or visitation always hurt your child.

For help in collecting child support, contact your county or district attorney's office. Your ex-partner can be traced through his social security number. If he lives in another state, or even outside the United States, he can be located and required to fulfill his legal obligations.

## Renegotiation

Divorce decrees are structured to fit the circumstances at the time they are awarded. In drawing up your divorce proposal, you try to anticipate future circumstances, but these can change dramatically: parents move and remarry, people change or lose jobs, children grow older and express their own needs. Changed circumstances may cause one or both parents to want changes in the divorce structure.

■ ■ ■ ■ ■ ■ ■

Attempts to control your ex-partner through money or visitation always hurt your child.

You don't have to go to court to renegotiate. If you and your ex-husband can agree on how you want to alter the divorce agreement, you can simply implement that new plan, though the new agreement is non-binding. If he defaults on the new agreement in some way, then you may want to see a mediator or a lawyer.

## Mediators

Negotiation can take place between just two people. If those two people cannot work out a satisfactory deal, a third party (consisting of one or more persons) can work with the two people to arrive at a solution that is satisfactory to everyone.

Anyone can be a mediator—a mutual friend or a professional. Though the information in this section refers to professional mediators, the same principles apply to non-professionals. In fact, some professionals who mediate do not call themselves mediators.

In the case of one divorcing couple, for example, two tax lawyers worked out a satisfactory property settlement without the participation of the former spouses. Each tax lawyer was a consultant for the primary lawyer for each partner. This was a safe and painless option for the divorcing parties; their financial mediators were thoroughly familiar with financial benefits and law. In order for both parties to make informed choices and fair compromises, their legal experts need to be familiar with the relevant aspects of the law. For divisions of property, a tax lawyer or a CPA could be appropriate, depending on the circumstances. Your primary lawyer should have a financial consultant, one that will keep your interests foremost.

A person may register with the state as a certified mediator, which means that she has completed a state-approved course in mediation. This does not make any statement about her actual ability to negotiate. She is not necessarily a lawyer. Often, certified mediators are psychologists, social workers, or members of the clergy. The aim of mediation is to avoid destructive litigation in favor of mutually acceptable resolutions to conflict. A mediator sits with both parties, listens, and offers options, alternatives, and creative solutions to potential areas of conflict. A mediator's fee is, on average, approximately 60 percent of a lawyer's.

The process of mediation is fundamentally different from litigation. In a court dispute, both parties face off against one another in adversarial roles; the court system defines their relationship. The lawyers present facts and arguments, and the judge decides the dispensation of children, property, and other matters. There is a winner and a loser. Judges do have their biases, so you never know how the decision will go until it is announced. The process may make you feel debilitated, dehumanized, and powerless. You have little control over the outcome; you can only select a lawyer you hope will present your case in the best way.

In mediation, however, the two parties come together to discuss the issues rather than opposing each other. They design their own solution, which must be mutually acceptable. The result is not win/lose, but win/win. Both parties are empowered, because both are in control of the outcome. Ideally, there is a spirit of cooperation and even mutual support. The children may be far less disturbed by a peaceful resolution than by a courtroom battle. According to a study by F. M. Margolin, court resolutions to conflict between divorcing parties are six times more likely to be appealed than are mediated settlements.

The California court system was the first to mandate that divorcing couples with children go through mediation before going to court when there is a custody dispute. The parents must work out a resolution with a mediator to avoid court conflicts and to avoid further litigation. Other states have similar mandates that require mediators to work with the lawyers representing both parties. At several points in the process, the mediators meet with the lawyers to obtain information and to offer the custody plan for approval. The lawyers then present the plan to the judge in court, who approves it.

Some lawyers do not approve of mediators and there are some good reasons—not just the potential loss of business. Because mediators are a new and unregulated service group, they may be viewed as highly risky. A mediator may not understand complex legal concepts, since she does not have a legal education. In matters of property, possessions, and children, a simple division of 50/50 often won't do. It is possible for two parties to go through mediation and feel satisfied with their resolution only to learn, later, that the real-life implications of their mutual decision are unworkable. Then they must go back to mediation or court, or carry on with a difficult situation.

In court, you are at risk due to your lawyer's skill and the judge's bias. In mediation, you are at risk from the legal knowledge of the mediator and her talents in human relations.

You and your ex-partner may meet with one mediator or you each may have your own mediator. Upon arriving at a mutually agreeable settlement, you should have a lawyer review and edit the agreement, if necessary, to conform to the law. It will also help to have a second opinion from someone who is an advocate for your interests and those of your child.

If you want to investigate working with a professional mediator, call counseling practitioners and mental health centers in your community and ask for recommendations. Interview mediators by phone and ask about their training, experience, and client references. Talk with those clients about the mediation experience and their response to the settlement before you decide on a mediator.

> ■ ■ ■ ■ ■ ■ ■
>
> "It takes two to make peace. It only takes one to make war."

## Going back to court

"It takes two to make peace. It only takes one to make war," says lawyer Mary Frances Lyle. The court system was intended to provide justice to victims. When you need to protect yourself or your child, it is an option. Many women do not go back to court for an appeal or for new litigation because they fear losing. They do not want to take the risk. That also means that they do not have the opportunity to benefit from a decision in their favor, and that benefit can be considerable. The choice may be costly, both emotionally and financially, but if you decide to go back to court, get the best attorney you can afford. If your ex-partner brings a case against you, of course, you have no choice.

## The cost of litigation

There are up-front costs as well as additional costs if you lose. Most attorneys require a retainer, but some may waive it, especially if they think a case is either a sure thing or challenging in some way.

Courts can award "frivolous" fees to defendants. One woman, for example, had multiple sclerosis and could not work. Her ex-husband was an optometrist. Two years after the divorce, he filed to terminate her lifetime alimony. He won. She appealed to a higher court. She was sick. She had no money and no way of making any. She stood up for herself. She took a chance. And she won. The higher court awarded additional money to the woman because her ex-husband wasted their time with a frivolous case.

Some lawyers will work with low-income people on a sliding scale basis; if your income is low enough, one may give you a break. Your local YWCA or other women's centers may have a list of lawyers who operate in this way. If they don't, ask them if they would create one as a service to you and other single mothers. In some cities, the local bar association may provide a free lawyer referral service to the community. (Look under "Attorneys" in the Yellow Pages.) Also consider calling a well-known, expensive woman lawyer; ask her to recommend a less expensive but competent lawyer, one whose courtroom record is very good but whose reputation does not yet price her out of your budget.

When you have compiled a list of lawyers who offer financial breaks, ask other lawyers about their courtroom reputations. The last thing you want to do is throw away your money or your rights. Call up a good family lawyer in your town; if you explain your situation, she might give you good advice about the lawyers on your list.

Legal Services is also available to those who meet their financial requirements. If your income is low, call them to find out if you qualify. If not, ask them for suggestions. If they say they do not recommend lawyers, ask them who does.

Federal, state, county, and city governments, and even small municipalities, provide community services and public information offices that can refer you to local agency sources or legal aid societies in your area.

## Finding a good lawyer

Word of mouth is the best way to find a new lawyer. Ask relatives and friends, especially women friends and those who have been through divorce. Call up your local newspaper office and ask to speak with the reader advocate, ombudsman, or legal expert. Call a law professor at your local university. Call a clergy member. Ask for a lawyer who is honest and who has good courtroom skills and an excellent record. Ask for several recommendations, because prices vary. (Lawyers can charge flat or hourly fees.) You need to shop around for someone you can trust and afford, who will listen to you, and whose language and reasoning makes sense to you.

You can ask a lawyer for a preliminary conference, at which you can ask questions about how he operates. This will help you get a feel for whether this would be a good lawyer/client relationship. Before you make an appointment, ask if he charges for a preliminary conference; some do, some don't.

Don't feel obliged to accept a lawyer's services after a phone call or a preliminary conference. You don't have to say yes. If you have any doubts or negative feelings about the lawyer and he asks if you are ready to commit, tell him that you always take time to think over a decision before you make a commitment. Tell him that you will call in a day or so with your answer.

## What to tell your child

Be honest. If you can tell that she suspects that something is up, tell her that you are going to court and what the general issue is. Try not to go into details. Tell her that it is OK for her to love her dad just as much as ever. You can tell your child that you are upset with her father, if you are, but that this problem is between you and him; your child should not feel she is the cause. Seeing their parents argue upsets children, so if you need to talk with your ex-husband and you know it is going to be an emotional conversation, do it while your child is not present. If he calls you when your child is at home, tell him you need to talk with him when she is out, and make a phone appointment. If he keeps calling, unplug the phone. Tell your child that the court is responsible for making a decision; this prevents her from feeling that she needs to solve her parents' problems.

## Go with a friend

If you go back to court, think about taking someone with you. When Dee went to court, she sat all alone in court with only her lawyer. Across the way her ex-husband sat with his new wife, who stroked his arm and looked concerned. Together, they looked like a loving, supportive couple. Dee looked friendless and forlorn. She *was* forlorn in that lonely courtroom, but she was not friendless. She could have asked a friend to accompany her to court, a move that would have supported Dee emotionally and might have impressed the judge.

## Plan time for healing your court wounds

It's tough living through the stress of litigation. If you win, it's stressful; if you lose, it's worse. You may feel completely drained and need to cry, to curl up in bed, to talk or celebrate with a friend, to walk off your frustration or energy, or to otherwise make the transition from court to routine life. You may want to take time off from work following your court date. You may want to arrange for a friend to be on call to take care of your child after you return from court. On the other hand, you may want your child with you. It's a good idea to plan for both options. This is a time when your support group, if you have one (see chapter 9), should be made aware of your court process and be with you, either physically or at least in spirit, thinking about you as you go through the experience.

Though you can expect the court process to be unpleasant, you can also expect that unpleasantness to pass. Time is on your side.

A good general resource for legal questions is *The Everything Divorce Book*, Mary L. Davidson, Adams Media Corporation, 2003.

# Raising Healthy Children

Aleen,
New red she machine
why your Mama carry you
ten months and smile smile
    smile?
Vomit then the runs every
    seven days
but she don't care. She
    happy.
Why she want you so bad?

Now you here
all wiggle, peep and suck
you do make a body smile.
Your Mama, you wear her
    out
she shake her head
her eyes black from no
    sleep.
You one little thunder
    horn.
Aleen, why you cry and cry?
What you see up ahead,
    child
that make you complain
    so?
Hush now. Let your Mama
    rest.

What you be ten years on?
You be young willow tree
You be mountain stream
You be girl with woman
    peeking out
long sun-brown legs
runnin' with the pack
so fast tryin' to get
    somewhere
you don't even know.

Your Mama, she know
    about the bomb
she know about flesh rot,
head rot, drug stuff, rape,
    tears.
She look at you and forget
    that trash.
She look at you and have
    faith.
She want a baby, that all.

## The friendship cake

Pauline Rawley of Mount Airy, North Carolina, made a friendship cake for her son-in-law. It takes thirty days to make a friendship cake. First you mix together the first batch of fruit and let it sit for ten days, stirring occasionally. Then you mix in the second batch of fruit and let that sit for ten days, stirring occasionally. Then you add the remaining ingredients, bake the cake, and let it sit for another ten days so the flavors will blend and age just right.

It takes a lot of attention to make a friendship cake. The process is spread out over time. Raising children is very similar. Their development and maturation doesn't happen overnight.

These days, many people appreciate a Betty Crocker cake mix solution to dessert and would love to have a quick-fix solution to raising perfect children instantly. It does not exist. The process will involve struggle, problems, mistakes, worry, and a lot of attention to details. The early years are significant in forming your child's values and behavior patterns. Once she reaches the age of fourteen, your child will make a lot of her own choices. As mothers, our job is to continue paying attention to the details, even as we gradually let go of the controls.

No mother I know is perfect, but we may feel we ought to be. Mothering isn't easy, and single mothering requires extra effort. In the end, we are all struggling to do the best we can. Perfection is a goal toward which we are working but which we must understand we will never attain. But we don't have to be perfect to be ideal.

## Unconditional love

Being a mother requires a high degree of constant responsibility. When you divorce, that responsibility intensifies. Even if you have joint custody with your ex-partner, when your child is with you, he is totally dependent on your time, your energy, your patience, and your love. Living with parents, a roommate, or a romantic partner can make your job more complex: you are probably having to run interference between your child and the other occupants of the house, trying to keep him quiet, trying to keep his "stuff" picked up from around the house, trying to keep him from destroying the other occupant's chair, CDs, books, china, or other possessions, trying to keep peace.

Children of divorce are automatically under stress. They have two parents in two homes, and they would like to heal the rift, to meld the family into one whole biological unit. It takes a long time for children to give up that fantasy.

According to Sara McLanahan and Irwin Garfinkel, in their book *Single Mothers and Their Children: A New American Dilemma*, children from single-mother households are less likely to graduate from high school and more likely to marry as teenagers, have children as teenagers, and divorce, than are those who grow up in two-parent households. McLanahan and Garfinkel's research shows that the negative effects persist even in cases in which the mother's income is equal to that of a two-parent family. Children are affected by their mother's stress as she adjusts to changes in her parenting responsibilities, economic standards, working conditions, and living arrangements.

Children can complicate a single mother's life; they require time and resources that are usually scarce. Children can call her away from work and social activities. They can sap her finances. They can handicap her attractiveness to men. They can misbehave. They can get into trouble at school and with the police. They can develop serious physical and emotional problems.

Children are also refreshing. They have energy. They are wide-open to the world at every phase of their growth process. They can be funny and fun. They can challenge your established worldview. They can bring new people into your life. As they grow older, they can be tremendous help around the house and, once they are adults, they can be supportive and enjoyable in many ways.

Above all else, children are family. They are someone to come home to after a day's work; someone to interact with on a daily basis, to rub smooth your rough edges, to give you polish; someone to share holidays with; someone to invest in and who invests in you;

and someone whose blood is your own, the bond that never breaks.

Nobody is perfect. Everybody makes mistakes—ex-partners, children, and mothers. It is important to allow ourselves to be less-than-perfect mothers and to know that we are not going to cripple our children in the process. You will make mistakes with your child, but if you handle them well, those mistakes may be great learning tools. Mistakes can allow children to accept their own imperfections and can strengthen the bond between you and them.

Margaret came home from work tired. Her daughter Debbie told her that she has a piano recital the next day at 4:00. "Why didn't you tell me last Saturday after your lesson?" Margaret asked. Debbie gave some excuse. Then Debbie spilled milk on the living room sofa, did a shoddy job washing the dishes, and forgot to feed the cat. Margaret yelled and sent Debbie to her room. Time passed, and Margaret reflected on the events of the day and evening. She regretted the yelling. She went to Debbie's room and said those magic healing and bonding words: "I'm sorry." Then Margaret told Debbie briefly that she had a bad day at work, which gave her a short fuse. She was able to talk calmly with Debbie about Debbie's responsibilities and how important they were in maintaining a sense of community within their household. Debbie could tell her mother what interfered with her doing a better job. Mother and daughter revealed a lot in this interaction, and together they had a better chance of understanding each other's concerns and supporting each other's efforts at harmony. Above all else, Margaret demonstrated true love and concern for her daughter.

> ▪ ▪ ▪ ▪ ▪ ▪ ▪
>
> In the end, love and concern, paired with parental control, provide a solid foundation for our children.

In the end, love and concern, paired with parental control, provide a solid foundation for our children. If a child feels unconditional love from a parent, mistakes will be forgiven. Mistakes can be learning experiences, and the bond between parent and child that results will carry them through many years and many transitions together. And when your child grows up and separates from you, that unconditional love will work like a shock absorber to cushion him against the harsher realities of the world. Your love will provide emotional sustenance, the greatest gift that a parent can bestow.

As a single mother, you need to ask yourself some important questions: *"Is my love for my child based on more than good behavior and good works?"* and *"Do I love the true identity of my child, that special part with which she was born and will die, and to which I respond in love, at some deep level, even when I am angry?"* If the answer to both of these questions is yes, then you can carry on with some assurance that your parenting, though sprinkled with mistakes, will result in a child who says yes to life.

While you are a strong influence on your child's life, you are not the only one. Other people influence your child as well—thank goodness. Your child is enriched by the love of your ex-partner and by the support of extended family, friends, teachers, and others.

But you have a limited amount of time and energy, and you have considerable needs of your own. That is why it can be comforting to recognize that your own unconditional love for your child is sufficient for now.

## Feeling guilty for being a single mother

Becky Simpson runs her own non-profit community resource center in Harlan, Kentucky, serving her poor Appalachian neighbors. Among other victories, Becky fought and won the first class-action suit against a coal company for strip mining a mountain hollow and displacing eighteen families, including Becky's brother's. Becky's legal and community work has been featured in national and even international media.

Becky has a third-grade education. As she puts it, "I thought for a long time that I didn't have no education and that I couldn't do nothin'. But then I said, 'Well, this ain't right, what the coal companies is doin' to our people. It just ain't right.' So then I started askin' questions and doin' things that I never thought I could of done in my life. I learned that if you don't have a education, you've just got to go on without it. You've just got to go on."

It's the same story with single mothers. Your child's parents don't live together with her. Her family is divided. She may relate to her father on a regular basis or she may not know who her father is. It's easy for you to feel guilty for being a single mother and "subjecting" your child to a broken home. But like Becky Simpson, you must go on regardless of your limitations. It probably means that you will have to shoulder greater responsibility in caring for your child, but you, like Becky Simpson, can prevail.

## Divorce adjustment groups

Many places offer periodic courses, workshops, seminars, lectures, and counseling to help people adjust to divorce. Some of the groups include children. Infants and toddlers would not benefit from these offerings, but as soon as your child is old enough to ask questions about your divorce, he is old enough to need some answers.

Divorce adjustment groups can help children by:

- teaching them what to expect from divorce
- giving them a place to ask questions and get answers
- introducing them to other children with whom they can share experiences.

Call your local mental health association, YWCA, a school counselor, social service organizations, or a clergy member to find a divorce adjustment group. Announcements are often made in newspapers and on library bulletin boards.

If you can't find a divorce adjustment group for children in your town, you can suggest to one of these organizations that they create one.

## The no-money guilt trip

You look at your sleeping child and think, "Poor baby. I can't afford the same lifestyle for you that we had when your father and I were together." What you're really thinking is, "I am failing to provide for you, and you are suffering for it."

Unconditional love is essential to the emotional health of your child, but it doesn't pay for designer jeans, tennis lessons, or prom dresses—or even diapers and good day care. A woman's standard of living often goes down after she divorces. That decrease often creates considerable financial strain for her and her children.

Dealing with a reduced income is never pleasant, but you can be creative about compensating for it. If you love to entertain, switch from preparing everything yourself to hosting a potluck supper, which will save both money and time Collaborate with your child to make handmade holiday cards, give gifts of time, and buy fewer clothes or fewer new clothes. If your teenager doesn't like the clothes you can afford to buy, encourage him to get a job so he can buy his own and learn useful lessons about the working world. In many small ways, you can economize to prevent a significant negative impact on family life.

The bigger ticket items often frustrate single mothers. Your child may have to move from a house into an apartment. He may not get the dance or art lessons you dream of and might not get to go on a school trip. If your child's bicycle is stolen, you may not be able to replace it this month—or next month, or possibly until next year. And God forbid that the refrigerator should break down. Or the car.

One evening, Liza spoke to a group of women about her anguish over her limited financial resources. Liza was a commercial artist. She had given up a job that paid well to go into business for herself. In spite of her high energy and hard work, the business failed. She was forced to move into a leaky duplex with her two children while she looked for another job. Meanwhile, she scrambled to meet her daily expenses.

Liza's ex-husband owned a spacious home in the country. A creek flowed across his property. The children enjoyed visiting him on weekends, exploring the small wooded area, going out to dinner, and riding with him on his motorcycle. Liza worried about the motorcycle, but in other respects, she felt, her ex-husband seemed to be a good father. "Sometimes I think I should just give him custody of the children," she said in despair. "He can give them so much more than I can."

The other women encouraged Liza to ride out her financial difficulties. She was a loving, caring mother. The children were as well off with her as with her ex-husband, the group maintained, because they were a family together. And the children needed Liza's mothering.

It is hard not to feel guilty because you can't provide all the material things you would wish for your child. But it is important to remember that we all live within limits. That father with the country home has his limits as well. Maybe he can't afford to go to Europe every year, drive a Porsche, or keep a winter home in Florida.

You may think, "Well, those are hardly basic needs." True. But life is full of many different kinds of struggles. One is learning to accept our limitations and to make the best life we can from our circumstances while we are working to improve them for ourselves, our children, and our communities. Our children need to learn to accept limitations as well. You can be an excellent role model in showing your child how to live within financial limitations and still maintain quality of life.

In the end, food, shelter, clothing, and love are our basic needs. If you can provide them for your child, you are doing your job. People live through good times and bad together, and they grow stronger for it. It's easy to dance and sing when times are good. The quality of resilience is measured in part by the woman who can dance and sing when times are bad.

My grandfather was a farmer in Nebraska. One year, all the crops failed due to lack of rain. My grandfather piled his family of six into the car and headed out to explore the Black Hills of South Dakota. Other farmers thought he had lost his mind, but he said, "Well, if you can't harvest the crops, you might as well take a vacation."

We can overcome the weight of circumstances if we can learn to accept limitations and take a vacation within the context of our limitations—a walk to the park, a shared meal with friends, dancing to the radio. Our lives together, our futures, and our potential are more important than a broken toaster, an overdue bill, or whatever may happen financially in the next six months.

## Questioning your competence as a parent

Joyce confided to a friend one day, "Sometimes I feel like I'm flying by the seat of my pants. I don't know whether I'm helping or hurting my kids." She had tough decisions to make about housing, about her job and how a change would affect the children, about what to do with a son who was bringing home failing grades, and many other issues.

> ▪ ▪ ▪ ▪ ▪ ▪ ▪
>
> We can overcome the weight of circumstances if we can learn to accept limitations and take a vacation within the context of our limitations...

When you don't know what to do in a situation, get more information. Call friends, read books, call up a school or a professional in a relevant field. If you have made a decision you are unsure of, get a second opinion.

After you have instituted a new rule, tried a new intervention technique, or initiated a new family tradition, take time out to reflect. Evaluate how successful the change was. How could it be improved? Formulate a new, revised action plan, and try that out. Reflect again on the situation. Are things getting better?

Learn to trust your instincts. If you sense trouble, confront the situation yourself or get help. If you sense your child is out of sorts, ask her, "What are you feeling right now? Do you want to tell me about it?"

From time to time, you can even ask your child, "How am I doing as a mother?" She will probably give you some interesting feedback. Reflect on that.

Give yourself a break; you're probably doing a good job. And when all else fails, call a friend.

## Self-esteem

Self-esteem is an important personal quality. People who feel good about themselves tend to do well in life. Those with low self-esteem are more likely to fail. Your child's self-esteem will play a critical role in how he performs in school, at work, and with his peers throughout life.

When you believe you are capable, significant, and successful, you have self-esteem. People who have low self-esteem feel unworthy, incapable, or unimportant. People who have high self-esteem feel they are liked, talented, and successful.

Some characteristics of high self-esteem are:
- feeling good about yourself
- being cheerful and friendly
- thinking positive thoughts, such as "I am who I am, and I am OK"
- having a sense of humor
- having a high energy level
- helping other people feel good about themselves.

Some characteristics of low self-esteem are:
- frequent anger
- destruction of one's own property or that of others
- inability to get along with others
- poor decision-making skills
- low energy level (also indicative of depression).

## SOME IDEAS TO HELP IMPROVE
## YOUR CHILD'S SELF-ESTEEM:

■ Celebrate his birthday or other important events: a new tooth coming in, a school performance, making the team.

■ Provide opportunities for her to help others. Older children and teenagers can participate in a regular volunteer activity. The choices are endless.

■ Ask your child to help you or his sibling or other family member.

■ Ask for and respect her opinions.

■ Spend quality time doing things with him, such as playing cards or other games, walking to a park, telling stories, and reading books.

■ Provide opportunities for her to succeed.  Give her manageable tasks around the house that she can learn to do well. Find out what she does well and encourage her to use those talents.

■ Be sensitive to his physical and personal needs.

■ Encourage her to perform at school or at events in your community.

■ Take time to visit his school. Most schools have evening orientation programs for parents in the fall. If you work in the evening, visit the school during the day. Some mothers work close enough to their child's school to have lunch with them from time to time.

■ Use high-esteem words and phrases, such as: great, good job, thank you, you're wonderful, I'm proud of you, I love you.

■ Avoid low-esteem words and phrases, such as: stupid, dumb, you can't do anyting right.

Children's self-esteem can take a major dive during and after divorce. Children of divorce question the stability of their family and, as a result, they question their own worthiness. As a single mother, you must provide tender, loving care to your child in order for her self-esteem to improve.

When we treat children with dignity and respect, they will find ways to solve their problems and face disappointments and setbacks. With high self-esteem, your child will have the courage and determination to achieve her goals in life.

## Affirmation

Children love positive attention, as do we all, but giving it to them is not as easy as it sounds. It requires enterprise in a way. For single parents, "Don't rock the boat" is often a basic and essential guideline. We want our children to pick up after themselves; keep themselves clean; refrain from crying, whining, failing, and fighting; do what we ask them on the first request and do it well; and give us some time and space of our own. When the children don't come through for us in these ways, they are "rocking the boat," and we have to deal with—or live with—the results. Often we deal with the problem the fast way because we have been confronting other challenges all day, at work and at home, and we are just plain tired.

If your children are fighting with each other, you might physically pull them apart and yell, "Stop fighting!" But what if they are not fighting, what if there is no problem? It takes some objectivity to realize, "Well, this is a nice quiet time," and some energy to say, "You children are playing so nicely together. Watch out, now, you may be growing up!" But do it. I guarantee you that your children will like the attention. You can almost see their chests puff out with pride.

You must take the initiative when your child behaves well. You are building self-esteem through positive reinforcement. You are providing your child with the motivation for future good behavior.

You can praise your child at the moment he behaves particularly well or you can save the praise until later. You can comment on his

**BUILD SELF-ESTEEM**
**THROUGH POSITIVE REINFORCEMENT:**

1. Make a request.

2. Wait for your child's response.

3. Offer affirmation/praise.

*Example 1*

1. *"Please do the dishes."*

2. Child does this on first request.

3. *"Thanks for helping out on the first request. It means a lot to me and to the family. You did a good job too."*

*Example 2*

1. Sibling A brings sibling B a glass of ice water without being asked.

2. *"What a nice thing to do! You're a thoughtful brother/sister."*

behavior when you sit down in the evening to relax and reflect for a minute. Invite a young child to crawl into your lap or an older child to sit next to you. Pick out some good behavior to comment on. You can also do this at bedtime when you say good night. If you always leave him with a positive comment about a specific behavior, his heightened sense of personal worth will make him feel as loved as a hug and a kiss do. Begin looking for opportunities to praise your child and the positive reinforcement will become a habit—one you'll enjoy and that will become one of your best tools to help your child feel good about himself. But keep the technique in mind: pay attention to your child when he's not rocking the boat.

## Fostering a sense of security

Sad things happen when children don't feel secure. They may tell lies because they are afraid people will not accept them if they are not perfect. They may become withdrawn because they question their own self-worth. They may become reluctant to form friendships because they are afraid that people will leave them or hurt them. They may become obsessed with consuming things, attention, and time because they feel a lack of something necessary in their lives—loving people who stick with them.

Giving your child a sense of security helps prevent these problems. Unconditional love is one element in building security. Here are some other ways to help your child feel secure:

> ■■■■■■■
> **You must take the initiative when your child behaves well.**

▪ Always let him know where you are and how to contact you.

▪ Make sure she knows how to contact her father or other available, caring person in case of an emergency.

▪ Always say goodbye to your young child when you leave him with a babysitter, his father, or anyone outside your home, even if it seems to make him sad.

▪ Talk about the importance of family with her.

▪ Let him have access to family photo albums. Look through them together from time to time.

▪ Frame a picture of her father even if he is gone from your child's life forever. Hang or otherwise display it somewhere in your home, perhaps in the child's room.

▪ Present his father in a positive light.

▪ Let her participate in some of the family decision-making, such as helping to choose a vacation spot.

▪ Give him a territory he or she can count on for privacy —a bedroom, a drawer, whatever. Let him control that space.

▪ Allow her to ask questions and answer them truthfully. Get more information if you need it. If the questions are painful, share the pain.

■ Always be honest with him. However, it is prudent to refrain from telling your child things that would be detrimental to his interests. What you do say should be the truth. He needs to trust you.

■ Try to keep your home life as stable as possible. Minimize the number of moves you make, the number of babysitters you call on, and the number of men you introduce your child to.

■ Always give your child a good night kiss and hug and say "I love you," even if she is eighteen years old. Do not wait for her to initiate this; you do it. Make it a ritual.

## School

Schools are bureaucracies, and most bureaucracies are still set up to deal with biological family units—Mom, Dad, and the kids all living together. All schools maintain records for each student. When your child enters a new school, check to make sure that the records accurately reflect your child's situation. If you have joint custody, for example, does the form show both addresses and, assuming there is a regular schedule, tell when your child is at each home? If you, your ex-partner, or the emergency contact, changes jobs or moves to another location, make sure to update records with new phone numbers and schedules.

Incorrect phone numbers and addresses cause major communication breakdowns that should be avoided for everyone's sake. For instance, some hospitals and emergency rooms will not treat minors without written permission from or the presence of a parent or legal guardian.

Your child's school performance may be affected as a result of her separation from her father, whether through death or divorce. If the separation results in tension between you and your ex-partner, your child may become occupied with her parents' problems to the extent that it affects her ability to concentrate in school; her grades may drop. She may also "act out," behaving in unsatisfactory ways.

If signs indicate that your child is in trouble at school, call the school right away. Talk with a teacher, the principal, a guidance counselor, or a social worker affiliated with the school—anyone who will listen. Find out what resources—people and programs—are available. Get to the source of the problem and work with school personnel to try to intervene. It is the responsibility of the school system to provide an education for your child that meets her needs for safety, social adjustment, and academic gain. The majority of educators believe in these goals, but they are busy people. You are busy too, but your child's performance at school should be your priority; she is in school six or more hours a day, and that's a lot of time to be miserable.

> ▪ ▪ ▪ ▪ ▪ ▪ ▪
>
> If signs indicate that your child is in trouble at school, call the school right away.

If your child is having a problem in school—and junior high school children are famous for this—it will usually take some effort to work things out. It will take patience, hope, love, charity, and time before the worst is over. You will have to have faith in the system, but also challenge it if it is not serving your child well. If she knows you are concerned enough to be working on the problem, she will know that you love her and will stick with her through thick and thin. Whatever else happens in school and out, your child needs to know that.

## School refusal

Some children develop physical symptoms, such as vomiting, that appear in the morning before school and lessen or disappear in the evenings and on weekends. These symptoms are usually caused by anxiety about school. Your child might be frightened by the experience, dislike his teachers, feel isolated from or pressured by his peers, or find the academic work too challenging. Most of these children are in elementary school, but school refusal also happens in seventh grade and the first year of high school.

■■■■ ■■■

**YOU SHOULD BE CONCERNED ENOUGH TO TAKE
YOUR CHILD TO A DOCTOR IF:**

■ There are recurrent, vague physical symptoms
(stomachache, headache, diarrhea, palpitations).

■ After careful evaluation, you can't find a physical cause of
those symptoms.

■ Symptoms are usually present in the morning on school
days.

■ Your child has missed five or more days of school
because of these symptoms.

## Too sick to go to school

Many school-age children try, at one time or another, to stay
home whether or not they are unwell. This is usually a minor problem, but it can be distressing to determine whether or not your
child is ill enough to stay home. If your child is recovering from an
illness, you also need to decide when she is well enough to go to
school. For these lesser health problems, pediatrician James W.
Cheek, M.D., offers the following medical advice:

### Objective Criteria for Keeping Your Child
### Out of School
■ fever of 101°F or more.

■ repeated vomiting, to the point that your child is
unable to keep down clear liquids, not single episodes that
may occur as a result of stress over projects, tests, or presen-
tations. In cases of stress- or anxiety-related nausea or vomiting, have a cool, rational discussion about the reasons for
the upset and reassure your child. This is a necessary part of

teaching him the importance of fulfilling even unpleasant responsibilities.

▪ other gastrointestinal upset, i.e., verifiable diarrhea.

▪ headache or other pain sufficient to prevent appropriate concentration in school-related activities, such as reading and calculations.

▪ evidence of contagious disease, like chicken pox, strep throat, or influenza.

▪ common cold, causing frequent coughing and sneezing, runny nose, or badly congested sinuses. This is a judgment call. If your child will not benefit from going to school in this condition, or if she will be an obvious health hazard to others, it would be better to keep her home.

▪ severe menstrual cramps or earache. Your child should stay home from school and you should call or see a health provider the same day.

*Activities:* When your child stays home from school due to illness, he should stay in bed. If he is well enough to watch TV, he should read or study school subjects so that he can keep up with classroom assignments and the overall aim of education.

*Extended illness:* Any illness that prevents pursuit of normal activities for more than forty-eight hours usually requires at least telephone contact with a medical provider, such as the family doctor or a hospital emergency room, to determine the need for a formal evaluation.

## Discipline

Children need someone to be in control and make decisions. You need to be that person. Above all else in dealing with your child, your word must be law. If not, you leave yourself and your child wide open for catastrophe.

Diane was a single mother whose son Scooter was three years old and out of control. Diane would say, "Don't throw the coffee cup." "Don't hit your sister." Don't. Don't. Don't. But Scooter would do it anyway. He was a charming and bright little boy who simply was not old enough to set his own limits, and Diane did not know how to help him.

Another single mother had a teenage daughter named Susan who stayed out all night whenever she chose to do so, against her mother's wishes.

Both Scooter and Susan were out of control, and their mothers clearly were not in control.

Discipline is a sensitive subject for parents. It is not punishment, but control; its ultimate

> ■ ■ ■ ■ ■ ■ ■
> Children need
> someone
> to be in control
> and make decisions.

aim is for your child to learn self-control. Discipline is a particularly crucial issue for a single mother; you may not be able to rely upon your child's father to reinforce your authority and to follow through with difficult interactions when you cannot.

When you have reached the end of your patience with your child, when he has crossed over the line of demarcation between what is OK and what isn't, when he has begun to push all your buttons and you are frustrated and angry, there are things you can do:

■ *Express anger.* It's OK to express anger, just be careful how you do. Use words that express your feelings instead of attacking the child. Say, *"I feel very angry about . . ."* instead of, *"You make me so angry when you . . ."* Try to find out how your child is feeling and why. After her feelings are out on the table, you can talk about the issues more calmly.

■ *Use Time Out.* This is an appropriate technique for both your child and for you.

When your child's behavior is out of control, say, *"I think you need Time Out. Your behavior is clearly out of control. You need to go to your room until you regain your self-control."* When you think you might lose control, say, *"I need Time Out from you. I've lost my patience and my self-control. Your behavior needs to change, because I can't deal with this. Go to your room until we both regain our self-control."* Separating yourself from your child gives you time to cool down and think about what you'll say when you see him again.

▪ *Take away privileges.* Make sure your child understands that there are consequences for her actions. *"You don't have to eat your green beans, but you can't have your ice cream until you eat your green beans." "You can't go outside to play right now because you hurt the dog." "No TV or telephone until you clean up your room." "Sorry, I don't feel like sitting by you right now. You can't be disrespectful to your piano teacher and then expect me to give you a hug. I love you, but I'm upset."*

▪ *Assign work consequences.* When you establish a rule and your child does not obey it, give him a work consequence. *"Since you didn't do the dishes last night, you can do them this morning before school, and after school you can scrub out the tub too." "Since you two are fighting, Jake, you can take out the garbage and, Laura, you can bring in firewood. You can both work off some of that energy in a more productive way."* It's a good idea to write the rules down, go over them with your child, and then post them somewhere.

If your child does a poor job with the consequence, say, *"Since you did a poor job with the garbage, you can clean up your mess and also sweep off the driveway."* Very quickly, your child will understand that the path of least resistance is to do what you ask. However, there may still be times when they choose to break the rules. No problem. They have to accept the consequence.

Consequences are appropriate for children ages five and above. You can post a list like this on your refrigerator:

- fold laundry
- set the table
- wash windows
- scrub out the bathtub
- vacuum carpet
- straighten bookshelves
- sweep walkways
- go to the grocery store
- take out garbage
- wash out the dog dish
- dust furniture
- wash baseboards
- empty dishwasher
- wash mirrors
- water plants

If you are unable to establish clear control over your child, seek help. Some sources are your child's school counselor (free), books on child care (free if you use the library), a private counselor (usually not free), or an organization called ToughLove (see page 114).

There is at least one primitive tribe that allows young children to crawl toward the fire when they get curious. They do this only once. The fire burns them, and they learn to respect their distance from it without an adult ever having to say, "Don't go near the fire."

In our society there are many hazards—from electrical sockets within reach of toddlers to habit-forming drugs available to teenagers. It would be dangerous to allow children free access to everything about which they are curious. Find situations where natural and logical consequences will teach your child a lesson; it will be a lesson well learned and you will not have to play the "bad mom." For example, if your toddler continues to ride her tricycle too fast, stop saying, "That's too fast!" Before long, she'll probably turn the tricycle over and scrape her knee. She'll slow down the next time.

Your child will learn on her own that her actions were not the best choice, and she will alter her behavior the next time. We all look back on lessons like these and say, "I learned it the hard way." And they are usually lessons well learned.

The problem with this method of discipline for most parents is that we want to protect our children from pain, rejection, and failure, and we would like to avoid our own embarrassment. You can say to your child, "I think you should do _____ in this situation. However, do what you think is best and take the consequences." The mother of a friend of mine used to say, "It's your little red wagon. You can pull it or push it, but if it breaks down, it is yours to take care of, not mine." In some situations, your child may make a good choice, regardless of the consequences you expected! Steve was a straight-A student who had some social problems. He wanted to go into the Army after graduation. His mother wanted him to go to college, but she accepted his decision. He enlisted and stayed in the Army for two tough years. He did a lot of maturing, and after he was honorably discharged, he was able to pay for his own college education. For him, it was a good decision, in part because it was his decision.

Allow your child to make some of her own decisions while she's still young. Remember, as an adult, she will be totally responsible for her own decisions and their consequences.

Some children have tantrums and otherwise rage uncontrollably from time to time. If that happens, isolate your child from everyone else and allow her to let off some of that emotional steam. A woman I know told her nephew, who growls and yells when he gets wound up, "It's OK if you need to yell. But you can do it in the back bedroom, and then, when you are finished yelling, you can come back out and be with us." He did go to the bedroom and yell until he tired himself out. Then he rejoined the group and was fine.

## Developing independence

The children of single mothers are usually more independent than children who live with both parents. They have to be; their mothers need their help. When a child can dress himself, care for his body and his possessions, and help with chores around the house, his mother's time and resources are extended. When a single mother asks her child to wash the car, it is a more serious request than when a married mother does. She has no husband to back her up or to do the job for her if her child fails to do it, may have no time or energy to do it herself, and may have no discretionary money to get it done at a carwash. Even a toddler who learns to put on a coat in the wintertime is making a valuable contribution. (And that is an opportunity for the mother to convey her gratitude to her child.)

▪ ▪ ▪ ▪ ▪ ▪ ▪

As single mothers, we need to encourage our children to be independent

But independence is more than learning tasks. It is also the confidence to launch out into the world separate from family, to risk failure in order to find success. Unconditional love and self-esteem give a child confidence to risk in order to succeed, and thus to become independent.

As a single mother, you may feel like you're in a tug-of-war regarding your child's independence. Sometimes, your child may be a responsibility that feels too heavy. Other times, they may be oh-so-wonderful company. They are a burden and they are a blessing. One single mother tells her children, "Just remember, when you're eighteen, it's up and out of this house!" She also tells them, "Oh, don't grow up so fast. Who is going to stay with me when I am an old lady?" She tells them this in humor, but there is an element of truth in what she says.

As single mothers, we need to encourage our children to be independent—to go to kindergarten, birthday parties, clubs, teams, jobs, proms, college, the world—when they are ready for each step. When you feel your child is ready for the next step, help him through it; you will be making his path in life smoother. He will carry on with or without your help, but your job is to let him go, to provide help when you can, and to wave him on with pride.

## Letting children be children

Sometimes we push too hard. We expect too much from our children. We need them to always be responsible. We need them not to make mistakes. But they will make mistakes. They will forget to take books to school, to tell you someone called, to pack their toothbrush for camp. They will wet their pants. They will spill, stain, break, be silly or obnoxious, and do so many things that you know they could avoid—if only. If only they were always careful, thoughtful, mindful, sensitive. Well, we need to remind ourselves that the job of children is to become careful, thoughtful, mindful, sensitive. Once they have done that, they are adults. Meanwhile, they have a lot to work on, and we have to give them some slack in what we expect of them.

If you find yourself snapping at your child a lot, if she makes you more angry than pleased in general, then you need to work on your relationship. Think about whether you are expecting too much of her. It's a question well worth asking from time to time, especially in regard to your oldest child, who paves the way for younger siblings.

Make sure that you do not allow your child to become your caretaker or your counselor. If you have a problem with alcohol, drugs, or your emotional health, you need to get help for yourself from a professional. To delay getting help is to burden your child with the responsibility of taking care of you, which may adversely affect her future relationships.

If you've had a hard day at work, it is fine to come home and say to your child, "I've had a hard day at work. I'm beat. My boss/secretary gave me a hard time." It is a mistake, however, to involve your child in your problems—at work, with her father, or whatever—if your child feels that you can't handle the problem and she has to find a solution.

Sometimes you can burden your child and not even know it. Bridgette had been having financial problems since she left her husband five years earlier. She and her daughter, six-year-old Kerry, were living in a house with a broken window, faulty plumbing, and other problems. Bridgette's dismal living conditions did not stop her from writing inventive romance stories, using her considerable imagination. Kerry was the practical one. She reminded her mother to lock the door. She reminded her mother where she had put and forgotten things around the house. She wrote out a Christmas list for Santa Claus that included a play sink, stove, and refrigerator, along with a tool set to fix things around their house. Had Bridgette inadvertently allowed her daughter to carry too heavy a burden? You call it.

## Male role models

Regardless of your relationship with your ex-partner, you probably will want your child to have male role models. Family, friends, and lovers are the three easiest options. Choose men who have a genuine interest in your child and who like to spend time with him. A single mother quickly learns which men enjoy her child's company, and which see him as an interruption or an irritation. Children know who likes them and who doesn't; you can't force friendly feelings. Keep your social relationships completely separate from your child when they involve men who do not enjoy his company.

Your son, especially, may need a relationship with a male role model. They may need to spend time together away from you. Identify a male relative or a friend and suggest that to him. A romantic partner may be uncomfortable with that kind of a responsibility because it hints of commitment for which he may not be ready.

There are also buddy programs in many cities that provide male role models for children, especially boys. Big Brothers International is one such organization. They will be listed in the phone book. They often have more requests for big brothers than they have volunteers, but you can ask that your child be put on a waiting list. This is a good opportunity to match your son with a caring man. Some of these relationships last for years. Make sure that the man who is paired with your son has been carefully screened; ask what the screening process entails. See also "Child abuse and neglect" at the end of this chapter.

Some boys who play team sports become very close to their coaches. Other boys find role models in scout leaders, their best friend's father, or an older brother. You might be able to find a teenage boy who can serve as babysitter and role model simultaneously for your son.

Fathers (or father substitutes) and sons share gender-based experiences and worldviews just as mothers and daughters do. While a boy relates to other boys as he grows up, it is beneficial to have a mature male from whom he can learn how to be a man—one whose values and motives you approve of.

## Homework without war

One Atlanta single mother who has adult children said this about homework for junior high and high school children:

"It's even more important for older children to do their homework before anything else, including telephone or TV, and that the groundwork has been laid for self-imposed good study habits before children are subjected to the incredible peer pressure that begins at eleven or twelve.

"Crack a textbook or two yourself so you can discuss the Magna Carta, isosceles triangles, and cell division. Keep kids talking and their worldview will reach to Tibet. You'll also end up discussing what Susan said about Karen, why all the guys hate the new phys ed teacher, and how gross the lunches are. You want curious, fired-up kids who love learning? Teenagers who are not secretive? Learn with them.

"The point really is, if your children's homework is interesting to you, if they perceive that their job—and school is their full-time job—is as important to you as yours, then they will take responsibility. Your job is to get them to that point, not to make them drudges or one-dimensional scholars, but to realize that their future really is in their own hands.

## HOMEWORK BASICS: WE WORK BEFORE WE PLAY

### For children

- Set up a study area, even if it's the kitchen table.
- Make sure the area is well lit.
- Choose the right time to study, then stick to that schedule. An excellent time is as soon as you get home.
- Get rid of distractions. Some people need quiet; others like soft music.
- Look for motivation, such as receiving praise from a teacher or parent or feeling good about yourself. Remind yourself of that motivation.
- Do the hardest work first.
- Repeat work out loud. Verbalizing helps you learn.
- Take breaks (after fifteen minutes for first graders, longer periods for older children). Stand up, stretch, get a drink or a snack.
- Check your work.

### For parents

- Help your child set up a system that works for him.
- Monitor your child's homework habits from afar, once the pattern is set. Avoid criticizing her methods as long as the work gets done.
- Let your child know that homework is a top priority in your home. It comes before friends, TV, or other recreation.
- Stop by your child's homework area and pat him on the back from time to time.
- At the end of each session, ask your child to show you what she has done, show genuine interest in her work, and praise her effort.

(Adapted from *New York Times* columnist Dr. Lawrence Kunter.)

"You can't preach educational values; kids instill them in themselves early on. Your part is to be the cheerleader, the self-esteem booster. Stress the knowledge, not the grades."

This same mother encouraged her own children to watch local and national news on TV, to read newspapers (beyond the sports page and comics), and to read books for fun.

## Child abuse and neglect

Child abusers harm other people, even people they profess to love. Many single mothers have difficulty maintaining personal control and balance in their lives. This, we know, is due in part to difficult circumstances at work, at home, and with their ex-partner. The pattern is often that the boss yells at the mother, the mother hits the child, the child kicks the dog. It's a pattern of violence that must be broken *before* it gets to the child.

Sometimes even the most rational of mothers feels dangerous and destructive urges toward her children. *"I felt like I was going crazy. I was sick of the kids, sick of talking to them, sick of seeing their faces."*

Children are an increased burden for single mothers. Your ex-partner is no longer readily available to help. You may have full custody of your child, and your inner resources may become stretched to the limit. Your child's constant needs can overwhelm you. You need only one irrational moment to lash out at your child—emotionally or physically—to damage her. And your own need for sexual intimacy may, in times of extreme fatigue and stress, cause you to reach out to your child for sexual gratification of one kind or another.

If you live with a man who takes on the role of stepparent as a result of his presence in your home, he may or may not have your child's best interests at heart. He may become an emotional, physical, or sexual abuser. You may suspect this but ignore it because of your own strong need for a companion.

The first function of a mother is to protect her children from harm. This includes hunger, overexposure to weather, and *abuse from others and from herself.* Child abuse and neglect creates emotional scars in our children, scars that will never go away. As adults, these children may fall prey to alcoholism, eating disorders, compulsive behaviors, or other addictions that begin as coping mechanisms.

Violent criminals often were abused as children. Adults who were abused as children are far more likely to continue the cycle of violence than adults who were not abused. It is too easy, in the privacy of your own home when no one else is watching, to verbally batter and denounce your child, to hit or beat your child, or to engage in inappropriate rubbing, hugging, and kissing. *It should not happen.*

**If you know or even suspect that you or someone else is abusing or neglecting your child, please get help today for your child and for the abuser. You can make an anonymous call to the National Foundation for the Prevention of Child Abuse (see Resources), and they will help guide you and your child to a safer, better tomorrow.**

▪ ▪ ▪ ▪ ▪ ▪ ▪

The first function
of a mother
is to protect
her children
from harm.

# CHAPTER 5

# Your Children
# And Their World

The family meeting

Having fun
   with your children

The family with others

Volunteering builds
   good citizenship

Getting your child
   to help around
   the house

Creating new
   family customs

Saying good night

Societal pressure

The haves and
   the have nots

Jobs

School—work—play

## The family meeting

Consider meeting once a week at a regular time with your children to go over business—perhaps Friday night. You and the children are finished with a week of work and school and are ready for the weekend. You can gather together, even if it's just you and one child, to discuss whatever is on your minds. If you run the meeting like a business meeting, you can also teach your children useful professional lessons.

Open the meeting formally. Designate a chairperson; it can be the same person for every meeting or you can rotate responsibility among family members so that everyone develops leadership skills and feels a sense of community and ownership in the meeting.

A simple agenda might include:

■ *Weekend and short-term plans* Give your children a glimpse into what you, they, and their siblings will be doing in the immediate future. Not only will they know what you are doing right now, but also where you are going to be in the next few days. They may have questions about your activities, and this is a good time to talk about them. When those activities occur, the children will have a better sense of what's going on.

■ *Old business* This includes anything discussed in a previous meeting. For example, if you and the children discussed a family vacation in the last meeting and you have more information now, bring it up for discussion. Or if a child is unhappy with a schedule set up last week for doing dishes ("I have to do them on Saturday and Sunday when we use more dishes. Cherrie gets to do them on Monday and Tuesday when we mostly use only plates."), you can reconsider the schedule based on the new information.

■ *New business* Now is the time to discuss anything that hasn't been brought up before. For example, Jeremiah might express his anger that his sister is going into his room and playing with his things when he is not at home. Or Natalie may want to stay up later at night, or receive a higher allowance, or feel angry about being yelled at on a particular occasion. Discuss whatever is on your child's mind.

■ *Bad news/good news* Each person should express one bad thing that happened in the past week ("Ronnie Meyers tripped me on the way to school this morning.") and one good thing ("I think my math grade is coming up this time, because I got an 86 on the test this week."). Some children have difficulty thinking of items to discuss. Often, if you give them a few minutes to think about it, they can come up with something. This part of the agenda gives everyone an opportunity to share the lives of family members outside the home.

■ *Adjournment*

■ *Refreshments and family activity* After the meeting is over, it is important to devote some time, even if only a few minutes, for the family to have fun together. Make it a tradition—have ice cream sundaes after the meeting, look through the photo album, play a board game, dance, read a story together, or whatever you like.

The family meeting can be a time to set rules and allow your children to negotiate with you a little. It gives your children a forum to discuss problems and feelings with you in an atmosphere that is more emotionally neutral. Your children must be able to trust other family members to listen to their concerns and discuss them without becoming angry. If you feel yourself becoming angry, table the matter at hand until you can discuss it calmly. This is a time to listen, negotiate, find consensus when possible, reach resolutions, and share.

Initially, your children will not understand what the meeting is supposed to accomplish. After a few meetings, they will catch on. You may hear some resistance from them. But if there is an atmosphere of love and trust, they will greatly appreciate the forum.

Here is one mother's agenda, the list she jotted down during the course of one week to bring up at the meeting. During that week, a couple of incidents involving her children's friends caused this mother to want to take a look at how and when her children related to friends and establish clearer guidelines with the children:

*Family meeting agenda items*
- bath rules
- rules for when Mom is not at home
  - how far to roam
  - having friends over
  - asking permission
- rules for having friends over (supervised)
  - by day
  - by night
  - how far to roam (with permission)
- mail rules
- other new business
- weekend plans
- hugs
- soft drinks
- dancing

## Having fun with your children

Kids bring energy, innocence, a fresh look at the world, skills, talents, dreams, and companionship to the family structure. They can be a lot of fun. Talking with them and spending time with them builds intimacy and teaches them how to be intimate with their own families when they are adults.

With this in mind, the Single Mothers Group of Vanderbilt University developed the list below for use in Nashville, Tennessee. Many of the ideas can be adapted for use in other towns:

*Free and Cheap Fun*
- Eat popcorn and watch movies on the DVD or VCR.
- Go to museums or historical sites; many are free or inexpensive.
- Watch planes at the airport.

- Attend story hour at the bookstore.
- Fly kites.
- Go to a pet store—the next best thing to a zoo.
- Feed the ducks at the park.
- Try ice skating, roller skating, bowling, or tennis.
- Play kickball, soccer, or badminton.
- Go to junk stores and flea markets.
- Take a bike trip with kid carrier and picnic.
- Scratch your child's back and let him scratch yours. Rub each other's feet.
- Go for a walk in your neighborhood.
- Attend a semi-pro, high school, or college baseball game.
- Play miniature golf.
- Go to the library.
- Tour a factory; many manufacturers offer free tours that are very entertaining.
- Play squirt bottle tag in summer.
- Wash the car together.
- Turn on the music and dance.
- Attend free outdoor concerts during the summer.
- Wade in a creek.
- Climb trees.
- Put on swimsuits and run under the lawn sprinkler.
- Cook together.
- Play card or board games.
- Attend craft fairs, street fairs, and festivals.
- Go jogging or walking together in the neighborhood or on a school track.
- Sing songs.
- Fish at a nearby lake.
- Go camping.
- Sit outside at night and tell stories.
- Go on a hike.
- Collect items for arts and crafts.

## The family with others

It's wonderful to have family and friends with whom to share your child. It's good for children to be part of a larger group and share its concerns. You can promote common goals and common values. It defines your family as part of a larger group.

Within the context of larger groups, you can play together, worship together, volunteer together, and sleep overnight together with family or friends. (Avoid including casual romantic friends.)

## Volunteering builds good citizenship

Volunteer work is an excellent way to teach your child to value her blessings in life as she works to make life better for others who are less fortunate. Contact United Way, your church, a social service agency, the mayor's office, or other organizations to find a place where you and your child can volunteer together. There are many one-time opportunities, if you and your child aren't ready for an ongoing responsibility, and many projects that can utilize people of all ages and abilities. Volunteers are almost always people who like children.

When your child reaches age thirteen, consider requiring her to do forty hours of volunteer work during the school year and forty hours in summer. Many private schools require volunteer work hours for their students at a charity of the student's choice. These schools know that voluntarism builds character; it paves the way for a child to become an adult who continues to practice philanthropy.

People who volunteer and donate to charities make the world a better place. You and your child working together can be part of that effort. And it just feels good.

## Getting your child to help around the house

Many daily chores, like feeding the cat, can be done according to a schedule and established rules. Your child may be resistant when you assign non-routine jobs. Explain to him that he is contributing to the community of his family. Use these guidelines to involve your child in household responsibilities:

■ Tell your child that you need his help; you can't do it all by yourself.

■ Let her know what specific tasks you expect of her with each job.

■ If you agree he can do a task later, get him to commit to a specific time and then hold him to that time.

■ Tell her to let you know when she finishes each task because you want to inspect her work.

> ■ ■ ■ ■ ■ ■ ■
>
> Traditions define
> who we are
> as family.

■ Praise him when he follows through with a job assignment and comment on the quality of his work, his contribution to the family, and his personal growth.

■ Give her a special reward when possible.

When these guidelines don't work, try assigning consequences. Remember that all children prefer a neat and clean house and a parent in control.

## Creating new family customs

Diane said, "The first Christmas after we split up, I went out and bought the kind of Christmas tree Dave used to get and put it up in the living room. I bought the same kind of lights that Dave used to put on our tree. I bought the same colored balls and tinsel. I started putting all this on the tree, and then I thought, 'I'm doing everything just the way Dave used to do it. This is absurd. I didn't like it then, and I don't like it now. I can set up a different kind of tree.' And then the whole holiday season took on a new sense of beginning."

Traditions define who we are as family. You may feel sadness and a sense of loss when your family traditions change. But this is also an obvious time to modify some of your traditions to suit the needs of your new family structure. And anything goes. Now you have complete freedom to design new traditions involving food, family, friends, decorations, and other details. If you and your child like to go for a bicycle ride every Sunday afternoon, you can do it. If you want to order pizza every Friday night, you can do it. If you want to invite a foreign college student to share your family's Thanksgiving meal each year, you can do it. Whatever heightens your pleasure in family and life, you can do. Your family will benefit.

## Saying good night

If you have pleasant childhood memories of a parent tucking you into bed, you know how important bedtime can be in conveying a sense of well-being to a child.

From babyhood to age eighteen, bedtime rituals usually decline. This is a shame; bedtime is a nice time for parent and child to share. Teenagers need attention from their mothers as much as infants do—not physical maintenance, but mothering. So here are a few things to keep in mind for your child at every age through high school:

▪ Read a bedtime story. Turn off the TV and allow time to read to her; as she gets older, the books just get more interesting. Have her read aloud to you. At age four, the book might be Margaret Brown's *Goodnight Moon*; at age seventeen, it may be Stephen King's *It*. Select a book you and your child can enjoy together.

▪ Tell your child about something he did during the day that pleased you.

▪ Give your child a kiss and a hug.

▪ Say "I love you."

▪ Tuck your child in. A teenager may prefer bedtime privacy in her room; save a bedtime tuck-in for when you sense she has had a bad day, then ask, "May I tuck you in bed tonight, just like old times?" Sometimes the simplest gestures

—like a hug or a tuck-in—are better than therapy or confession.

## Societal pressure

Social pressure is part of everything from country club membership to toys advertised during cartoons. Our society is full of over-consumers who shop until they drop. Teens and preteens cruise the malls ceaselessly. Window shopping is an acceptable date activity for adults. When our clothes go out of style, we discard them; garage sales feature yesterday's treasures that have become today's trash. Yesterday's high-tech computer has been bumped by the new generation. On and on it goes, the buying and selling of merchandise that quickly becomes outdated.

Fast-paced consumption of goods works against the typical single mother who is struggling to meet financial commitments. Valuing people above things helps to simplify our lives. It is important to:

▪ recognize the areas of our lives where we over-consume and try to cut back

▪ value things for their function first and their newness second

▪ be creative in making our environments attractive and in maintaining quality interactions with family and friends that are not dependent on heavy outlays of money.

## The haves and the have nots

You don't want your child to suffer in any way. She may already have suffered through the divorce or separation process, and you probably feel some regret about that. But to the extent you can protect her from harm and deprivation, you will. This includes keeping her from feeling poor, even though your income may have been reduced after you separated from your ex-partner.

This probably sounds familiar to many single mothers: "Mary Beth's birthday is coming up, and I've got to give her a big party.

We always give her a big birthday party. But I just paid a car repair bill, and I'm a month behind on two other bills. I don't know how I'm going to pull off that party, but I'll find a way."

It is a tribute to single mothers that they manage to hold their families together financially through hard times, especially in the first five years following divorce. Somehow, children continue to receive their allowances, dance lessons, camps, travel, and new clothes. Meanwhile, their mothers brown-bag their lunches, use fingernail polish to stop the runs in their nylons, skip some haircuts, do not go out at night, and cut corners and juggle finances in order to make sure their children do not go without.

Five to eight years after you become a single mother, you may be in better financial shape because you will be over the initial financial hump of setting up a new household. You may have received promotions or raises or found a better-paying job. You may have formed a romantic relationship with another man, and you might be benefiting financially from that relationship.

But during the initial difficult years, you may feel guilty when you have to say no to your child. Maybe you can't get the allowance together one week, and you have to ask her to wait. (If you ask her to wait until the next paycheck, you must be sure to pay her at that time. Demonstrate that you follow through on your word, so that your child will become someone who does the same.) Maybe you have to reduce her allowances for a while. Maybe you have to buy ice cream at the store instead of taking her out for dessert. The best thing you can do is to explain calmly that you need to cut a few corners to ensure that you have enough money to meet all the family expenses.

Jennifer told her children that, due to her reduced income, the children could only pick one new item of clothing for the new school year. The daughter chose a pair of designer jeans. The son chose a jacket with the right brand name and look. The mother purchased the other clothes they needed at discount stores and used clothing stores. The two children valued their chosen clothes

## HOW TO FIND CHEAP CLOTHES:

▪ Investigate discount stores.

▪ Shop the February and July sales, when you can find new clothes 50 to 75 percent off.

▪ Check out Goodwill and consignment stores. These places always carry some designer label clothes that were given away by an affluent family. To be successful, you have to go once a month or so, and it helps to have an eye for good design so that you can find the diamonds among the coal.

▪ See if you can get hand-me-downs from relatives or friends.

▪ Approach someone you know and suggest a barter arrangement, trading clothes for skills.

▪ Put up a note, with your name and phone number, at a grocery store in a wealthy area of town. State that you would like to buy used clothes and which sizes you need. Do the same in the newspaper classified ads one Sunday; this costs money, but if you connect with someone, you save a lot of money very quickly.

▪ Pass on your child's good clothes to another single mother.

much more than the whole wardrobes they had been able to buy before the divorce.

An eight-year-old boy was embarrassed by a tan, secondhand raincoat bought at a used clothing store across town. He was somewhat mollified when his mother explained it was highly unlikely that any of his friends had previously owned the raincoat. She stopped worrying when, the next morning, he raised one arm á la Peter Falk and said "Well, Mom, here goes Columbo!" and ran out the door into the rain to catch the school bus.

I remember another mother, Maxine, who seated her two oldest children, ages twelve and ten, at the dining room table and showed them on paper what the monthly budget was. The children saw that every month their mother fell $25 behind in basic expenses. After that, there was much less "I want" this and that and "Why can't I have that?" It was one of the best economic lessons the ten-year-old girl ever learned. She began to respect not only the power of money but also the effort her mother made every day when she left for work. That little girl grew up to be the author of this book.

Children are both vulnerable and resilient. If your child is well fed, warmly dressed, safely housed, and well loved, doing without for a period of time can teach her about economics, sacrifice, the value of love over things—and the strength of riding through tough times together.

## Jobs

When your child gets to be about ten years old, he may want to start earning his own money. At first, he may think any money he makes is a good deal. Then when he starts comparing his earnings with his friends, he'll find that some jobs pay more money than others. Another good economic lesson.

The first question he may ask is, "How much do I charge?" He can ask around at school and get the latest information on fees. Or he can call up businesses listed in the Yellow Pages and ask how much they charge for the same services; these businesses usually employ adults, however, and can charge higher fees.

There are many jobs that children can perform:

■ *Babysitting.* The American Red Cross has chapter offices in many towns that offer a six-hour course called Babysitting. Girls (and some boys) age eleven and up are taught basic safety, diaper changing, children's activities and games, and other skills. Some chapters offer a referral service to match babysitters with prospective clients who have been screened by the Red Cross. Cost of the course is minimal.

As the mother of the babysitter, you must screen your child's potential employers—name, address, phone number, occupation, ages of children, and references from another adult whom you know and trust—before you let her babysit for them. When you don't know the people, meet them first and decide if the family is suitable. As a parent of a minor, you have the right and responsibility to monitor your child's activities, including her jobs. If the first time goes well, then your child can operate on her own.

Your child should know not only to contact 911, but also where to reach you and the parents at all times while babysitting. Laura was babysitting one night about five houses down from her mother's house. When she arrived, the older of the two boys had a white cloth wrapped around his hand. The parents left almost immediately to go to a party about 30 minutes away. After they left, the son showed Laura a gash across his palm that bled badly whenever he opened his hand; he had been afraid to tell his parents for fear of punishment. The parents were still in transit and couldn't be reached, so Laura called her mother, who told her to call the emergency room for advice. They told her to bring in the boy for examination right away—but his parents must be in attendance. Laura called the parents at their party. They returned and took their son to the emergency room, where his wound was stitched shut. (Apparently, he was a frequent visitor.) Even though Laura knew to call 911, her first call was to her mother. It was fortunate that Laura had three numbers to call in case of an emergency: the hospital, the party the parents were attending—and her mother's.

Your child can find babysitting jobs by calling family friends (or having you call on his behalf) or advertising in your workplace and in your neighborhood. For safety, do not let your child go to the homes of strangers.

■ *Yard work.* Raking leaves, mowing lawns, and other yard work is good exercise and can be good money for a

teenager. Your teen can go through the neighborhood looking for the lawns that need mowing, and offer his services.
Teenagers should have had some solid practice at home
before attempting to do someone else's yard. It's also a good
idea to find out if your teen might be expected to do heavy
lifting beyond her musculoskeletal capacities. Teenage boys
do not have the strength that men in their twenties have.

▪ ***Teenagers can design their own summer job*** so that
they can work and play on their own schedule. Many jobs
require unskilled labor; they may be time consuming, and
(in the summer) hot, and some adults are happy to have
someone else do it, such as:

- Walking dogs
- Feeding pets while owners are on vacation
- Making grocery deliveries to senior citizens
- Washing windows and screens
- Hauling away junk
- Painting fences.

Your teen should avoid overstraining (especially macho
boys ages fourteen to eighteen), second-story ladder jobs,
roof work, working with chemicals and power tools, and
overexposure to the sun. Be sure your child has adequate
health insurance in case of a work accident.

▪ ***Working for an employer.*** Federal law permits children to start working at age fourteen for minimum wage or
more. They can work in non-hazardous jobs (such as retail
work and offices) for up to three hours per school day and
up to eight hours per non-school day, up to eighteen hours
per school week and up to forty hours per non-school week.
They must work between 7:00 AM and 7:00 PM.

At age sixteen, they can work unlimited hours in any
non-hazardous job.

At age eighteen, they can work in hazardous jobs.

In addition to the federal laws, each state has child labor
laws that protect your child from possible labor abuse. Both

state and federal labor bureaus deal frequently with employers who break the child labor laws, either by design or through ignorance. It's a good idea for you, as a parent, to know the laws and make sure your child's employer adheres to them.

## School—work—play

Some teenagers, especially those who are sixteen to eighteen, can get caught up in working too many hours per week, to the detriment of their schoolwork. *If your child's grades start slipping, put a limit on her work hours until her grades come up.* That's a strong incentive for your child to pay more attention to schoolwork.

▪ ▪ ▪ ▪ ▪ ▪ ▪

Schoolwork first,
job second,
play third.

For your child's benefit, instill in her early the system of time-management priority that helps people get ahead in life: schoolwork first, job second, play third. These priorities will help your child stay out of trouble and do her best in life in many ways.

# CHAPTER 6

# Teenagers

The challenges and joys
of teenagers

Get to know your
teenager's friends

Teenagers need limits

Touching

Personal expression

Experimenting
with values

Sex

Just say "No"

Listening
to your teenager

Signs of trouble

A happy ending

The clock keeps ticking

## The challenges and joys of teenagers

Teenagers—many books have been written on the life and times of these wonderful creatures. Sometimes it seems like they come from another planet. All their glands are set on high ooze. But their energy, ready humor, and eagerness for life can be contagious.

In this stage of life, their friends take on an almost supreme importance. The herd instinct is strong, and they want to dress like, act like, and talk like their friends. They want to be with them, sometimes day and night. And when they aren't with their friends, they want to talk with them on the phone.

## Get to know your teenager's friends

Make your teenager's friends feel welcome in your home, even if you only see them in the kitchen and on the way to his bedroom to listen to music and talk. If your child goes over to a friend's house, get the friend's phone number and his parents' names. Call them up, introduce yourself, and tell them that you think it is a good idea for the parents to provide a support network for their children. Having the contact information for your child's friends and their parents will come in handy if he turns up missing one day (which can happen for any number of reasons, innocent and otherwise) and you have to track him down.

## Teenagers need limits

They need to know what is expected of them—how much work they have to do around the house, how late they may stay out, and how often they may use the car. Mothers need to maintain those limits in order to have peace of mind, keep their teenagers safe, and let their children know they love them. Limits support love.

## Touching

Many U.S. teenagers, especially boys, don't get touched much by their parents. Withholding touching is really withholding basic communication. Family therapist Virginia Satir has stated that people need twelve hugs a day for maximum emotional health. There are other acceptable kinds of touch: hair tousling, a hand resting on a shoulder, a playful punch in the arm, a shoulder or back rub, a foot massage, a kiss on the cheek, even a handshake. Teenagers get the same kick out of being touched by someone who loves them that we all do. It means, "I love you, I like you, I care."

### Personal expression

Crazy hair, dress, behavior, and music can be irritating. But what looks crazy in your home is quite ordinary at school. You can fight it or not; that is a personal decision. But if you can allow your child to express her individuality (or her group identity) through dress, hair, or music, you can save your energy for larger battles—such as grades, drugs, and sex. Consider this rule: as long as it doesn't hurt your child or someone else, or violate your moral standards, she is free to experiment. And that is, after all, what she is doing. If she confines her experimentation to dress, hair, and dance, then count yourself lucky.

A real estate agent was unhappy when his son dyed his hair blue after school got out for the summer. With tremendous personal restraint, the dad agreed to let his son keep the blue hair until school started in the fall. The son, age fifteen, had a volunteer job at a summer school for at-risk children. All the kids called him Mr. Blue. He loved it. At the end of the summer he shaved his hair to about half an inch He was cheerful, his dad was relieved, and everything ended happily ever after.

### Experimenting with values

Your teenager loves you, but it is his job to create a separate identity from his parents, so he will probably withdraw emotionally at this time in his life. It is easy for you to let go too soon, to stop monitoring your teenager; he seems so able to take care of himself. If he is showing signs of trouble, it's tempting to hold your breath, shield your eyes, and hope whatever it is will go away. But while teenagers are able to care for their own bodies and get around town by themselves, they do not always make wise choices about how they spend their time, experimenting with alternatives to your value system.

Laura was a straight-A student; her parents were divorced with joint custody. One day she brought home a report card with an F. Her father was astounded. Grades were very important to him; his world was turned upside down. When he asked his daughter why she failed, she told him, "I just wanted to know what it was like to get an F." He was not amused. Her mother was more curious than angry. Both parents were concerned. They met with Laura's teachers and the school counselor, who said, "Many of our students run into problems in junior high. Sometimes it seems like it is a normal part of the passage into high school."

> ■ ■ ■ ■ ■ ■ ■
>
> Like measles, some adolescent difficulties simply have to be borne...

Her father arranged for regular counseling for Laura, insisted she do more homework, bought her organizers, and did all he could think of to help his daughter get back to her straight As.

It did no good. She made poor grades for most of the year, to her father's frustration. She was frustrated with her situation at her father's house. Near the end of the year, her teachers told her that if she did not pick up her grades, she would not be able to continue to participate in the program for gifted students. Like magic, her grades went back up and she was back on track. Eventually Laura and her father resolved their communication problems, and she started eighth grade in better shape all around.

Like measles, some adolescent difficulties simply have to be borne; some children will suffer more than others. Beginning in junior high, teenagers can have problems.

Teenagers' biggest concerns are:

- pregnancy
- sexuality
- sexually transmitted diseases (such as AIDS)
- relationships
- birth control.

They are looking for guidance in these areas. Become knowledgeable and informed about these issues and look for opportunities to bring them up for discussion in a natural way—in response to a television program, a newspaper article, or a popular song on the radio.

## Sex

Each parent handles this subject in a different way.

Many adolescents have their first sexual encounter before they graduate from high school. As a result of this high level of sexual activity, it makes sense to give your child solid information on venereal diseases (especially AIDS), condoms, safe sex, birth control, and every parent's favorite—abstinence.

According to the National Campaign to Prevent Teen Pregnancy, 40 percent of teen girls become pregnant once before age twenty; there are almost half a million teen births each year. The United States has the highest rate of teenage pregnancy in the industrialized world.

Planned Parenthood can be a helpful organization; they have specialized in sex education for years. Local offices have free brochures available, and classes are offered from time to time on sexuality and communication.

Before you have Planned Parenthood, a church, or any other organization offer your child sex education, please investigate its perspective. It should not violate your values and it should be factual. Be aware that in some places, the curriculum for sex education classes can include subjects such as the joys of sex, the use of condoms, homosexuality, and other concepts that you may not want your child to learn. You will never know what goes on in a sex education class unless you ask. Your child is worth that investment.

Ina May Gaskin, writer, lecturer, and director of The Farm Midwifery Center in Summertown, Tennessee, writes, "From my perspective, there seem to be three distinct ways of dealing with sex education . . . *you don't tell them anything* and they learn what they can from the barn; *you don't tell them anything* but let them watch "Dynasty" and "Dallas"; and you tell them a lot."

The best way to make sure that your child gets the sex education—spiritual, emotional, physical, and social—with the dignity and protectiveness and truth that he deserves is for him to hear it from his parents.

## Just say "No"

Peer pressure is strong during adolescence, strong enough to override what your child knows you want her to do. Your child is going to make up her own mind about sex and drugs. Once you have outlined the physical dangers, the legal risks, the moral teachings, and the societal consequences, you've done all you can do.

When your child is under pressure to have sex, one of the best responses she can give is, "I'm not ready for that yet." No matter what her partner says, she can simply reaffirm, "But I'm not ready for that yet." It's a nice way of saying no. If someone rejects your child because she says no to drugs or sex, then that person does not respect her right to make her own decisions and is not a worthy friend. Your child already knows the risk in losing a friend by saying "no." Foster your child's self-esteem, listen to her, and praise her efforts to question authority (which in this case is her peer group). You are supporting her efforts to achieve autonomy, and you are increasing her chances of becoming a strong, healthy, and independent adult.

## Listening to your teenager

The best way that you can encourage your child to open up to you is to take what he says seriously and respond with respect for him. Try not to be personally offended by what he says. A Washington

State mother says of her daughter's teenage years, "I learned not to let her bait me." If you disagree, state that calmly and coolly, along with the reason why. By the time children are fourteen, they are making up their own minds about things, and all you can do is continue to present your values, your reasons, and your life view in a calm and consistent manner and hope that you and your child can maintain an open line of communication. Where teenagers are concerned, as one father said, "Make every effort to keep up that communication with your child, 'cause you can lose it quickly."

> ■ ■ ■ ■ ■ ■ ■
> Traditions define
> who we are
> as family.

It helps to keep your own sense of inner balance through these years when your teenager seems so serious about life, so emotionally charged, so cocky, and so frightened. Both you and he need that balance—plus a little humor wherever you can find it to lighten the atmosphere and enjoy each day just a little more. (See the resource section, page 322, for the book *How to Talk So Kids Will Listen and Listen So Kids Will Talk*.)

## Signs of trouble

When you can't get your teenager to behave in acceptable ways, you've got trouble. Parents typically agonize over low grades, lying, friends who are bad influences, drugs, sex, materialism, skewed values, and not knowing where their children are or what they are doing.

Here is a letter from a woman to her friend whose teenage son was showing signs of trouble:

> *I know many junior high and high school kids who have a hard time. My neighbor's daughter, for example, good-time Kimberly, has been arrested for shoplifting, has been suspended from school, and has sneaked out of the*

*house to spend the night with friends on the prowl. Her mother is afraid she will pair up with her friend and run off to another city for an adventure at some point. The mother is talking about the painful possibility of her daughter moving to a home for troubled youth because she can't control her.*

*The majority of prisoners with whom I work were hot-blooded young men when they got into trouble. School was a bore. Warm-hearted women and fast money were strong on their minds. They were looking for short cuts and were willing to take big risks and break rules. They were not asking "What's right?" or "How will this affect my loved ones?" but "How can I have a good time, get what I want and not get caught?" They made mistakes because they weren't willing to walk away from trouble—but that's the price of freedom.*

*A few of the inmates are very bright. Prison is a kind of time out to reflect on how they intend to live their lives in order to achieve their goals. That's somewhat idealistic, but operative. But as one of my favorite inmate friends says, "Hell, after I was in here for a week, I knew I wasn't going to do something to get me back in prison again. They could have let me go." He has been incarcerated four years and is up for parole next month. In so many ways, he's a nice guy.*

*All I know is that teenagers have to go through their own processes. They are making their own decisions. By age sixteen, they are already set in their world view until a pivotal experience comes along to jar them into rethinking that world view. I think one of those pivotal points is moving out of their parents' house. Another is having a child. It all works on us to sand off the rough edges. Here I am, forty-one years old, and I'm still learning, still trying to fine-tune my own process.*

If you suspect your child is headed in the wrong direction—"acting out," withdrawing from family and friends, or refusing to go to school—explain your concern and get information from a school counselor, your child's physician, the police department, drug testing centers, a shelter for runaways, or other residences for troubled youth. Professionals who are used to dealing with troubled youth will be able to give you some immediate feedback about your problem and give you some helpful options in dealing with the situation. Keep on calling different resources until you get some answers that make sense.

*TOUGH*LOVE is an organization for parents who are having trouble controlling their children. The organization has published several books, which have sold hundreds of thousands of copies. They have support groups in many locations across the nation as well as a website, www.toughlove.com. The philosophy of the organization is that being tough is sometimes the best expression of love: "Tough Love may not work for every child, but it works for every parent." *TOUGH*LOVE has some answers for children who will not abide by house rules. Parents receive support from other parents and learn techniques that have worked for other parents: behavior modification, methods for enforcing loving limits, and much more. Some members even provide contact information so that you can get in touch with them in an emergency.

Your troubled teen can benefit from talking things through with other troubled teens, expressing his anger, sorting out his values, and admitting his problems. There are teen support groups led by competent counselors in many towns. Call your local mental health agency to find a group in your area.

### A happy ending

Gina was out of control. By age sixteen, she had been in trouble at home, at school, and with the law. Her mother was unable to set effective limits. After the third time Gina ran away, her mother had the courts declare her uncontrollable. She became a ward of the state's Department of Human Services, and a social worker was assigned to her case. That same day she was given a drug test; she tested positive. Her social worker placed her in an in-patient drug rehabilitation facility in a rural area, paid for by the state. Gina completed the program (including some school make-up work) and was moved to a highly structured group home where she attended school and received intensive counseling, which the hospital determined was the next important step. Gina told her mother, "If I had not come here, I don't know what would have happened to me. I felt like I was going crazy. I didn't know how to stop."

Gina's mother had to entrust her daughter to the care of professionals who were able to help. Though mother and daughter both missed each other, they also knew that Gina had to go through a process of recovery. Giving up custody did not mean giving up loving or giving up communicating. Both mother and daughter benefited from the process.

## The clock keeps ticking

By the time your child is a teenager, you have only a short time left with her. Your goal is to raise her to lead an independent life, which means that she will probably leave you eventually, either to work or to attend college. Sometimes remembering how soon she will be gone gives you a little more patience, a little more understanding, and a little more grace under fire.

Where teenagers are concerned, as one mother said, "It's amazing how smart I'll be by the time they are twenty-five." Another mother says, "My children put me through the grinder and polished off all my rough edges. I'm a different person and a better person for it. Now I'm in good shape to enjoy my grandchildren too." For most of us, it all happens in a blink. Enjoy your teen.

# CHAPTER 7

# Child Care

## Choosing a preschool or child-care center

Without child care, a single mother with young children can't work outside the home, but finding quality care at an affordable price is difficult. Many single mothers are forced to choose child care on the basis of 1) price; 2) available space; and 3) quality—in that order.

True stories:

▪ When Mandy went to pick up her daughter one evening, the babysitter said she was closing down her operation immediately. Mandy would have to find another sitter; the babysitter had a new job outside her home.

▪ Neb worked nights at a convenience store. She was in danger of losing her job if she couldn't find a sitter for her daughter right away. A friend told her about a family on her street who babysat. Neb took her daughter over there that night. There were no other children. She felt funny about it, so she called two hours later to check on her daughter. No one answered the phone. She left work to check it out. When she got there, a neighbor told her that the people "took the little girl and left in the car." Neb panicked. She called the police. Later, they found the couple at another house in the neighborhood. Neb snatched her daughter and left. To this day, she feels that the couple was planning to sell her daughter through a black market adoption.

> ▪ ▪ ▪ ▪ ▪ ▪ ▪
>
> As mothers, we need to shift our priorities and look for quality care first and an affordable price second.

As mothers, we need to shift our priorities and look for quality care first and an affordable price second. If you have to settle for less than ideal care initially, then keep looking around for another caretaker that offers better services.

**HERE ARE SOME WAYS TO LOCATE CHILD CARE:**

■ Make a list of child care centers and providers you already know of in your community or near your work.

■ Ask for recommendations from neighbors, friends, and coworkers.

■ Call the Department of Human Services for a list of providers in your area.

■ Check the Yellow Pages.

*When you call a potential caregiver, find out:*

■ availability (There may be a waiting list.)

■ hours

■ fees (There are often discounts for a second child.)

■ additional costs, such as those for supplies or overtime.

Make appointments to visit the child-care centers in which you are most interested. After you find a program that you like, drop in unannounced and review the facility again. Plan an extended visit to the center or home with your child before his first full day so that you and your child can get to know the caregiver. This visit will ease your child's adjustment into the new program.

## Evaluating the facility

Make sure to consider the following:

■ *Licensing Programs* that provide care for five or more children are required to be licensed by the state. These standards are for your child's protection. You can find out what constitutes minimum standards in your state by calling the

Department of Human Services. Make sure the center you are looking at is currently licensed.

Centers with fewer than five children are usually operated in private homes. Some of these caregivers apply for licenses, as well, for business reasons. If you are considering a home setting that does not have a license, you will have to monitor standards yourself.

▪ *Staff* Check the education and experience of the director and staff. Ask about annual training, staff development, turnover, and employee references. Day-care staffers rank in the lowest ten percent of U.S. wage earners; this contributes to an average turnover rate of as much as one-third of the staff per year.

▪ *Adult-child ratio* State licensing requirements vary. A guiding principle is the lower the ratio, the better. The State of Tennessee offers the following:

| Age | Required | Recommended |
|---|---|---|
| 6 weeks–15 months | 1:5 | 1:4 |
| 15 months–35 months | 1:8 | 1:6 |
| 3 years | 1:10 | 1:8 |
| 4 years | 1:15 | 1:10 |
| 5 years | 1:25 | 1:15 |
| 6+ (after-school care) | 1:25 | 1:15 |

| Group sizes | | |
|---|---|---|
| 3 years | 20 | 10 |
| 4 years | 20 | 15 |
| 5 years | 25 | 15 |

▪ *Operations* Look for posted menus, planned activities, and daily schedules. Ask about written policies, discipline guidelines, and emergency procedures. Ask to see the kitchen while a meal is being prepared and check out the bathroom the children use.

▪ *Outside play* Inspect the playground and equipment for safety and maintenance. Ask if children go outside each day. Make sure they are never left unattended outside or inside.

▪ *Field trips* Ask if and how you are notified before each field trip or activity away from the center. Check transportation safety. Are there seat belts or car seats? There should be twice as many adults supervising as there are children.

▪ *Parent involvement* Investigate opportunities for parent involvement and communication. Do you feel welcome when you drop in early? Can you have lunch with your child? Are parent conferences encouraged? Is there a newsletter?

▪ *Special activities* Many large programs offer dance, music, gymnastics, computer classes, and other activities. Are the teachers in these enrichment programs trained to work with children?

▪ *Your child's temperament* Will he enjoy the benefits of a larger program with more activities, or will he be more comfortable in a smaller environment?

▪ *Your impressions* Does the caregiver seem like a competent, dependable, and caring person with whom to trust the care of your child? Trust your instincts.

## ASK THE FOLLOWING QUESTIONS
## OF ANY CHILD-CARE PROVIDER YOU ARE CONSIDERING
## FOR YOUR INFANT OR TODDLER:

■ Is a professional—someone who knows about infants and their development—overseeing the facility?

■ Is there a high rate of staff turnover? It is important for an infant to have a consistent relationship with one adult. Positive bonding and attachment will provide her with the emotional security and energy she needs to develop well. High staff turnover is detrimental to bonding.

■ Is physical punishment of any type used? If so, look elsewhere.

■ Are bottles propped or lying in cribs or playpens? Feeding in this manner can result in ear infections, strangulation, and an insufficient food intake.

■ Are parents required to label bottles, food, and clothing to avoid mix-ups?

■ Is there a refrigerator in the room so caregivers don't have to leave children unattended to get bottles and food?

■ Are the crib sheets changed and laundered as needed?

■ What is the procedure for toilet training? Children should not be forced to sit on the potty for long periods of time.

■ Is there a specific area for diapering? Is it located in the same room as a hand-washing facility?

■ Is there a tightly covered container with plastic liners used for diaper disposal? Is it inaccessible to toddlers? Is it emptied twice daily into an outside, covered garbage receptacle?

## ASK THE FOLLOWING QUESTIONS
## OF ANY CHILD-CARE PROVIDER YOU ARE CONSIDERING
## FOR YOUR THREE- TO FIVE-YEAR-OLD CHILD:

■ Are positive self-concept and independent growth promoted through self-help skills, decision making, and problem solving?

■ How is language development fostered? Children should be encouraged to participate in conversations and discussions, offered activities with books and flannel boards, and given opportunities for dramatic play and questioning.

■ Are children allowed creative expression through arts, music, exploration of environment, and play?

■ What techniques are used to teach art? The ideal program will involve creative exploration of materials, with limited use of worksheets and teacher-made products.

■ Are there opportunities for community awareness through field trips, parental visits, and teacher use of community resources? Have the teachers, through observation of children, developed a curriculum that is challenging and based on individual and group needs, interests, and abilities?

■ Does the program emphasize sharing, waiting turns, and the enjoyment of being an active participant in a group?

■ How do kindergarten and first-grade teachers in public schools rate this facility in terms of other children's school readiness after having attended the facility? Call or visit with the principal of one or more schools in your area to find out.

## ASK THE FOLLOWING QUESTIONS
## OF ANY CHILD-CARE PROVIDER YOU ARE CONSIDERING
## FOR BEFORE- AND AFTER-SCHOOL CARE ASSESSMENT:

■ What are the hours of operation?

■ What provisions are made when school is closed because of holidays, snow, school vacation days, and teacher professional development days?

■ Does the care center provide transportation for the child to and from school?

■ What are the fees? Is there an extra charge for extended days (when the center is open all or half of a normal school day due to early school dismissal)? Is there a late fee when you pick up your child after the center closes?

■ What is the daily schedule? How does it change on extended days?

■ What are some of the planned activities? Are children required to participate in planned activities or do they have a choice about how to spend their time at the center? Are they encouraged to do their homework before they play? Can they watch TV? If so, what programs do the children watch regularly?

■ Are there toys, games, and books available that interest your child, and are they age appropriate?

■ Are there opportunities for learning new skills? Taking responsibility? Being involved in community activities such as Scouts, sports teams, music, or drama lessons? Doing homework? Being alone? Choosing between active and quiet activities?

*(Source: The Nashville Association on Young Children in cooperation with the Department of Human Services)*

## Health care provisions

Find out about any child-care center's policy for children who become ill on the premises. Is there an area where staff can isolate a sick child from others? Are children encouraged to wash their hands, with increased frequency for those with runny noses? Are all parents notified when communicable diseases become apparent among children who attend this program?

## Sniffles day-care programs

More and more cities are offering day-care facilities for children who are mildly ill with earaches, stomachaches, colds, and sometimes—when children are no longer contagious—flu, chicken pox, and measles. A registered nurse oversees the children. Regular day-care centers will often know of the sniffles program, if one exists in your area.

## Babysitters

Professional babysitting services are expensive, but there are other options. If you are lucky enough to have relatives to help with babysitting, treat them like solid gold. A lot of babysitting is done by junior high and high school girls and boys; this is usually more affordable than a professional adult babysitter.

If you need to find a babysitter, consider the following approaches:

- Ask teenagers who live in your neighborhood.
- Look for advertisements posted on bulletin boards at local grocery stores or apartment complexes.
- Advertise for a babysitter on the same bulletin boards.
- Ask for referrals from other parents in your neighborhood.
- Call the junior high or high school in your school district; the guidance or vocational counselor may keep a list of students who babysit.

■ Call job placement offices at your local college or university; this is usually more expensive, but can be a reasonable option.

Your community may have a babysitting exchange—a group of parents who agree to babysit for each other for free. Participants agree to a system under which each family provides and receives an equal amount of babysitting services. Depending on the exchange rules, you can take your child to the sitter's home, have the sitter come to your home, or use a combination. The sitter may or may not bring her children along if she comes to your house. While time-consuming, this is a family-oriented and free way to approach babysitting. The children get excellent adult care by experts—other parents. Fathers as well as mothers often provide care. If your community does not have an exchange, think about starting one. You could even set up an exchange with just one another parent.

## When is a child old enough to stay alone?

Single mothers often feel considerable pressure to leave their school-age children without adult supervision because child care can cost so much. Many of them—often called "latch key" children—stay by themselves after school before they are really ready; their mothers often feel guilty. Many parents believe that their children are ready to stay alone once they are in seventh grade. Even more affluent families, for whom money is not the deciding factor, may feel this way.

Regardless of your family's financial status, the decision to allow your child to stay home alone should be based on the best interest of your child, not financial consideration or peer pressure. This decision will depend on your child's maturity, the time of day, the length of time he will be alone, and your comfort level. Your child needs to be emotionally ready to handle being alone; if he is afraid, he is not ready. You can test the waters by leaving your child alone for half an hour during the day on the weekend. Gradually increase that time until you stay away for the amount of time that your child would be alone on a typical school day. Always do this during the day. Children, even teens, often fear staying alone at night.

## When your child begins staying home alone

Teach your child appropriate safety precautions based on where you live. You may want to cover some or all of the following subjects:

- strangers: at the door and on the phone
- fires
- knives and scissors
- tornados, earthquakes, and any other natural disasters
  that may occur where you live

More importantly, your child needs to learn to deal with "What if..." situations. Ask her a variety of questions, such as *"What if a man with a briefcase asks you to open the door?"* or *"What if a woman and a child come to the door?"* This strategy will help you and your child develop strategies for similar situations, should they occur.

As soon as your child gets home, she should call you at work. You need to know where she is at all times. Keep in regular contact by telephone. Post emergency numbers at the telephone and make sure that your child knows which number to call for what: 911, your work, her father or another relative (if appropriate), and perhaps an adult friend. It is best if that friend is a neighbor who lives nearby and is usually at home in the afternoon.

Emergencies will not be your child's greatest problem—loneliness and boredom will be. Develop a list of activities with her that she can do to keep busy; after-school centers have a daily schedule of activities for the same purpose. Limit the time that she can watch TV. Reading, drawing, working on the computer, fixing a snack, washing the dog, putting away the dishes, talking on the telephone with a friend—these activities and more will keep your child occupied and happy.

Be clear on rules about having friends over, playing outside, and fighting with siblings. When two or more children are in the home after school, decide whether or not the oldest child is in charge. Is she ready for this responsibility?

## Summers: beyond day care

Start forming your summer plans in January, regardless of what those plans are. Talk to your ex-partner about his vacation plans and how the two of you can work together. If your ex-partner is the type who says, "I don't even know what I'm doing next week, let alone next summer," you've got to work with that. Make your plans and double-check them with him before you put your money down.

When your child no longer goes to after-school care during the school year, he may resist going to a day-care center in summer. Explain the difference between staying alone all day long, day after day, all summer long and staying alone for a few hours after school. Your word should be final; if you've decided on day care, that's it.

You have options. You can split up day care and self-care, putting your child in day care on Mondays, Wednesdays, and Fridays, and allowing him to stay home alone on Tuesdays and Thursdays. Some centers will allow this, especially if you can pair up with another parent whose child needs care on Tuesdays and Thursdays. This compromise works well because it offers your child some variety in his schedule.

Think about the summer as an orange—in sections. Fill each section with a different activity so that your child won't become bored with his routine. Besides day care, self-care, and paid jobs, consider volunteer jobs, camps, visits with relatives and friends, and family vacations.

■ Volunteer jobs offer good opportunities to serve other people, which also promotes self-esteem. Hospitals, day-care programs, museums, and other organizations use teenagers and sometimes younger children as volunteers. To identify volunteer opportunities, contact the American Red Cross, your mayor's office, the YMCA and YWCA, your child's school counselor, and some county or municipal agencies. Think about your child's interests and how he might apply one of them to a volunteer situation. Some volunteer jobs turn into paid part-time jobs as the child gains experience.

■ There are many options for camps, including day and overnight; prices vary from affordable to expensive. You can find out about opportunities in your area by talking to other parents. The YMCA and the Boy Scouts and Girl Scouts all offer summer camps. Area churches and synagogues often have summer programs and some of them are free. Many day-care centers offer summertime activities that are more like day camps than babysitting. Children go swimming, attend movies, visit zoos, and play sports and other outdoor activities—all at prices that can be lower than those for private camps.

When considering a camp for your child, think about these variables:
- price
- number of campers
- gender and age of campers
- length of stay
- activities offered
- facilities (cabins, tents, river, ocean, mountains, bathrooms, etc.)
- structured and non-structured time
- adult-child ratio.

Some camps hire former campers to return the following summer as Counselors in Training, with a reduction in fees in lieu of wages.

Look for *The Summer Camp Handbook* by Thurber and Malinowski, which is very helpful when preparing for overnight camp (see Resources, page 322).

■ Your child can stretch her travel wings in a supportive environment by visiting relatives and friends. Airlines are wonderful about supervising children who travel alone. Bus and train travel can work well for teenagers for short trips. Check websites or call companies' toll-free numbers for more information on age and other restrictions for children traveling alone. Fully explore safety requirements and assurances.

■ Family vacations offer opportunities for bonding. Everyone needs a vacation, a time to get out of town, away from the telephone and heavy responsibilities—even you. If you are low on cash, borrow a tent and take a two-day trip to a state park with your children and perhaps another family. Let the children help plan the details, pack for the trip, and pitch the tent! For a list of your state's parks, e-mail, call, or write your state tourist information bureau. While you're at it, ask for other opportunities in your state. Your local Chamber of Commerce and the American Automobile Association may also have information.

Traveling can be stressful. To maximize your pleasure:

• Prepare well in advance.

• Notify your employer as early as you can.

• Don't overload yourself with extra work before or after the trip; leave notes for others to handle your projects while away.

• If you have to leave a phone number where you can be reached, make it clear that you should be called only in an emergency and define an emergency.

• Resist the urge to call the office to check in.

• Allow a day before you leave to pack and another day before you return to work so that you can unwind and relax.

# CHAPTER 8

■ ■ ■ ■ ■ ■ ■

# Life with Dad

Life without Dad

Talking about
  your ex-partner

Your relatives and
  your ex-partner

Love game

Tales of two houses

When your child
  doesn't want
  to visit Dad

Maintaining
  communication
  when the children
  are away

## Life without Dad

Fourteen-year-old Michael said to his father, "My life has been kind of rough—you and Mom arguing and all, and then you left us." Michael's mother actually left his father and took Michael with her. So even though Michael actually moved out of the house, his perception is that his father left him. Even though Michael sees his father every weekend, he still feels that his father, in some way, is gone.

Seeing your father is not the same as living with your father. There is a justifiable sense of loss when a child has a part-time relationship with a father. This feeling is intensified if his father lives in another town, if visits are few or irregular, or if there is no communication at all. It is natural for your child to feel abandoned, to feel cheated, to feel unloved and unlovable. It is so important for a single mother to find ways to support the relationship between her child and his father.

## Talking about your ex-partner

When you talk about your ex-partner—and his new wife, if there is one—separate your view of him from your child's. If you bad-mouth your ex-partner, you will hurt your child. As long as he's not dangerous to the children, you can scrape up a positive image—not perfect, necessarily, but positive—for your child. Even if he has abandoned your child, you can say, "Who knows why people leave? I know it wasn't because you are not lovable. Sometimes, people like your daddy have problems that take them away from people they love."

## Your relatives and your ex-partner

When you met the person who is now your ex-partner, you were a package deal, the package being you, your history, your friends, and your relatives—your connections to these people that preceded your ex. Enter Mr. Right, who then became Mr. Wrong.

Now you deal with the leftovers. He is the father of your child and, ideally, one of the two most important people in your child's life. He also has a relationship with your relatives.

That relationship may be negative. Perhaps they view him as more of a liability than an asset. They may wish he were not a part of your life and the life of your child. Whatever help and support your relatives give you is good news. However, their advice on how to deal with your ex-partner should be taken with a grain of salt. If they pressure you to take your ex back to court, to deny him visitation, or to interfere with his communication with your child, then they may be encouraging behavior that is counterproductive to your relationship with him. If you feel your relatives are doing this, tell them that you have heard their advice, that you will make up your own mind, and that you consider the topic closed. Hold the line. Look into the face of your child, know that he needs a father in his life, and make a few reasonable sacrifices and compromises toward that end. Yes, even if he doesn't reciprocate. Building bridges is always better than building a war zone. Take the high road.

▪ ▪ ▪ ▪ ▪ ▪ ▪

> Building bridges is always better than building a war zone.

What if your relatives *love* your ex-partner? Maybe they didn't want you to separate. Relatives! You can't live with them and you can't live without them.

P. J.'s parents embraced her husband from the day they met him. After the divorce, they repeatedly urged P. J. to reconcile with him. They would invite P. J. and her children to dinner and she would discover that they'd also invited her ex-husband. They honestly believed that their daughter had made a terrible mistake. He was a good man and a good provider and father in every way—except that he had affairs with other women. Ooops! P. J. loved her parents dearly and supported her ex-husband's relationship with her children; she had to stand firm for a few years before her ex-husband and her parents got tired of trying to engineer a remarriage.

Sometimes a single mother finds herself dancing the star role in a tragi-comic ballet. All the players—her children, ex-partner, and her relatives—are onstage, but they're each dancing a different ballet. The dancers keep bumping into each other. Over time, they get tired of the bumps and bruises and realize that they have to work together. The dance becomes a smoother and more enjoyable performance.

If your relatives do not like your ex-partner and are pressuring you to behave in a way with which you are not comfortable, don't talk about him with them. If they do like your ex-partner, encourage them to develop their own relationship with him apart from you.

## Love game

Your child may try, consciously or not, to play you and your ex-partner against each other. He might say, *"Daddy lets me ride my bike across the street [so why don't you?]." "Daddy takes us to get ice cream cones every day [so why don't you?]." "I never have to make my bed at Daddy's house [so why do you make me?]."* The unfavorable comparisons can go on and on, and the underlying implication is, *"I like life with Daddy better than I like life with you."*

One way to deal with that is to acknowledge the differences. *"Your daddy and I both love you, but we are different people, and we make different choices about what is best for you. Your daddy has his rules; I have mine. We both love you. Meanwhile, you get to experience two different ways of doing things. When you're grown, you can raise your children using some ideas from each of us."* Your child may grumble, but she will know that you cannot be manipulated in this area. Regardless of how they respond, children like parents who have the last word.

## Tales of two houses

Your child may stretch the truth about what Daddy does or doesn't do. That's one reason it's wise to communicate well with your ex-partner. Your child might be doing the same thing with him. The next time you talk with your ex-partner, you can ask him about any conflicting stories. Together you can confront your child with the discrepancies. False statements will become less frequent if he knows you are double-checking.

## When your child doesn't want to visit Dad

*I hate it over there. There's nothing to do.*

*All my friends are here. And there's going to be a great party at Jennifer's house Saturday night. Do I have to go?*

*Dad just doesn't understand me. It's like I never do anything right over there.*

*Sometimes I feel like my head is going to burst over there and I just can't take it anymore. I've thought about, maybe, hiding.*

It's painful to think about your child going into a situation that is boring, unsatisfactory, or even hurtful. It throws you into confusion. On the one hand, you could use a parenting break and your child needs to spend time with his father. On the other, you want to protect your child. Immediately, questions arise. "Is he neglecting our child?" "Is he mistreating our child?"

What you need is more information. Get it from your child and from your ex-partner.

When your child doesn't want to visit Dad, ask questions like:
- Can you give me specific examples?
- How often does this happen?
- When do you remember feeling this way the first time?
- Are there things about your father's house that you do like?

Tell your ex-partner what your child has said and ask for his response. Consider giving him some support by saying something like, "Look, I'm not trying to criticize you, I'm just aware of a problem with Rick, and I think we need to find out more about it so that we can help change his attitude for the better. What do you think?"

Your ex-partner might make a few trial changes based on what your child has said. He might want to talk with your child about the problem. You and he might agree to reduce the length of visits temporarily to see if that helps or to break up a single long visit into two shorter visits. You might reschedule the visit to allow your child to accept another invitation. Your child might bring a friend along the next time for a change of pace. Help your ex, if he can accept help, by offering him a list of suggestions of activities to keep your child from being bored. A list is a good idea because it is unemotional; it can be a permanent reminder of things he can do to keep his child happily occupied. Sometimes we all need to be reminded of simple things to do, such as playing computer or board games, taking bike rides, making dinner together, climbing a tree, and so on.

Children and parents sometimes go through spells during which communication becomes difficult. These pass. Remember: part of being a family is living through the tough times together. The bad times count too. During those times listen to your child, sympathize with his feelings, and don't make a judgment against the father. Instead, say something like, "I need more information. Maybe there's a way we can work this out. I know your father loves you, and that you need to be with your father."

At some point counseling may be necessary for your child and his father. Try whatever works. If nothing works and you feel strongly that it is warranted, deny visitation and see a lawyer.

The goal is not to separate your child from his father, but to promote a family relationship in his father's household, as well as in your own. It cannot be said enough: children need fathers.

## Maintaining communication when the children are away

We all like to get mail and phone calls from loved ones who are far away. When your child is away from either parent for an extended period, he needs to hear from them.

Here are a few suggestions that have worked for other mothers; they can work for fathers as well:

■ Call your child, and be sure she is allowed to call you—collect if necessary—when she wants to. It is important for her to hear your voice. If she is too young to talk, sing to her or recite nursery rhymes. While her father may initially resent this intrusion, without some opportunity for contact with you, your child can feel cut off.

■ Send books, T-shirts, and other gifts.

■ Write letters. One parent puts four letters in one envelope so that each of her four children will get a letter at the same time.

■ E-mail your child, regardless of his age; include the address of a website offering fun activities for children.

■ Send postcards from each place you go with a little story about what you have seen; your child may want to collect these cards.

■ Draw stories in pictures with simple captions to send to a young child who's just starting to read.

■ Cut pictures from magazines, glue or tape them to paper, and make up a story to go with them, perhaps offering a choose-your-own ending. This is a good project for birthdays and holidays.

■ Choose a theme, such as bears, and send a series of cards featuring different images of bears every few days.

■ Send a photo of yourself. One child said on the phone to her mother, "Mommy, I can't remember what you look like!" Her mother sent her picture to be put by her bed.

■ Record yourself. If you send a book, accompany it with a recording of you reading it aloud. For older children, read a "letter" to them into a tape recorder. They can send you one back on the same tape.

■ Film yourself. Get someone to run the camera to shoot you, then take over for a film tour of the house, or something else of interest. Schools often have video equipment and sometimes they will loan it. You can also borrow one from a friend or rent one. Check in the Yellow Pages under Video Rental.

■ Visit him for a few hours or overnight. This is especially important for a preschool child if he is gone for more than two weeks. It's important for him to see you so that he will know you have not abandoned him.

■ Write letters and don't send them; keep them. These letters are like journals; they allow you to bare your soul to yourself and to your child—even if she is too young to understand. It helps you feel connected with your child. Ten or twenty years later, share them with her.

> ■ ■ ■ ■ ■ ■ ■
>
> In your child's heart, there are no territorial privileges.

It is important—for both you and your child—to communicate with him in person and while he is away. This goes for fathers as well. In your child's heart, there are no territorial privileges. There is ample room for everyone who loves him. Whenever you find a useful new idea to promote communication between you and your child, share it with his father, for the child's sake.

# CHAPTER 9

# Taking Care of Yourself

"No wonder
I'm frazzled!"

Support group

Self-esteem

A sense of self

Euphoria

Grief

Loss and depression

Turning around
a blue day

Anger

Assertiveness

Stress

Action/reflection
cycle

Fear

Defining your needs
and goals

Learning to say "No"

Asking for and
accepting help

Crisis times

Journal writing

Counselors

Spirituality

Ritual

Exercise

Nutrition

Alcohol and drug abuse

AIDS

Other sexually
transmitted diseases
(STDs)

Breast exams

Pap smears

Healthy body/
healthy mind

Fourth of July—
bombs boom in my ear.
Firecrackers crackle and dance.
The street zings alive with freedom.

I'm waiting for tomorrow.
Light up the sky with L-O-N-E-L-Y.
Let the chemicals of my frustration
burst upon the sky in green orange red.
Send up a rocket for my children to ride
high beyond the limitation of their mother.

Fire cracker snapper
spill your pungent smoke
upon the wide-open black night
and FREE Free free ME Me me NOW Now now

**"No wonder I'm frazzled!"**

A typical single mother's day might look like this:

■ Get yourself and the children ready for work / day care / school. (*"Who left their dishes on the table?" "Have you brushed your teeth?" "Where's your other shoe? Has anyone seen Joey's shoe?" "We're late. Hurry, hurry, hurry."*)

■ Overload at work: gossip, misunderstandings, meetings.

■ Go to Kmart on your lunch break to pick up a couple of sale items, then on to the bank, even though you are due back at work.

■ Rush to the day-care center after work to pick up the kids.

■ Stop at the gas station to fill up so you won't have to do it in the morning. (The kids are saying, "I'm hungry, Mama, what's for dinner?" and you don't know yet.)

■ Drive home, pick up the mail, and get everyone and everything inside the house.

■ Dump the mail and the packages and think, "I'll deal with that later." (Meanwhile, the children are dumping their coats, shoes, and school items in the same manner.)

■ Figure out a quick-fix dinner in the kitchen and get it going.

■ Sit down to eat thirty to forty minutes later. The kids are talking over their days, laughing, fighting, spilling, or saying nothing. In ten minutes, they are done and gone from the table. You eat on in silence. "Can we watch TV?" the children ask. "Yeah," you answer.

■ Still left to do: dishes, children's baths, bedtime routines, maybe laundry and ironing. You may or may not do these, depending on how you feel.

■ When the children are in bed, the house is quiet. Maybe peaceful, maybe lonely.

Throughout the day, you have been planner, organizer, manager, and support staff. You have been mother, father, teacher, nurse, chauffeur, detective, judge, employee or employer, consumer, and friend. You are tired. And tomorrow you will get up and do it all over again.

Thank goodness mothers are often young, because they need all the energy they can get to handle all of their responsibilities. And, of course, single mothers usually shoulder those responsibilities alone. On some days, your energy ends before your responsibilities do. It happens to everyone, though we all try to prevent it.

In order to maximize your energy level for every day, you need to understand and take care of your most important asset: yourself. In order to do your best, your emotions, your spirit, your body, and your mind must work

▪ ▪ ▪ ▪ ▪ ▪ ▪

But there is great strength in belonging to a group.

in harmony. If you can say at the end of the day, "I did my best," then you have prevailed. We all have to live just a day at a time.

## Support group

Our society has overdosed on the "I, me, my, mine" philosophy. "I get mine first, and if there's any leftover, you dogs can fight for it." We are urged to be strong and told, "Do it yourself." Commercials plant self-indulgent appetites in us. TV programs and movies push violence and sex. These aspects of our culture promote the individual as opposed to the group.

But there is great strength in belonging to a group. When you are weak, the group can carry you until you regain your strength. You can find companionship in a group, people with whom to share the events we all experience. Being part of a group makes the journey of a single mother so much more comforting, like salve on a burn.

Single mothers often feel isolated. Their need for group support is as strong as at any other time of their lives but they often remain isolated, not knowing how to locate a support group. They suffer needlessly.

For a solid support group, identify five or *more* good people with whom you can spend time, even by phone, and talk over your problems. Ideally your group should include at least one man and at least one other single mother. He'll give you the male perspective, and she'll know exactly what you're going through. Write their names down; if you can't come up with five, then keep your eyes and heart open for opportunities to recruit a few more. Look at people in your community who warm up to you, people who have befriended you in the past, people whom you trust. Approach them and start a conversation. If they listen to what you say and seem genuinely interested in you, and you respond in kind, you are already developing a support relationship. If you have five supporters, then when one is out of town, one is sick and one is not at home, you still have two to call.

These are people with whom you can share your deepest, darkest secrets, your fears, your questions, your complaints, and your uncertainties, and they will not turn you away or turn away from you. Because they care about you, they are willing to invest in you, and you will invest in them as well. They will act as your emotional shock absorber, so that if you feel high or low, you can ask them to listen and give you feedback. Use them for emotional burdens, friends to go places with, one to exercise with, one to worship with, all *to* call on in case of an emergency—whatever your support needs are.

## Self-esteem

If your self-esteem did not take a severe dive when you separated from your partner, you are the rare single mother. In all likelihood, much of who you were—your sense of personal identity—was tied up with the life you led before. You probably need to redefine yourself. When you can let go of the past and redirect your view to the present and the future, then you can define your important new roles. The healing process takes time. Allow yourself time. Learn to value the little things you do. Sometimes just getting out of bed in the morning is an accomplishment.

## A sense of self

Educator and theologian Howard Thurman talked about a healthy sense of self being composed of two dimensions of experience:

■ *Self-image:* what we get from interpersonal relationships, seeing ourselves as others see us, and

■ *Self-fact:* that immutable piece of self that undergirds all of our life processes; who we are when we strip away our partner (or ex-partner), our family, our friends, our job, our home and car and all our possessions; who we are that does not change with the years.

> ■ ■ ■ ■ ■ ■ ■
>
> Often we hear more from other people about who we are than we hear from ourselves.

A healthy sense of self is really these two parts—the self-image and the self-fact—pulling against each other. We can go too far in either direction, relying too much on other people's opinions of us or engaging in narcissistic "navel gazing."

It can be a worthwhile exercise to spend two hours all alone and without distractions meditating on the question "Who am I?" After a two-hour session of reflection, one woman's description of herself was, "I am a person for whom truth and beauty are essential. I love art. I need gentleness and peace in my life. I shy away from people, but I watch them all the time. I believe in the goodness of people and that, in the end, goodness will prevail. I am not very disciplined, but I have a strong will. I am a strong person. I have certain talents. I care about other people."

Often we hear more from other people about who we are than we hear from ourselves. But only you can define your self-fact to balance your view of yourself. And knowing more fully who you are enables you to better experience and appreciate your unique personhood and to make life choices that are in harmony with yourself.

## Euphoria

Immediately after they split from their partners, many women often feel free, with the wide wonderful world just waiting for them. There is no doubt you are walking into adventure, but the territory is totally new for you in many ways, and you may miss the familiarity of the old, which is now gone forever. And you may be glad that it is gone forever, but you will grieve for it anyway.

## Grief

Every woman who loses her partner goes through a painful, yet standard, process of coming to terms with grief. She may also have lost her home, her car, her neighborhood—her entire way of life. Elisabeth Kubler-Ross, a psychologist who studied and wrote about grief, lists five basic stages of the process in her book *On Death and Dying*.

1. Denial
2. Loss and depression
3. Anger and ambivalence
4. Establishing a new identity and lifestyle
5. Acceptance of self and others.

This behavior is to be expected, and it may be helpful to know that in going through this grieving process, with all the accompanying feelings—hurt, rage, frustration, futility—you are reacting normally. There are, at the time of this writing, 9.9 million American women who are going through, or have already gone through, the same intense emotional experience.

The many changes and losses that follow the end of a relationship take an emotional toll. You will probably experience tremendous mood swings. It's similar to the physical consequences after a terrible car wreck. You go to the hospital and get patched up, but you've been broken and bruised and must heal before you are strong again. The process of grieving and healing is normal and takes time. Sometimes years.

## Loss and depression

Janine came to a meeting of single mothers. An attractive, professional woman, she was recently separated from her husband. The time came for Janine to share whatever was on her mind with the group. After three words, she burst into tears and said, "I'm so sorry. I don't mean to be going on like this. I don't usually behave like this. I don't really understand what's happening to me."

Episodic depression is one part of single motherhood. It comes and goes, depending on the big changes in your life. Some symptoms are:

- lack of appetite or overeating
- insomnia or wanting to sleep all the time
- difficulty functioning—can't get out of bed in the morning, can't change from one activity to another at work, can't get going
- somatic complaints—symptoms for which the doctor can find no cause (Internalizing stress, for example, can cause stomach cramps and migraines.)
- feeling sad and hopeless.

What can you do about it? Take it one day at a time. Sometimes just a step at a time, literally. If you feel you can't move, but you have responsibilities to fulfill, just take that first step, put one foot on the floor. That will get you up and moving.

Find or create a support group of people with whom you can share your emotions—ideally a group of people who are going through the same experience.

Give in to your need for periods of isolation. It's a part of the healing process. You may feel numb, like a sleepwalker, not emotionally there but going through the motions. Spending some time alone to reflect on life will help you sort out your experiences and give you some breathing room.

Make sure you also interact with others during this time. Participating in a faith community may help to heal deep wounds. Have a regular social life so that you can create new and good memories.

You may want to see a counselor for a while to dump all your problems in confidence and get helpful feedback. For more information on this, see Counselors, pages 161–162.

## Turning around a blue day

If your day turns blue long before your responsibilities are over, try turning it around:

■ Take a break and think. What are the good things that are happening in your life right now? What do you look forward to in the future? What are your plans and your dreams?

■ Telephone a family member or friend and say, "I need someone to tell me they love me." Unload your troubles for a few refreshing minutes.

■ Laugh. Call someone who has a good sense of humor. Ask her to tell you a joke. Laughter is wonderful medicine.

■ Go for a brisk walk for some exercise and fresh air.

■ Do something totally different. If you usually drink coffee, get a cup of tea. If you usually take a break from work with a certain person, invite a few other people to go with you and declare a ten-minute party. Call up a Porsche dealership and ask the price of a brand new car—loaded.

■ Take a mini-vacation on the Internet to anywhere in the world. Search the name of an intriguing place along with keywords like "vacation," "food," "culture," "tourist attractions," or any others that come to mind. Jennifer's mother was planning a trip to the Panama Canal, so she found the official Panama Canal website and watched the ships travel through the locks. She said it was fascinating.

## Anger

Depression is anger turned inwards. Women brought up in the United States are taught that it is acceptable to be depressed and to cry and that it is not acceptable to be angry. They may believe that angry women are bitchy women, and bitchy women are not attractive. Unexpressed anger—at your ex-partner, your boss, whomever—can have negative consequences such as somatic illnesses, depression, kicking the dog, abusing your child, and abusing yourself.

There are probably ample reasons for you to be angry—at the losses you have to endure, at your ex-partner, at what it means to be a single parent in our society.

Allow yourself to feel angry, but not guilty. Anger can be useful to motivate us and to clarify issues. Accepting your anger can help you simplify and shorten the healing process; look at that anger carefully as the first step to resolving it in acceptable ways. Only you can precisely define the source of the hurt behind your anger—the loss of your ex-partner, loneliness, money problems, work issues, etc. Ask yourself, "What can I do to make myself feel better?"

> ■ ■ ■ ■ ■ ■ ■
> Allow yourself
> to feel angry,
> but not guilty.

First of all, let go of your past life. Stop letting the man and the house and the rotten things that happened turn into hate; like acid, hate will eat you alive. Comedian Buddy Hackett said, "Don't carry a grudge. While you're carrying the grudge the other guy's out dancing." Give it up. Let it go. You need your energy so that you can look at where you are in life now and form new hopes, new dreams, and new plans. These are the bricks from which you will build your future.

Exercise and hard physical work are excellent outlets for anger. One therapist tells her clients, "Get out your lawnmower and whack off every blade of grass as if it were your ex-partner's head. Go bowling and try to knock down all the pins." Working out your anger, depression, and stress through physical energy feels tremendously empowering. One single mother got up in the middle of the night, full of anger, and attacked the kitchen floors on her knees, mopping, waxing, and polishing. And it worked. She was exhausted, but she had also gotten past her anger, and was happy with her clean floor, pleased with herself, and able to sleep like a baby.

## Assertiveness

Anger can be extremely useful in helping us function. It enables us to stand up for our own rights rather than be pushed around by other people. Many people give single mothers advice—lawyers, family members, counselors, friends, store clerks, strangers on talk shows, even authors—and much of that advice is probably well intentioned. But you must ask yourself, "What do I want? What do I need?" And when the advice doesn't match your answers, you need to stand up to everyone and say "No, thank you."

If you see something you want, or something you need fixed, you should confront people about it. If you have trouble standing up to people, you can learn to be more assertive. Many communities have classes in assertiveness training—programs that will teach you how to get your own needs met without stepping on anyone else's toes. See also Resources, page 321.

## Stress

Stress is a physical response to crisis; it sends adrenalin pumping through your body to give you the strength to handle whatever problem has arisen. This response is what allows mothers to lift cars off their children in order to save their lives. It can be a helpful surge of unusual energy. But adrenalin can also work against you—such as when your boss has dropped another special project on your desk—because you have no physical outlet for it.

Stress can manifest itself in stomach problems, Irritable Bowel Syndrome (severe abdominal pain, bloating, constipation, or diarrhea), migraine headaches, lower back pain, skin problems, and other physical discomforts.

When you feel stress, you need to identify its cause and come up with a plan for how to handle it. If you find yourself facing problems at work, for example, try to distribute your workload over a period of time, scheduling it at a pace you can handle. Tell yourself to relax, breathe slowly, move slowly, and carry on. Try a whole-body relaxation exercise in which you lie flat on your back and tighten and relax all your muscles, starting at the top of your head and working down to your toes.

■ ■ ■ ■ ■ ■ ■

Even in the midst
of war,
the generals
plan strategy
for the next battle.

Ask your doctor or counselor for more information about relaxation exercises, or search the internet. There are even mini-exercises that you can do at your desk. At home, take a bath instead of a shower, sit outdoors, take a walk, or try another form of physical exertion.

## Action/reflection cycle

Even in the midst of war, the generals plan strategy for the next battle. Sometimes single motherhood feels similar to war, and there seems to be too little time to do anything but rush around. But there is great value in taking time out to reflect on what you are doing, how you are interacting with others, and how you could do it better next time.

Consider using an action/reflection cycle to grab control of your life and move forward. When a problem arises:

- *Stop:* Get together with a friend or your support group.
- *Look:* Identify your problem.

■ *Think:* Ask yourself, "How can I do it better next time?" Get new information at this point, if you need it.

■ *Plan:* Identify your next steps.

■ *Act:* Implement your plan.

Perhaps your boss repeatedly asks you to stay late to finish last-minute projects for her; up until now, you've complied. The next time it occurs, discuss it with your friend or support group. With their help, look for options and brainstorm different possibilities such as:

■ Tell your boss you are sick.

■ Tell her that your day-care center will charge you a late fee.

■ Tell her you can work overtime twice a month (or whatever works for you) but not on a regular basis; see if you can get her to agree.

■ Check with your boss around noon to see if she anticipates any afternoon rush projects; try to get them early enough to finish by 5:00.

From these options, you might pick the last one to try next time. That's your action plan. You implement it at next opportunity. If it works, you have solved your problem. If not, you try another option. Keep trying options until something, or a combination of things, works, up to and including getting another boss.

Make time to reflect so that you can think, plan, and act.

## Fear

Some time after you split from your partner, you may feel afraid. Anything can trigger it—a movie, a story someone tells you, an unfamiliar sound. That fear may mushroom until you are overwhelmed by it. You curl up in bed; you hug yourself and rock back and forth; you experience a panic attack.

Whatever form this fear takes, it is real. It's a sign that something inside you needs some attention. In order to get rid of the fear, you have to name it. You can get out a piece of paper and write down all your fears. Everyone's list of fears is different, but perhaps yours looks like this:

- loneliness
- never having enough money to do more than get by
- something happening to the kids
- growing old alone
- illness
- losing the house
- somebody breaking into the house
- rape.

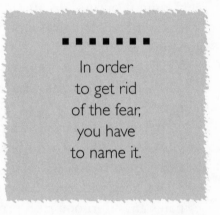

In order to get rid of the fear, you have to name it.

Look at your list and think about each item. From the list above, you could combine loneliness and growing old alone. Identify solutions to your fears. What might help your with loneliness and growing old alone? Count your friends. If you don't have enough to suit you, recruit more. A man may or may not appear, but friends will always be there for you. Every potential problem has practical solutions. While we can't always prevent tragedies, we can take preventive measures and have plans in place in case they do happen. Life goes on. People survive low points and overcome difficulties. Our friends, our minds, and our spiritual faith are powerful life tools.

## Defining your needs and goals

Mothers often operate on other people's agendas. When someone tells a mother, "I need something," she says, "What is it, and how soon do you need it?" Chances are good that she will do whatever it is, even if it means she will have to drop what she wanted to do "just this once." When you add up all the just-this-onces, you get a woman who meets other people's needs and neglects of her own.

One woman's needs list included:
- some time by myself every day
- art and music
- time to be with friends
- an exercise program
- sleeping late once a week.

Her goals were:
- to have my master's degree in five years
- to buy a condo in seven years
- to get one song recorded (She wrote songs as a hobby.)
- to get the kids through college
- to find a man.

In order to meet her own needs and achieve her own goals, she had to know what they were. So she wrote them down. Then she had to learn to focus on the goals, say no, and ask for help.

## Learning to say "No"

It's easy for us to say "no" to ourselves, but it's much harder when it's our children, our families, our friends, our bosses, and sometimes even total strangers who are asking. We want to say yes. We want to be liked. We want to help the other person; when we do, we feel good.

Instead of saying no, try saying, "I have other plans." You want to kick off your shoes and read the Sunday newspaper. It doesn't matter—that's your plan. You don't have to have a reason, just a phrase with which to say no.

A general statement like "I have other plans" is handy in many situations. It prevents the other person from trying to convince you that his need is more important than yours. Other handy turn-downs:

- I need to be at home / be alone / go out that night / rest right now / cook dinner. (Whatever your need is, state it clearly and repeat it if necessary.)
- I'm already booked solid that day.

■ I can't commit to that kind of a responsibility at this time.

■ I have to pick up my kids in fifteen minutes.

■ I don't give out my phone number.

■ I can't receive calls at work.

■ No, thank you.

■ I can't possibly afford that. (This always ends the request.)

■ I'm not interested.

No one will set limits for you. Only you know what those limits need to be, and only you can tell other people when enough is enough. Not everyone will be gracious when you say no, but that's his problem. When you meet your own needs first, you will be better able to meet other people's as well. This doesn't mean that you can't sacrifice your own needs from time to time for the benefit of someone else. But consider it a rare and precious gift. On a regular basis, sacrificing your own needs drags you down and keeps you from being the healthiest person you can be.

And the other people to whom you say no? They find other ways to get their needs met. If your child wants you to drive him across town to play with a friend, he can talk with the friend on the telephone or find another friend to play with or activity to do. Schedule a trip to the friend's house at a future time when it fits in with your plan. If a parent from your child's preschool wants you to telephone six other parents about a school program, tell her that she caught you on a booked-solid evening.

Often it's not the case that the people or the causes aren't worthy. But your needs are worthy too. If you have time and energy left over after your basic needs are met, you can use them to say yes—or no—to others.

## Asking for and accepting help

People often believe that a family should take care of its own. If they don't, then the family somehow has failed and should be ashamed. A single mother may be unable to handle every need and crisis that comes along by herself. If she becomes ill and cannot care for her children, then she needs help. If she believes she has to be a superwoman, then, even when she knows she needs help, she may be unable to ask for it.

But we don't need to be isolated from the world. If we have a support group or supportive extended family and friends, then we should be able to call on these people for any emergency.

When I was in college, I would go over to my grandmother's house to rest and relax. Grandma would hug me, feed me, love me, and let me go. Cokes were in the refrigerator, cookies in the cookie jar. It was perfect. At the end of each visit, she would hand me a five-dollar bill as I was leaving. I would protest, though I always needed cash. One day, she told me that I should take the money—she was passing on the help that had been given to her by others. She told me that a time would come when she would need my help and that she hoped I would give it. She said there would be other people, all through my life, for whom I could do something, and there would also be times when I would need to get help from other people, family or not.

> ■ ■ ■ ■ ■ ■ ■
> Ask for help
> and accept that help
> graciously …

Ask for help and accept that help graciously; it allows others to give and it makes them feel good. You don't have to wait until you are down and out to ask for things. What are your needs? Do you need a hug? Ask for one. Do you need to hear a joke? Have some fun? Find a sitter while you do spring cleaning? If you don't ask, no one will know that you need help. Translate your needs from feelings into real words that real people can hear. When you ask, give people a clear option, such as, "I need someone to keep the kids while I do some spring cleaning. If you have the time and energy, let me know. But it's OK to say no, because I have other people I can ask." This will give them an easy out, and you won't feel that you are imposing on them.

Your child is included in the group of people you can ask for help. Children over five will understand "I need some privacy." One mother drew a rough picture of herself sleeping in a bed and wrote, "Nap time for Mama." When she needed a nap or some time alone, she would tape the picture to the outside of her bedroom door, and her children would leave her alone. It takes some energy to ask your child to do things for you, but helping someone else is good for his self-esteem.

It takes courage to ask someone outside your family for help. But it is essential for you to enlarge your definition of "family" to include non-relatives who are also supportive people.

## Crisis times

You are never alone. When you feel that you are—when there is a death in the family, when you lose your job—wipe away the tears long enough to call someone. Many towns have crisis centers staffed with volunteers who are ready to listen to you and to provide you with sound advice and reliable resource people to go to if you need them. Your local police department will know the number.

For assistance with parenting problems, search the Internet, using terms like "parenting questions," "teenagers," "toddlers," or other topic-specific words.

And as always, your friends can be your best resource. If you are a religious person, a crisis time is a great time to pray.

## Journal writing

One way to get in touch with your feelings, express anger, work yourself out of a blue mood, and improve your self-esteem is by keeping a journal. When you let whatever is on your mind flow out onto paper, you find out a lot about yourself. You can clarify your thinking and make decisions. Any old notebook will do to record your thoughts and feelings. A few paragraphs a day are plenty. Even writing once a week will benefit you, though it's easier to keep at it if you try for once a day.

After some time has passed, look back through your entries. You will be surprised by how vividly you can recall events you thought you had forgotten. You will also see the progress you have made in your personal journey during a period of challenge and growth.

Caution: do not let your ex-partner find your journal; he could take it to court, which has happened more than once to other women. Put it away where your child cannot find it and read it.

## Counselors

One man says, "I went to a counselor when I was married to my first wife. We were having some problems, but by the time he got through with us, we were in the biggest mess you ever saw. I've done that once, and that's the last time I'll do it."

A woman says, "After I left my husband, I started seeing my counselor. I could tell her anything, and she helped me figure out some things. I was so confused. She even talked on the phone to my ex-husband. He wouldn't listen to a thing I said, but he listened to her."

There are all kinds of people in the world and all kinds of counselors. There are a number of different theories of counseling too.

When you look for a counselor for yourself or your child:

▪ Ask for recommendations from friends, health care professionals, and others.

▪ Find someone whose personality you like. Interview a potential counselor over the phone; after the first session, you should know if you can communicate well with him. If not, change counselors. Why throw your money away?

▪ Ask what the counseling procedure will involve and how each session will be conducted. Will the counselor give advice, just listen, confront you, or use another approach?

■ Find out how many sessions the counselor recommends, based on your stated need. Some counselors will say, "As long as you feel the need." Others might say, "Let's do eight weeks and then take a look at the situation." Short-term therapy—six to eight weeks—is more often covered by insurance.

■ Ask the counselor about her credentials—does she have a Ph.D.? An LCSW? In what area? From what institution? (Note: A degree does not necessarily mean the person is the best counselor for you. A few good counselors have no psychology degrees at all. But insurance companies will not pay for counselors without certain degrees; check with your company's policy before proceeding.)

## Spirituality

Spirituality is a part of the public and private lives of the people of every culture. The heart hungers to be filled with something beyond self, to communicate with something larger than humankind, to experience the divine in ourselves, in others, and in all of creation.

Becoming a single mother is a time of transition, full of losses and new challenges; it is natural to turn inward. You have the opportunity to reevaluate everything in your life; it's a great time to consider your spiritual nature, to look for the divine within yourself. Normally, you are probably too involved with the routines of life to reflect on your spiritual beliefs. When your routine is disrupted, you have an opportunity for deepened awareness.

There is a common bond. Soldiers living through days of life and death struggle, prisoners in concentration camps, parents with terminally ill children, and other victims of tragic circumstances speak eloquently about the meaning in their lives that is provided by a belief in something larger than humankind. It can be the greatest source of strength, ever present, limitless, and bonding us with the rest of humanity in a community of the divine.

How do you cultivate spiritual experience? You could worship with others in a church or synagogue. Allegiance to an organized religion is a way of sharing a personal credo and life values with a community of like-minded people, though spirituality is a fuller experience and a more powerful resource than simply going to religious services.

For some people, spirituality does not include public worship. Some use the earliest waking hour to read, meditate, and pray as a way of preparing themselves spiritually for the day.

Experiencing nature, music, art, and even play can allow you to focus on the connection between the human and the divine. Any activity that focuses your mind and your spirit on the expressive wonder of creation is a spiritual communion; it strengthens your life.

## Ritual

Ritual is a powerful tool; it allows us to express our feelings and our needs in community as we mark milestones in our lives. Weddings and funerals are rituals. Divorce is not a ritual; it is a legal process. There is currently no widely practiced ceremony recognizing divorce, but some women are creating their own rituals to fill this need. On the anniversary of her wedding, one newly divorced woman hosted a freedom party surrounded by friends who gave her the love and attention she needed at a difficult time.

Another woman invited her friends to a Celebration of a New Beginning following her divorce. People sat in a circle and talked about what she had meant in their lives or about how they had made transitions to their own new beginnings. It was a time of intimate sharing complete with singing, prayer, and Holy Communion.

A third woman left her partner and moved back to her hometown. She held a "House Blessing" event, which was both a party and a worship experience. People shared their hopes for her, as she began a new phase of life in a new home, and their gratitude that they could renew their friendship with her.

Some people create their own wedding ceremonies; you can also design a ritual for any event that is important to you. Your celebration can include words, music, dance, food, and anything else that best expresses the meaning of the event to you. This is one way to transform a potentially sad and self-defeating time, such as the remarriage of your ex-partner, into a meaningful and memorable occasion. You can also commemorate markers in the lives of your child as well, such as a symbolic passing into adult-hood (like a bar mitzvah) or a separation ceremony when she goes off to college.

## Exercise

Low-intensity, aerobic exercise for 45 minutes or more at a time releases endorphins, naturally produced chemicals that are similar to morphine; they can help counteract depression. To maintain your physical health, try to exercise three times per week. To improve your physical and mental health, aim for six or more times per week.

If you have trouble sticking with an exercise program, identify an exercise partner. You can help each other with discipline and make the experience more fun.

Your personality will match some sports better than others, according to an article by James Gavin, Ph.D., in *Psychology Today*. The better the match, the more likely you are to stay with your exercise program.

Before you begin a new exercise program, it is always a good idea to see your doctor for advice on recommended rates of increased activity.

## Nutrition

You should pay attention to several different aspects of nutri-tion that can affect your health and your mental state.

■ *Caffeine* can cause anxiety, jitters, nervousness, or depression when large amounts are consumed. The amount necessary to trigger such a response varies with the individ-ual; if you consume more than your body is used to, you may experience negative effects. Caffeine also keeps you awake, which is why offices usually have supplies of coffee, tea, and other caffeinated beverages. People who have migraine headaches should maintain their caffeine intake every day—weekdays and weekends—since varying consumption can contribute to a migraine.

■ **B Vitamin** deficiency can contribute to depression. Caffeine, alcohol, sugar, and stress all result in a loss of these important vitamins. A well-rounded diet, high in complex carbohydrates, should provide you with enough B vitamins for good health.

■ **Chocolate** has a physiological tranquilizing effect. Unfortunately, it also contains caffeine, sugar, and lots of calories. If you eat chocolate, the most beneficial form is dark chocolate, which should be consumed in moderation.

■ **"Too much protein, fat, sugar and salt"** is the title of a chapter in *Jane Brody's Good Food Book: Living the High Carbohydrate Way.* But that just about sums up the American diet. Fast food is fat food. But when time is short and the kids are hungry, you may have to fry up a meal in a hurry or stop by the local burger window. Life goes on. When you do this, enjoy it, but remember that our bodies are one of a kind; the better we treat them the longer they will last. Many physical and emotional problems are affected for better or worse by the fuel we put in our tanks. And, of course, our children are learning their dietary habits from us.

■ **Eating habits** can become problematic for single mothers. Make sure you don't neglect feeding yourself while you look after everyone else. Snacking can be pleasurable, but it can also become a bad habit.

Many people skip breakfast, eat a light lunch and a large dinner, and then snack in the evening. You can lose weight and feel better if you eat breakfast, a full lunch, and a light dinner and avoid evening snacks.

The best summation of weight-loss theory I have heard is simply to eat less, exercise more. A possible improvement on that formula is to eat right, exercise more.

The regular misuse and abuse of yourself does not do you or your family a favor. Make yourself a priority.

## Alcohol and Drug Abuse

Johns Hopkins University Hospital in Baltimore, Maryland, asks these questions of patients who suspect they may be alcoholic; they apply to drug abuse as well.

1. Do you lose time from work due to drinking?
2. Is drinking making your home life unhappy?
3. Do you drink because you are shy with other people?
4. Is drinking affecting your reputation?
5. Have you ever felt remorse after drinking?
6. Have you gotten into financial difficulties as a result of drinking?
7. Does your drinking make you careless of your family's welfare?
8. Has your ambition decreased since drinking?
9. Do you crave a drink at a definite time daily?
10. Do you want a drink the next morning?
11. Does drinking cause you to have difficulty in sleeping?
12. Has your efficiency decreased since drinking?
13. Is drinking jeopardizing your job or business?
14. Do you drink to escape from worries or trouble?
15. Do you drink alone?
16. Have you ever had a complete loss of memory as a result of drinking?
17. Has your physician ever treated you for drinking?
18. Do you drink to build up your self-confidence?
19. Have you ever been to a hospital or institution on account of drinking?

One YES is a definite warning that you may be an alcoholic.

Two YESes suggest that you are an alcoholic.

Three or more YESes should alert you that you are definitely an alcoholic. You should seek help immediately.

If you are not ready for Alcoholics Anonymous or Narcotics Anonymous, call up a drug and alcohol treatment center in your area and ask for phone counseling to help you decide what your next step should be.

Substance abuse is a crutch that people try to use when life becomes overwhelming; ultimately it doesn't help with the problems it is intended to address. Ask any recovering alcoholic. The first step is to admit you have a problem. The next step is to find out what your options are. You don't have to commit to a program or plan, but it's good for you to know what's available when you decide to throw away your crutch.

At the close of every AA and other twelve-step meeting, people say the Serenity Prayer: "God grant me the strength to accept the things I can't change, the courage to change the things I can, and the wisdom to know the difference."

## AIDS

As a single mother, you must protect yourself from AIDS.

One day, thirteen-year-old Lauren overheard her mother talking with a friend about death. After a while, Lauren broke in and said calmly but firmly, "Just don't die before we grow up." Since Lauren's brother Jake was ten, theoretically their mother had about twelve years to practice safe sex; then she could start playing around with risky sexual encounters. That would take Lauren and Jake through college, at which point they would be grown and able to let mom die from her risky behavior.

Morbid though that scenario is, it points out the heavy-duty responsibility that single mothers shoulder, every day, to protect and raise their children until they are grown. The National Women's

Health Network in Washington, D.C., recommends the following precautions:

■ Always use both a condom and the spermicide nonoxynol 9, found in contraceptive foams, jellies, and creams. It kills the AIDS virus on contact.

■ Use a latex condom for vaginal and oral sex. When a latex condom is used properly and does not break, the AIDS virus cannot get through. Be sure your partner is wearing the condom *before* penetration.

■ Never have anal intercourse. Condoms are more likely to break, and the delicate rectal tissue is more likely to tear; both increase your risk of infection.

■ Unless you know your sex partner is not infected, don't allow his semen, urine, feces, or blood to enter your body.

■ Do not use intravenous drugs. If you do, never use a needle someone else has used.

■ Your risk increases with each additional partner. Ask a potential partner questions about his past sexual history and drug use. If he has used intravenous drugs or had a sexually transmitted disease, he is at higher risk of carrying the AIDS virus.

■ Take every precaution against this deadly disease. Your life is much too precious to risk.

## Other sexually transmitted diseases (STDs)

The more sexual partners you have, the more you increase your chances of one of them having a sexually transmitted disease. Latex condoms protect you from some—but not all—STDs. Some common STDs are syphilis, gonorrhea, NGU (nongonococcal urethritis), chlamydia, herpes, trichomonas, and venereal warts. Of these diseases, some are a nuisance but not permanently damaging; others can cause serious and even life-threatening problems. Some are easy to detect; others have few detectable symptoms. Like cancer, the longer an STD goes untreated, the more dangerous it is to you.

The American Social Health Association says that the earliest signs of STDs occur "on or near parts of the body used in sexual activity. These include the penis, vagina, anus, mouth, or throat, depending on how one engages in sex. These early symptoms almost always will be one or some combination of sores, discharge, pain, swelling, and itching."

If you suspect that you or your partner might be infected, you should see a doctor immediately. Public health clinics are often much more familiar with STDs than a family doctor, who may see one case of gonorrhea in five years. Consider going to a facility that deals frequently with the range of STDs. You should be treated with complete confidentiality; be sure to ask about that beforehand. The laws regarding AIDS are changing rapidly, so it's best to find out for sure what your rights are. Wherever you go, make clear to the medical staff that you want to be checked for STDs; there are examination procedures and tests specifically for them.

If you need help in finding out where to go, you can call the toll-free VD/STD National Hotline at 1-800-227-8922.

## Breast exams

Breast cancer kills more women than any form of cancer other than lung. Your chances of getting breast cancer increase with age. The American Cancer Society recommends that you:

▪ Undergo yearly mammograms starting at age forty and continuing for as long as you are in good health.

▪ Have a clinical breast exam (CBE), as part of your periodic health exam, approximately every three years when you're in you twenties and thirties and every year when you're forty and over.

▪ Report any breast change promptly to your health care providers. Starting in your twenties, perform regular breast self-exams (BSE).

▪ Talk with your doctors if you are at increased risk of breast cancer (due to family history, genetic tendency, past breast cancer, or other causes). Find out about the benefits and limitations of starting mammography screening earlier, having additional tests (e.g., breast ultrasound or MRI), or having more frequent exams.

## Pap smears

When you have a Pap smear, your doctor will place a sample of your cervical mucus on a dry slide and examine it under a microscope for evidence of abnormal cells. It can be used to detect cervical cancer and some, but not all, sexually transmitted diseases; syphilis and gonorrhea cannot be detected using a Pap smear. The American Cancer Society recommends the following:

■ All women should begin cervical cancer screening within three years after first vaginal intercourse and no later than age twenty-one. Screening should be done every year as part of the regular Pap test or every two years using the newer liquid-based Pap test.

■ Beginning at age thirty, women who have had three normal Pap test results in a row may get screened every two to three years with either the conventional or liquid-based Pap test. Women who have certain risk factors, such as diethylstilbestrol (DES) exposure before birth, HIV infection, or a weakened immune system due to organ transplant, chemotherapy, or chronic steroid use, should continue to be screened annually.

■ Women over thirty can be screened every three years (but not more often) with either the conventional or liquid-based Pap test, *plus* the HPV DNA test.

For more information, visit the website of the American Cancer Society and search their site using keywords "cervical cancer."

## Healthy body/healthy mind

The fact that you have this book is one indication that you are open to growth through reading. Look for other opportunities. Keep a paperback in your purse for those occasions when you have to wait at the dentist's office or at the bank. Books and magazines in the bathroom and at your bedside are wonderful temptations. Join a monthly book club to share reading with others socially.

New ideas, new information, and critical thinking activities can be energizing and fulfilling. They make you a more interesting and attractive person to others. Many people will tell you to exercise your body, but few will suggest that you should also exercise your intellect. Make it a priority for yourself.

...exercise your intellect.

Turn off the TV one night a week and do something else. Listen to music. Write letters. Play a board game with your child. Read the newspaper, and note local lectures and art exhibits to attend. It is too easy to let whole months and even years go by without challenging your brain, occupied as it is with your work, your family, your household, and your life.

Shakespeare wrote in *The Tempest*, "O brave new world, That has such people in't." The world we live in—the seven continents and the seven seas—beats Disneyland any day. There are opportunities for excitement, adventure, and enrichment. Go, see, do, enjoy. Do yourself a favor and make time to explore your Mother Earth.

# CHAPTER 10

■■■□■■■

# Working

"What am I going to do with the rest of my life?"

Who are you?

The master résumé

Look at the possibilities

Temporary work

Plunge in somewhere and then upgrade

The minimum wage trap

Wanted: secretary

Two fallacies

Money versus meaning

Going back to school

Job searches

Creating your own opportunities

Résumé

Interview

You don't have to say yes

Taking risks

Wanting to stay home with your child

Part-time work: a stepping stone

Dealing with your emotions

Sexual harassment

Do's & Don'ts of sexual harassment

Working two jobs

The working single mother as victim

Jumping ship too soon

Time for a new job?

Loyalty

**"What am I going to do with the rest of my life?"**

Perhaps you've just decided to leave your partner (or he to leave you) and you haven't worked outside the home for a few years. Or your job doesn't pay enough to support you and your family, or your boss is on your back, or the hours are too long. The list of possible horrors goes on. You need a job—or a new job. One woman was stuck in the same boring position, with the same company, at basically the same salary, for three years. She wanted to make a change, but she couldn't decide what her next move should be. If you don't know which move to make, stay where you are until you can figure it out.

> ■ ■ ■ ■ ■ ■ ■
>
> Money alone does not provide job satisfaction.

Making good career choices is essential for a single mother. Ideally, you want a job that suits your personality and your talents, one that provides a comfortable living for your family. And you would like to accomplish this with a minimum of stumbling around in the slush of the newspaper's classified ads. If you make wise choices initially, you are less likely to want to change jobs frequently—"job hopping" does not look good on a résumé. In order to make good career choices, you need to understand who you are and then analyze your aspirations, your resources, your family responsibilities, and the mechanics of the working world.

**Who are you?**

Studies have shown that the women who are happiest with their jobs are those who like what they are doing; money alone does not provide job satisfaction. Most single mothers spend about eight hours a day sleeping, eight hours working outside the home, and eight hours with family, friends, TV, errands, or whatever. That means that, five days a week, you spend half your waking hours at work. That's about 2,000 hours a year when you can be either happy or sad.

Nancy Ransom, former director of the Vanderbilt University women's center, gave the following career advice to her three children. I have thought about it many times:

> *Find out what you like to do, and then find out how you can make money doing it.*

To find what you like to do, you need to know who you are: your personality, your talents, and your stamina. What are the tasks in life that give you satisfaction? If you do not clearly know the answer to these questions, then career counseling is the best investment you can make. It will cost you time, and it may cost you money, but find a way to get it, because good career counseling can pay personal and financial dividends for the rest of your life.

Many counselors, tests, and books are available to help you with career development. Inquire at the YWCA, the public library (which will have many books on career planning), the personnel office of your employer, or a university counseling office. The career planning process often involves self-reflection, standardized tests that assess your interests and abilities, and counseling to interpret the results of the tests. It can be a tremendous help in determining in which direction you want to move.

## The master résumé

At this point, you may want to put together a summary of all your work experience to date. Include everything, even the babysitting you did in high school—you can always take it out later. Don't worry about dates; just put everything down in chronological order, in four categories: 1) Education; 2) Paid Work Experience; 3) Volunteer and Community Work; and 4) Personal Hobbies and Interests.

Even if you already have a résumé, this master document will give you the most comprehensive view of your assets, and you can draw from it to pull together specialized résumés tailored to specific job opportunities. Always keep a copy in your files.

## Look at the possibilities

Once you have determined your abilities and interests and which jobs require them, you can identify those positions or fields that appeal to you the most. Let's say you would like to do research. Look at your master résumé and identify which jobs and interests you've held that relate to research. Perhaps you are trained as a nurse. You don't like working with patients who quickly come and go, and rotating hospital shifts do not lend themselves to easy child-care arrangements. Your master résumé lists a summer job as a research assistant for a psychological study at your university; you loved that job. You can't afford to go back to school for a Ph.D., which would allow you to become a college professor and do research. One solution would be to do medical research with a doctor at a medical school. Both your nursing training and your summer research experience would be assets.

Try to look at your experience critically and creatively to see how it can work for you in putting together an attractive résumé for a specific job. That's the first step to getting that job.

## Temporary work

Women sometimes find themselves in a crisis situation in which they realize, "I've got to have a job . . . any job." One way to work immediately is to work for a temporary employment agency. In most cases, that means clerical work, but not always. Call an agency (look under Employment in the Yellow Pages) and ask them what kinds of work and how much money they can offer you. Should they choose to work with you, the agency will place you in different temporary positions. You may be able to register with more than one agency so that you could work full time if you need to.

Often these jobs just barely keep you off food stamps (which is unfortunate, since food stamps expand your monthly food budget), but sometimes they can lead to a permanent position. If the company wants to hire you on a permanent basis, you will probably have to continue to work through the temporary agency for three months before they will release you to the new employer; then you get the higher salary and benefits. There are two problems with temporary work: no benefits and no time to interview for new jobs.

## Plunge in somewhere and then upgrade

Perhaps you've taken a position as a secretary for a company with many different departments. You do your job well, but you know you will want to make a transition to something else as soon as possible. Analyze the company. Perhaps there is a department within the company that would better use your abilities and interests.

Get to know the people in that department. They may tell you about the job responsibilities and the department atmosphere. Each department has its own personality; while yours may be tolerant or even nurturing, another, even within the same company, may be tough. Management usually sets the mood. Develop good relationships with the people in your target department; the better you know them, the easier it will be for you to break in. They might even tell you when an opening is coming up.

If you have a job but want to change employers, make sure you are improving your job situation in one or more of the following ways:

■ *Job description:* you are getting closer to the job that will allow you to use your talents and interests to the fullest.

■ *Pay:* it usually takes a 10 percent increase in pay to offset the benefits you lose in changing companies.

■ *Environment:* Investigate things like employee turnover and the reputation of your prospective supervisor to make sure you're improving your environment.

Whatever change you make, upgrade your job situation. No job need be a dead end.

## The minimum wage trap

A mother of two children who is paid minimum wage at her job is living below the federally defined poverty line. She is eligible for food stamps. After forty hours of work per week, she has little, if any, discretionary income. With the added cost of child care, a single mother working for minimum wage does not fare well.

One simple economic principle is that the lower your income, the less you can buy. If your income decreases, you have to start making choices. Do I need a car to get to work, or can I do without one? Can I get along without a telephone? Many minimum wage jobs do not offer health, dental, and life insurance, paid vacations or holidays, or retirement plans. We're talking about fast-food employees, dishwashers, baggers at grocery stores—"the working poor."

## Wanted: secretary

Have you ever heard someone say, "I'm just a secretary"? That's a woman who is not comfortable with her working image. Either she needs to change her job to one that she respects, or she needs to change her opinion of the worth of a secretary. Unfortunately, "secretary" sometimes carries a second-class connotation in our society.

This catchall job description—also known as administrative assistant or clerical worker—is a broad category. More women work in this area than in any other. The pay can be lower than many other white-collar jobs, but if you have good clerical skills, being a secretary will offer you many different kinds of opportunities.

There are many kinds of clerical jobs in many different environments—even the Foreign Service! You can earn a Certified Professional Secretary rating by going through a challenging process that requires considerable skills and carries much respect. Salary varies tremendously and is determined by the individual employer.

One woman, who had worked for years as a secretary for the same company, was offered the position of company cashier. The salary was better and the greater prestige appealed to her. She accepted. Her new job responsibilities included controlling the entire payroll for the office and factory workers, making monthly, quarterly, and annual tax reports, and doing other complicated accounting procedures. She found it very stressful and bemoaned the day she had said yes, longing for her old secretarial position that better suited her interests. Finally she retired early just to get out of a stressful situation.

> ▪ ▪ ▪ ▪ ▪ ▪ ▪
>
> If you can identify a mentor in your company who has the power to promote you, pay attention to that relationship.

While working as a secretary can be a launching pad to bigger and better things, make sure you are not moving to bigger but worse things. Investigate first, and then make a move.

## Two fallacies

Many of us are taught to believe these statements, which sometimes turn out not to be true:

▪ *"If you work hard, you'll get ahead."* You can work hard and well in your job but not get credit, in either status or salary. If you want to expand your responsibilities in your company, talk with your supervisor. If she will not develop a plan for growth with you, think about a move.

▪ *"You can't get something for nothing."* People get free rides all the time. A supervisor may promote an employee even if his job performance does not merit it, even above another employee with more skill and experience.

Make things easy on yourself. If you can identify a mentor in your company who has the power to promote you, pay attention to that relationship. When you are looking for a job, investigate the reputation of a potential employer; make sure that employees are treated fairly. Take pride in what you do and in doing your best. Take advantage of any opportunity that will make life easier for you as long as it's not illegal or unethical. You might as well work for an easy boss as for a difficult one.

## Money versus meaning

Diane was trained in a field she did not enjoy but that paid a living wage. Following her divorce, she worked for two years at an interesting part-time job while her children were young; eventually she needed a full-time position to keep it all going financially. Since she hadn't found a career she enjoyed, she said that she felt she was "evading developmental milestones. I feel like I'm in a pressure cooker. There is no time to pay my dues [retooling in school or working at entry-level positions]. The credentials I've accumulated are part of a lifelong effort to please other people. What do I want to do? How can I be me?"

Diane faced a difficult choice between using her degree to make good money in a job she did not enjoy or earning too little money at a low-level job in a field she did enjoy. She and her children lived in a cramped, old apartment. She worried about college tuition. In the end, she chose to work in a well-paying job for which she had been trained, hoping to be able to move within the institution, in time, to a job that offered greater satisfaction.

## Going back to school

Lorraine was twenty-six years old, going through a divorce, and had a three-year-old daughter. She planned to find an apartment near her job or on a bus line so that she could sell her car and live on her income as a secretary for a city real estate banking firm. Her husband had not paid child support during their separation.

Lorraine's employer offered her a sizable raise if she would complete night courses in business management and accounting. The cost of tuition, child care, and transportation forced her to moonlight, typing reports on weekends at home. She was a straight-A student. She got up at 5:00 A.M. each weekday to have two hours to study. Her daughter complained, "Mama is always too tired to play with me."

When single mothers like Lorraine go to school to upgrade their skills, they encounter problems with financial aid. There is a lack of stipend money or work-study options for a woman who must support her children while going to school. The cost of child care, transportation, books, and equipment is usually not covered in aid money. Women who need to work part time and study part time have little access to financial aid. And loan regulations are overly stringent.

Getting a degree does not guarantee you a better job, but it can help. If you want to pursue a degree or certification, there are library books that list financial aid opportunities for women. Many single mothers have made the time and financial sacrifice to go to school; once they have changed or upgraded their career opportunities, they have found greater personal satisfaction and financial reward. Keep this in mind: if you accept financial aid, you have to pay it back. If you leave school with thousands of dollars in debt, repayment will take a while.

## Job searches

Anyone who has ever tried to find a job knows that it is hard and often frustrating work. The higher the salary you need, the fewer jobs there are and the harder your search may be. If you are hunting for a new job while holding down a full-time job, you may become exhausted. But dogged persistence pays off in finding a position that is right for you.

Instead of classified ads and employment agencies, consider a more focused investigative approach. If you know what position, location, and environment you are looking for, then you can identify specific companies to investigate. Think of family, friends, bookstores, and the public library as sources of information. To help you

▪ ▪ ▪ ▪ ▪ ▪ ▪

## JOB SEARCH VARIABLES:

▪ *Type of job:* Know what you want.

▪ *Salary:* A new employer should offer you an increase in salary of at least 10 percent to offset the loss of benefits from your current job. Like moving to a different home, moving to a different job can be expensive.

▪ *Hours:* Is there flexibility? (This may be important because of your child.) Will there be overtime? If so, how much will you be paid for it?

▪ *Benefits:* Is health, life, and dental insurance offered? Tuition payment? Retirement plan and profit sharing? Generous vacations and sick leave? Child-care? On-site, free parking?

▪ *Environment:* Corporation or small office? Hectic pace or relaxed atmosphere? Formal or casual? Dress code? Windows?

▪ *Management style:* Does your prospective new boss's style match yours?

▪ *Location:* How far from home in distance? In time?

▪ *Opportunities for advancement:* Does the company promote women?

in this type of search, get the paperback book, *What Color Is Your Parachute? A Practical Manual for Job-Hunters & Career-Changers*, by Richard Nelson Bolles.

## Creating your own opportunities

Some people envision a job that simply does not exist. When Karen separated from her husband, she began looking for a full-time job. She had not worked since the birth of her son, ten years before. Karen was a La Leche leader. She dreamed of working with teenage mothers, very few of whom breast-feed their babies, in a low-income prenatal clinic. She would instruct them in the health benefits of breast-feeding and bonding with their babies. She decided to write a grant to cover her salary, but she felt she needed to set up a relationship with a clinic first. She approached a downtown hospital women's clinic and they were interested in her project. It turned out that they had grant money coming in soon for a somewhat different, but related project. The clinic director hired Karen.

Look for opportunities to affiliate with someone who is doing work in the field that interests you. If you can sell the organization on your idea, you can write your grant, possibly with the assistance of an affiliating organization.

Getting a grant depends on the quality of your proposal, the availability of money, and luck. You are competing with other people, just as if you were applying for a job. From the time you write your proposal to the time you get your money, six to eighteen months may pass.

## Résumé

Résumés come in all forms. With few exceptions, such as higher education or medicine, it's a mistake to create a résumé that's three pages or longer. You do not need to tell your whole life history. An employer uses résumés to screen out unlikely candidates for a position. If you can keep it to one or two pages, you will get a better reading.

Your résumé should be a thumbnail sketch of you—an appealing introduction that is designed to get you an interview. At the interview, you can go into detail about your capabilities and describe how you can offer something special to the company. It's hard to crystallize yourself onto one or two pages. Identify the highlights, but be concise. Make sure your spelling and grammar are flawless. To write your one- to two-page résumé, work from your

**SAMPLE RÉSUMÉ**

Laura A. Swanson
115 Cannon Street
San Lorenzo, California 94580
615-555-1212

## Objective

A challenging opportunity with career potential in sales, especially trade shows, telemarketing, and specialty advertising.

## Profile

Enterprising, goal-oriented individual
- Solid communication skills, including sense of humor
- Quick to grasp and develop scope of projects
- Creative—an idea person

## Education

Associate of Arts, May 1984, Hayward Community College
- Business major
- Dean's list 1982, 1983, 1984

## Experience

Sales representative (August 1986–November 1988)
Bethany Michael's Cosmetics, Inc., Oakland, California
- Expanded sales markets in central California
- Broke sales goals in 1987 and 1988
- Demonstrated and sold products at regional department store promotions
- Reorganized and expanded retail client files for more efficient contacts
- Suggested and developed in-house newsletter for better interdepartmental communication and for morale enhancement

Executive secretary (1982–1986)
American Can Company, Oakland, California
- Carried out daily administrative operations for office of CEO
- Managed factory tour bookings and trained tour guides

## Personal

Enjoy travel, people, and gourmet cooking. Excellent health. Native Californian. Two children.

*(Note: Bring your references to the interview rather than listing them on résumé.)*

master résumé (page 176). The job for which you are applying will determine what information you pull from the master résumé.

After you develop your résumé, write a one-page cover letter to each prospective employer to whom you want to send it. In this letter, you can include a few details that you did not put in the résumé, ones the employer might view as advantages. If you include information about the employer, you will win points, Example: "SMS stock held steady in 2003, a year when the majority of stocks lost value. I am attracted to a company that obviously is doing things right, and I want to contribute to that kind of effort."

After you type your résumé and cover letters, have at least one person read them for errors and general comments.

Some people pay professional résumé companies. (Look under "Résumés" in the Yellow Pages). The company will take the information you provide and organize it (if it needs it), format it, and print copies. The result is usually slick looking. Maybe a little too slick. Before you pay to have professionals do your résumé, make sure you see a sample of a finished résumé and that you like it.

Creating your own résumé is not hard; you can create an excellent version if you follow a consistent format. Your résumé should be created on a computer, neatly formatted, and printed on good quality paper. If you photocopy your résumé, make sure the copies are clean and sharp.

## Interview

People get understandably nervous about job interviews. Let that extra adrenalin work for you to keep you alert and focused on your task. A few tips:

■ Do your homework. Know the basic facts about the company where you are interviewing: how long it has been in business, its history, how many people it employs, what products or services it offers. Check out their website or call the company and ask them to send you information. Many larger companies have brochures, annual reports, and other information they can send you, or you can pick them up.

▪ The day before the interview, think through things you have done in the past that directly relate to this job. Write them down. This will help you remember them in the interview.

▪ Write out a script of possible questions and answers. Practice your responses in front of a mirror, with a friend, or with your child. Do not try to memorize your answers. You want your responses to be informed but fresh.

▪ If you can visit the company unnoticed before the interview, observe how women at your job level are dressed and wear something similar but conservative. A simple medium-to-dark suit with a skirt, blouse, and mid-level heels works well for most interviews. Avoid showy jewelry, colored hosiery, sexy clothes, and perfume. Do not smoke.

▪ Be squeaky clean and well groomed in every way.

▪ Identify a friend you can telephone after the interview; let that be a reward you can look forward to.

▪ Take either a small purse or a slim briefcase, but not both. You may want to take a few notes, so carry notepaper and pen.

▪ Before you enter, pause and take five slow, deep breaths. Relax.

▪ Go to a restroom and comb your hair.

▪ Find your interviewer. If you have to wait, do more slow breathing.

▪ Give a firm handshake, smile, and introduce yourself.

▪ If there are photos in the interviewer's office, you might ask, "Is this your family?" This may put your interviewer at ease.

▪ You may be asked a wide variety of questions: Expect anything and be ready to answer anything. Some people like to throw you off guard to see how fast you think. There is nothing wrong with saying, "That's a good question, but I

need some time to reflect on it rather than give you a super-
ficial answer now."

▪ Be honest. Be sincere.

▪ Keep your answers brief—no more than three or four
sentences, if possible. Expect the interview to last about fifteen minutes. You may get thirty or more, if they are interested.

▪ Take your cues from the interviewer; try to determine
if she is pressed for time or can move at a more relaxed
pace.

▪ Remember that you can also ask a prospective employer questions during an interview, so that you can find out if
you would be happy working for this company.

▪ Ask about whatever is important to you in management
style, environment, hours, and opportunities for growth
within the company. Often an interviewer will ask, "Do you
have any questions?" This is your chance, but keep it brief.
Do not ask about benefits until you talk about salary.

▪ You may be asked, "What kind of a salary are you looking for?" Do your homework ahead of time; know what the
going range is for this level of job. (*The Occupational Outlook
Handbook*, published annually by the Federal Government,
will give you an idea about this. You should be able to find it
in a public library.) If you can postpone answering this question, do so until you get closer to being offered the job. You
might try a response like, "Money is a secondary consideration at this point. Let's talk more about the job, and I'm sure
we can come to an agreement about salary later on."

▪ Remember that your goal is to present yourself as having something unique to offer. Look within yourself and find
those qualities that will translate to fresh ideas, high energy,
or whatever the company might want. Again, keep your
responses brief.

▪ Ask what the next step will be in the hiring process.
You will want to know how soon to expect word from them.

If your interviewer says, "We will finish interviewing this week and will let you know something by next Wednesday" and you don't hear from him by Wednesday, call on Friday morning and say, "I hadn't heard from you, and I'm just calling to say I'm still very interested in the position." You may get an update on the process.

∎ After the initial interview, write a thank-you note on plain paper or a note card and mail it as soon as possible.

> ∎ ∎ ∎ ∎ ∎ ∎ ∎
>
> . . . you can decide yes or no. Keep your options open.

## You don't have to say yes

Judy had been trying for some time to transfer to another job within her own company, which had three divisions. She liked the company and wanted to keep the benefits she had built up over five years. But no jobs opened up. A friend suggested that she apply for a good middle-management position in another company. Judy said she would, but then she hesitated. Her friend told her that even if they offered Judy the job, she didn't have to say yes. With that, Judy decided to submit her résumé. She was nervous going into the interview. When it was over, she called her friend on the phone and said, "I loved the interview!" The board that met with her must have been impressed, because they offered her the job, and she accepted.

If you have questions about a job, the interview is the place to ask them. On the basis of what you hear, you can decide yes or no. Keep your options open. There's no risk in just going to an interview; you don't have to accept an offer.

## Taking risks

Life doesn't usually offer sure things. Marriage certainly isn't one, and neither is job satisfaction. You give it your best shot. Often women don't take risks until they are in emotional or financial crises. They tend to be more conservative than men. They want to hedge their bets or they want a sure thing.

Sometimes that means they stay too long in bad situations. They worry about what will happen if they make a change. Change is stressful, and who needs extra stress?

Theologian Paul Tournier wrote about what he called the "trapeze bar" experience in his book *A Place for You*. The trapeze bar experience is a leap of faith. You throw yourself into the process, whatever it is, and go as far as you can, then let go. There is a mid-air breathlessness, an anxiety effect, when you let go of one bar and grab onto another. You have to believe you are going to connect.

The opposite of the trapeze bar experience is an approach called "the brick wall that isn't there." Some people create imaginary barriers in order to avoid facing some unpalatable truth—lousy job performance, misplaced loyalty to an employer, a stressful change, limited opportunities. Whatever your brick wall is, it inhibits your freedom of rational choice. You need to knock it down and look honestly at your choices, naming your fears but holding them in check. Once our emotions build the brick wall, our minds say, "Well, as long as that wall is there, I really can't get beyond it." It's a stalemate. We can put ourselves through major grief, enduring an unnecessarily bad situation.

## Wanting to stay home with your child

You may want to stay home with your child, especially when he is a preschooler, to care for him like no one else can, to watch him develop at close range daily, to introduce him to the world with you at his side. Money is the key.

Welfare is not an attractive option for most single mothers; you have to put up with poor neighborhoods and a severely reduced standard of living. But there are single mothers who have done and are doing a good job of raising their children on welfare checks. It is just an unending financial strain.

Living with your parents is rarely a satisfactory long-term solution. But for the short term, it can be an opportunity for you to save some money to put down on an apartment or to pay off some bills.

Nancy became a single mother when her boys were six months and two years old. Her ex-husband paid her $700 child support each month. She felt committed to staying home to care for her children, and she met all her expenses out of the child support money and food stamps. They lived in subsidized housing and did not travel or spend a lot of money on entertainment. But Nancy was rich in friends and led an active social life. By the time the boys were four and six, Nancy felt she was ready to go back to work; she got a research job at a local university which paid her enough to move into a duplex in a neighborhood near her friends.

Some women are able to make a living working at home. This offers some advantages: you have fewer office interruptions, you have flexible hours, you may have attractive tax breaks, you do not have to lose time commuting to work, you may save on child care, and you can be there for your child. But at home you will be your own boss. It is tempting to do housework or other errands instead of working. If you can handle self-discipline, you may be able to make some money at home, either full-time, or part-time.

Some working-at-home options include:
- bookkeeping/accounting for small businesses
- cake decorating for weddings and other occasions
- catalog sales
- child care in your home for the children of other working women (generally low pay)
- computer software development and consulting and/or programming
- graphic arts
- independent sales representative
- marketing research
- photography
- tailoring and dressmaking

- teaching music, dance, or English as a second language
- telephone answering services
- tutoring
- typing, editing, and copy-editing dissertations, résumés, and manuscripts
- writing.

Working at home requires concentration for blocks of time, which can be difficult when you also need to supervise a child under four years old. However, the women who manage to do it say that it is worth the effort. If you are enterprising and have a skill to offer, look into starting your own business out of your home. This is a major financial risk; to avoid failure, consider starting small by moonlighting. When your home business arrives at a point at which it can support you, you can give up your outside job with greater confidence.

If you are interested in starting a home business, the Federal Government's Small Business Administration can help you in a number of ways. Search the web for "Small Business Administration SCORE program" to begin investigating this resource.

## Part-time work: a stepping stone

Part-time work can work to your benefit in several ways:
- If you have not worked in a while, it can allow you to enter the work force at a slower pace. You can often use volunteer experience to get a part-time job.
- It can give you a steady income while you are building up a part-time business at home.
- It can allow you to be home with your child more—a plus for children of any age.

## Dealing with your emotions

Like death, separation and divorce provoke strong emotions. You may find yourself at work feeling like your nerves are exposed and raw. You are under a lot of stress; you may cry easily. If your co-workers understand that you are going through tough times—

and these days, most people understand divorce—they will understand why you might be more easily upset than usual. Talk with your supervisor about your separation; tell him that you know that it is normal for you to be under stress, that you will make every effort to continue as normal, that you know this phase will pass, that you would appreciate his continuing support through the process, and that you welcome feedback at any time.

### Sexual harassment

Sexual harassment is illegal. It violates Title VII of the Civil Rights Act of 1964, which states:

> *Unwelcome sexual advances, requests for sexual favors, and other verbal or physical conduct of a sexual nature constitute sexual harassment when 1) submission to such conduct is made either explicitly or implicitly a term or condition of an individual's employment; 2) submission to or rejection of such conduct by an individual is used as the basis for employment decisions affecting that individual; 3) such conduct has the purpose or effect of unreasonably interfering with an individual's work performance or creating an intimidating, hostile or offensive working environment.*

Women constitute 97.1 percent of the reported cases of sexual harassment. Single mothers are prime targets, as they are less able to leave a difficult situation due to financial and family constraints.

*No woman should tolerate sexual harassment.* Her work will suffer, her self-esteem will drop, and the unhealthy atmosphere created by sexual harassment will affect everyone. But what can you do?

#### Do's & Don'ts of sexual harassment

- Do stare the harasser in the eye.
- Do use a direct and honest approach.
- Do deal with the situation immediately so it won't continue. Do say "No!" emphatically to the harasser.

**EXAMPLES OF SEXUAL HARASSMENT INCLUDE**

■ verbal harassment or abuse of a sexual nature

■ subtle pressure for sexual activity

■ sexist remarks about your clothing, body, or sexual activities

■ unwanted touching, patting, or pinching

■ leering or ogling at you

■ brushing against your body

■ demanding sexual favors accompanied by implied or overt threats concerning your job, grades, promotion, pay, or letters of recommendation

■ physical assault

■ inappropriate display of sexually suggestive or porno-graphic materials, including e-mail. (Keep copies.)

■ Do keep detailed records of each incident.
■ Do demand respect.
■ Do report the incident immediately.
■ Do ask for help!
■ Don't smile at the harasser.
■ Don't look away from the harasser.
■ Don't let someone lean on you or get too close. Stand up and move away.
■ Don't worry about the harasser's ego; worry about your self-respect.
■ Don't think that if you ignore the problem it will go away.
■ Don't let anyone ask you questions of a sexual nature, especially in an interview.

(*"Sexual Harassment: Vanderbilt University Guide for Faculty, Staff and Students,"* Margaret Cuninggim Women's Center, Nashville, TN.)

Even if you feel your job would be on the line if you confronted your abuser or reported the abuse to a higher authority, seriously consider taking that risk. If women do not confront abusers, the abuse will continue for you and possibly others.

## Working two jobs

If you have to work more than forty hours a week to keep yourself financially afloat, try to find a job that pays you more or make every effort to decrease your consumer appetite.

Working a second job or working overtime regularly while you have custody is difficult for your child. Child care is OK for an eight-hour workday, but no one can replace you in your child's life. No one has your child's interests at heart more than you do, and good or bad, mistakes or not, you need to interact with your child as much as possible and on a regular basis for her to feel secure.

When Purdue University professor A. Charlene Sullivan surveyed six hundred married couples that either moonlighted or worked overtime regularly, she found that these couples were depressed about their budgets. As compared to couples who did not moonlight, these "superworkers":

- were having more trouble repaying their debts
- felt more strongly that they were too deeply in debt
- felt a greater need to borrow to keep up their lifestyle
- were more likely to have no extra money at the end of the month
- were less likely to pay off their credit cards in full every month
- thought that credit cards did more harm than good.

Single mothers sometimes find themselves in a similarly leaky financial boat, killing themselves to pay their bills and never getting ahead. They get into compromising positions and have to rely on family or friends to bail them out. These are women who have a fulltime salary with benefits plus child support, whose homes are charming and whose cars are new, but whose financial life is a mess. Difficult as these situations are, a second job is not necessarily the answer. It may be a symptom of an inability to set realistic financial limits.

## The working single mother as victim

Carol was a single mother with two children. She and Sharon, who was married, were secretaries in the same department. Their two bosses quit within one month of each other, leaving Carol and Sharon to run the department. The president of the company told them that they would have increased responsibilities until new management was hired. They got immediate changes in their titles. If they did a good job, they would get salary increases after three months.

They both assumed much of their former bosses' work (though at a third of the salary), and they made plans to move up the ladder together. The president's evaluations of their first month's work were very complimentary. Then Carol went out of town on business for a week. While she was gone, Sharon talked with the president of the company about Carol's alleged poor performance. By the time Carol returned, the president's secretary was avoiding her, and the president seemed noncommittal. On Carol's next business trip, she returned to find that she had been demoted to secretary at her original salary, while Sharon had received a $7,000 raise and a second change in title. No one would eat lunch with Carol. She was isolated and miserable. She had gone the extra mile for the company and her reward, she felt, was a stab in the back by her former best friend. Carol hung onto her job, her self-esteem slowly sinking, for another four months. She could not afford to quit because she had no husband and, therefore, no financial backup. When another company offered her a better job, she took it gratefully.

Whenever there are people in vulnerable positions, there are also people who will take advantage of them. As a single mother, you are vulnerable. It may be hard for you to confront someone who is abusing her power; you may not be able to risk losing your job. Perhaps you feel that you cannot defend yourself when your boss complains about your taking time off to be with a sick child. You feel that you cannot argue about unpaid overtime. Single mothers will remain victims as long as they remain in low-paying, powerless positions, living on tight budgets with children whom they must protect without the support of a partner. And the result is too often silence in the face of injustice.

## Jumping ship too soon

Maybe you hate your job—it's boring, demanding, involves too much overtime, pays too little money, offers terrible working conditions. You are nervous, tense, bursting to move on. You fight to control your emotions. One day, you reach the breaking point and submit a letter of resignation. In two weeks, you're gone. But what next? Temporary secretarial work will not come close to paying your former salary, but you think you can get by on it until you find another, better-paying job.

This is Russian roulette. There are many people vying for the same jobs as you are. Some of them do not have children and, therefore, look a little more attractive. The job search process is so time-consuming and complex that no one—*no one*—who is not independently wealthy should leave a job without another job to go to.

Long before you reach the breaking point at your job, listen to your head, not your heart. When you begin to feel real dissatisfaction, take a look around and make an assessment.

## Time for a new job?

Whether because of office politics, boredom, or claustrophobia, one morning you may have that sinking feeling, "Oh, no, I have to drag myself to work today." And you realize that lately you have been having that feeling every morning.

Possible trouble signs are:

- You got a lower raise than others the last time around.
- You received a lukewarm job evaluation.
- Your ideas and requests are dismissed.
- You are cut off from office gossip or socializing.
- You are depressed at work.
- You are regularly stressed and feel you cannot handle your job load.
- You feel trapped or at a dead end with nowhere to go in your career.

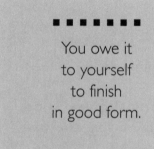

■ ■ ■ ■ ■ ■ ■

You owe it to yourself to finish in good form.

An unhappy job situation can become overwhelmingly depressing and stressful. Change the way things operate at work—or start looking for a new job.

The best thing you can do is to confront the situation, whatever it is. Do not drift. Talk with your supervisor. Find out how he can help you become more challenged and define and solve problems with co-workers. Discuss the supervisor's own problems regarding your performance. Your supervisor may say, "That's the job. Take it or leave it." Or, "If you aren't satisfied here, you may need to make a change." In that case, it is better to leave before you become entrenched in mediocrity or are fired.

## Loyalty

Taking care of your child and yourself must be your highest priority. Keep it business only where company loyalty is concerned. If you have to leave an employer after years of service or after only three weeks, do it. You are not indispensable; there are a lot of people who would love to do your job and would do it well. You are probably making a lot less than the supervisor to whom you feel this sense of obligation.

When you quit your job, give at least two weeks' notice—even if you are leaving a bad situation and would like to get revenge, or don't think you can hang on. You owe it to yourself to finish in good form.

Your strongest loyalties and commitments should be to you and your child. That's where your greatest investment will bring you the greatest return.

# CHAPTER 11

■ ■ ■ ■ ■ ■ ■ ■

# Finances

Living within
your means

Knowing how
you spend

Insurance

Establishing credit

Credit crunch

Chapter 13 bankruptcy

Identity theft

Filing taxes jointly
with your ex

Claiming dependents

Head of household

Earned Income Credit

Tax forms

Tax helpers

A home of your own

The down payment

Shopping for
mortgage money

Retirement

Making your
money grow

Rich Mom, Poor Mom

Financial advisors

College funds

Ready-cash funds

If it's hard
for you to save

Wills

Feeling rich

*Wolves prowl in my head*
*hungry for me*
*watching me at the bank*
*at the grocery store*
*at the gas station.*

*There must be no mistake.*
*I have been careful.*
*I have stretched taut my desires,*
*my wishes for marmalade*
*and sometimes for bread.*
*Still it is not enough.*

*Tomorrow is a living standard away.*
*Today the phone bill is due,*
*The mortgage is due.*
*Gas, electricity, water.*
*The hedge needs clipping.*
*My nails need clipping,*
*My mind needs ironing*
*to get out the humpbacks of the wolves*
*who howl and wait.*

## Living within your means

In 2001, the annual median earnings for full-time, year-round work for men was $38,275; for women it was $29,215, according to the U.S. Census Bureau. There's a difference of $9,060 between those two figures—for every dollar earned by a man, a woman earned 76 cents. This disparity has remained fairly constant for over two decades.

However much you earn, money certainly makes life easier, especially when you manage it so that you have enough each month to pay the bills, play a little, and make provisions for emergencies. One man used to say of his wife, who managed the family money, "She can get 40 nickels out of a dollar." You might not be *that* good at managing money; few people are. Lawyers, CPAs, investment brokers, and others have made oodles of money helping other people manage theirs. This chapter will cover some of the basics of money management, a tool that can dramatically affect the quality of life for you and your child.

Many single mothers must lower their cost of living when they have to live exclusively on their own salaries. You make some decisions about what is important to you and your child, and how you can hold onto as much of it as possible. Ask yourself, "What provides quality in our lives? How can we maintain that with our budget?" Instead of thinking consumption, think conservation, making do, recycling, being creative with your assets, and sharing resources and skills with other people.

You may have big-ticket plans to purchase a car, buy a home, go to school, take a trip, and save for your child's college education. If so, you must keep today's expenditures lower than you would like while planning for tomorrow.

## Knowing how you spend

Keep a record of your expenses for a three-month period; it will tell you how you spend your money. Keep all of your receipts for every purchase and note on each what you purchased and for whom. At the end of the period, put each expenditure into one of two categories: basic needs and optional purchases. Rent, food, utilities, transportation to work and school, medical expenses, clothing, and repayment of credit purchases are basic needs. You may have additional basic needs, but many other purchases you make are optional, such as household items, gifts for family and friends, entertainment and travel, and hobby items.

Group your expenses into categories—utilities, entertainment, etc.—and add up the totals for each category for three months. Divide each category by three, and you will have the average of how much you spent each month for that category. Clothes, for example: you spent

$ 20  in June
$180  in July (back to school sales)
$ 10  in August
$240  **total**

divided by 3 months = $80 per month average for clothes.

If you want to limit your monthly expenses, look at all of your basic needs items. Housing is usually the biggest item. You could consider moving to less expensive housing to reduce this cost. Perhaps you can limit your expenses for food by eating out less often, buying fewer prepared foods, or cooking in bulk. You should work conscientiously to reduce credit payments every month, until you can pay off your entire bill at the end of each month.

You may not want to reduce most of your basic needs items. Add up the total amount of money needed in an average month for your basic needs. Subtract that from your salary and other income; that is the amount of money you have left over for optional purchases. For example, one single mother's financial report looks like this:

$2,400 salary and child support
$2,000 basic needs
$400 left over for optional purchases.

In each month in which she spends more than $400 on optional purchases, this woman goes over her budget and borrows, in one way or another, from another month. This "borrowed money" will have to be paid back in future months, leaving her with less money for optional purchases in those months. But when she spends less than $400 on optional purchases in a month, she can apply that money to pay off debts or to save.

Living on a budget allows you to understand where your money is going and make informed choices about how you use it for short- and long-range planning.

> ▪ ▪ ▪ ▪ ▪ ▪ ▪
>
> Living on a budget allows you to understand where your money is going and make informed choices …

## Insurance

A newspaper carried a tragic story of a nine-year-old boy, son of a single mother, who was walking on the side of the road when he was hit and killed by a drunk driver. The article said, "Funeral expenses for Carter will be paid by Big Brothers. . . . 'I didn't have any insurance because I couldn't afford it,' the mother said. 'It took every penny I had just to keep a roof over his head and clothing on his back.'"

It is a struggle for many single mothers to stretch their income to meet the bills. But because we have children, we have to make sure to plan for the emergencies, to make sure that we can take care of our children and ourselves. Ask yourself: What will happen if I die? If I am disabled? If I have health problems? Where will the money come from? Here are some things you should keep in mind when planning for unfortunate circumstances:

▪ *Life insurance* is cheap for adults under thirty-five years of age. Term insurance is like renting your insurance by the month. It is pure death protection, and it is the least expensive life insurance. Perhaps you can get group term life insurance at work; if so, take advantage of it, but bear in mind: when you leave that job, you leave the insurance.

■ *Disability insurance* is offered by many employers. If you are disabled, each month you will receive a percentage (usually 60 to 75 percent) of your working wage at the time you left work. It is relatively inexpensive.

AFDC and Social Security benefits are also available to you in case of disability, but it is very difficult to survive on that income alone. But if you become disabled, you should know that there are many support programs available to women on AFDC, programs that are seldom used because women don't know to ask about them. Social workers, tax lawyers, the mayor's office, and other resource people can tell you about these support programs.

■ *Health insurance* is available at many different levels—Cadillac, Honda, or Ford Pinto. Your employer may pay all or part of the cost of your health insurance. The higher the deductible, the cheaper the monthly insurance premium will be. You probably need catastrophic coverage—for organ transplants and major accidents and other possible big-ticket items—most of all.

Some states offer health insurance plans for people who have been turned down by other companies because they are considered to be poor risks, such as people with AIDS or other chronic or fatal illnesses. The premiums are higher, but you are insured. Check with your state department of Commerce and Insurance or whoever regulates insurance in your state.

■ *Auto insurance* is essential; without it, you will lose your privilege to drive. "Minimum limits" payments enable you to pay in twelve monthly installments, with a slight fee for processing the payments. Your insurance costs will depend on your driving record and the model and year of your car.

■ *Other kinds of insurance* you need include home owner's or renter's insurance (for property and household goods), and dental insurance (sometimes offered by an employer).

When you are looking for a new job, remember that insurance benefits from your employer can add two thousand dollars or more per year to your salary.

## Establishing credit

If you do not have credit in your own name at the time of your divorce, open a savings account at your bank. Even if you deposit just the minimum amount permitted, you are establishing credit. Next, find a locally owned store in your area—a department or specialty store, for example—which will set up a credit account for you. Charge something and pay the bill before it is due.

It's usually easy to get a gasoline credit card. Some have to be paid in full each month, but others do not. If you don't have a major credit card, you must have some way of covering emergency car repairs and tires. Save your gas card for these large outlays and use cash to buy gas.

When you apply for a major credit card, you must provide information about your personal life and your financial situation. If you have paid all your bills on time for at least six months (ideally including your local store credit card), you may receive credit. Your application will be reviewed by a credit officer, who will make a judgment based on how she interprets the information you have given. If you are denied credit, call the bank and find out why. Request a copy of your credit report to ensure that it is accurate. Reapply when you have straightened out any problem you can identify or apply for a different credit card.

Some people collect so many credit cards that they could play poker with them, but just one major credit card can allow you to charge yourself into bankruptcy court—which, of course, you want to avoid. Keep your number of credit cards to a minimum; it will make it easier to keep track of them, result in fewer monthly bills, and give you fewer companies to contact if your purse is lost or stolen.

## Credit crunch

Denise kept buying things on credit until she could not pay her bills when they came due. One by one, the credit companies canceled her credit; some things were repossessed. Denise was nineteen. She married, and her husband, a successful plumber, spent thirteen stormy years with her struggling to bail her out of one financial problem after another. Denise and her husband briefly separated; during that time, her house and car were nearly repossessed. She spent $600 on new clothes for a three-day training program she attended. She gave her parents new dining room furniture, for which she could not pay, and she somehow managed to borrow $20,000 from the Small Business Administration for a business that went defunct within a year. In every case, Denise's husband paid bills he did not agree to in order to avoid financial disaster for both of them.

Credit is a handy way to borrow money temporarily, but if you can't pay back one loan before you borrow more, you may soon find yourself owing large amounts to credit companies, with interest charges of 18 percent or more—a bad use of your money.

Compulsive shoppers buy things—sometimes useless things like clothes that don't fit—out of an uncontrollable need that overrides financial considerations. Like overeaters or alcoholics, they can't help themselves. It's a sickness, the root cause of which may be low self-esteem; these people need help to change their buying habits.

We are a nation of people that live on credit; the average individual's credit debt is around $8,000. "Everybody's doing it," so it may seem impractical to carry no debt, but is it the best use of your money? If you carry a balance on a credit card, paying out 10 percent to 24 percent in interest charges, your purchases actually cost that much more than the prices of the things you're buying. Paying cash provides such a feeling of power, particularly if you have ever had to dig yourself out of a credit hole. The last car I bought, I paid for in cash—something I never thought I could do (read *Rich Mom, Poor Mom* below). The sales person and I had agreed on a price. She said, "Now I will take you to Mr. \_\_\_\_, who will help you arrange for payments." I said, "Oh, that won't be necessary. I'll just write a check." I whipped the checkbook out of my purse and said, "To whom shall I write this check?" while she was still recovering from the shock. It was a beautiful moment.

If you have trouble paying your entire balance each month, consider leaving your credit cards at home so that you can avoid impulse buying. If that doesn't work, cut up most of your cards, keeping one for emergencies. During the next month, try to limit your credit purchases to things you truly need (not clothes or entertainment or other extras). If you can, keep the card. If not, cut up that one too. Once you've reduced your debt to a level that you can manage, you can acquire one more card, and gradually build back your card collection, if you chose, slowly and with caution.

You can pay off credit accounts with high interest rates by taking out one large loan, called a debt consolidation loan, at a lower interest rate. Once you've used this loan to pay off your credit cards, it is tempting to use them again; if you do, then you'll have to pay back the debt consolidation loan *as well as* your new debt. Filing or destroying your credit cards can help you resist the temptation to use them.

If you are more than sixty days overdue on a credit card bill, the creditor will report you to the three major credit bureaus, which will record this blot on your financial record; the credit bureaus provide information on your credit history to any business that requests it. The creditor, or their collection agency, will send letters and call you, which is both annoying and embarrassing. If you know you can't pay your bill, do not avoid the creditor. Write a letter or telephone to explain your circumstances; suggest a repayment plan that you can manage. The company may not like it, but they will probably be receptive to any offer, because they want to collect their money. Many people do this. When you and the company agree on a repayment plan, ask them to write to the credit bureaus to take your defaulted payment off your record; make sure they send you a copy of the letter. If you don't get it, keep calling the company until you do.

## Chapter 13 bankruptcy

If you cannot meet your financial commitments, bankruptcy may be an option. Many people must do so, through no fault of their own, when they incur unexpected medical bills or lose their jobs or support. As long as you have a fixed income—whether from a job, alimony, or investment income—Chapter 13 bankruptcy can help you get back on your feet financially without losing everything you own. Here's how it works:

You hire a lawyer who has experience with bankruptcy law. She files a petition on your behalf. You and your lawyer meet with your creditors. You specify how much money you need to meet your basic monthly expenses. You promise to pay what is left over from your fixed income to your creditors. Together you negotiate the value of your property (i.e., car, clothing, furniture, and other assets) and the principal and interest you can pay your creditors. You keep your property, but you can't use credit without the court's permission for the duration of your repayment plan (usually three to five years). You, your lawyers, and your creditors present the plan to a Chapter 13 trustee of the court. Only if one or more creditor objects to the plan do you have to go before a judge; usually this does not happen because no one wants to pay the additional lawyer's fees.

There is a reasonable filing fee, which can be incorporated into your repayment plan along with your lawyer's fee. You need no up-front money to go through the Chapter 13 bankruptcy process.

Though the process is relatively easy, bankruptcy goes on your permanent credit record, which will discourage creditors from loaning you money in the future. There is also a social stigma against it.

If your paychecks are being garnished to pay debts or you are threatened with foreclosure on your house or repossession of your car, get advice from a lawyer regarding bankruptcy and other options.

## Identity theft

In 2002, identity theft cost almost 10 million Americans about 5 billion dollars, according to a Federal Trade Commission survey. In one example, an attorney's wallet was stolen. Within a week, the thieves had ordered a cell phone package, applied for a credit card, been approved to purchase a computer on credit, received a PIN number from DMV to change the attorney's driving record information online, and more. Here are some suggestions from that attorney to help make you a less likely victim than the next person:

Before a theft occurs:

■ Have your checks printed with your first initial and last name; don't use your first and middle names. Continue to sign your checks with your first and last name; a thief would not know that you do this, but the bank will recognize it as your standard signature.

■ Put your work phone number on your checks instead of your home phone.

■ If you have a post office box, use that address instead of your home.

■ Do not have your social security number printed on your checks.

■ Photocopy the contents of your wallet; copy both sides of your driver's license, credit cards, and any other pieces of identification. Everything. You will have a record of what is in your wallet, and who to contact if it is stolen. Keep the photocopies in a safe place.

After a theft occurs:

■ Immediately call and cancel all of your credit cards. You should have the toll-free numbers on the photocopy you made.

■ Immediately file a police report in the jurisdiction where the theft occurred. This will prove to credit providers that a crime occurred and you have been diligent. It is the first step in an investigation (if one occurs).

■ Immediately call the three national credit-reporting organizations to place a fraud alert on your name and social security number. Any company that checks your credit— which must happen before additional accounts can be opened—will know that you have been the victim of a crime; they have to contact you by phone to authorize any additional credit accounts. Here are the current numbers:

- Equifax, 800-525-6285
- Experian, 888-397-3742
- TransUnion: 800-680-7289
- Social Security Administration fraud line: 800-269-0271.

## Filing taxes jointly with your ex

You cannot file your taxes jointly with your ex-husband for the tax year during which you were divorced. If you are separated but not yet divorced, you can file jointly with him and it may well be advantageous for you to do so; joint filing usually offers the highest return on your money. If he makes considerably more money than you do, then you may be better off filing alone. You can even use that as a bargaining chip with him.

Let's say that if you file alone, you would get $300 back on your taxes. If you filed jointly, your husband would have to pay $700 less on his taxes. That's a $400 difference. The two of you can split that and receive $200 apiece. He gives you the $300 that you would receive as a tax refund, plus the $200 that is your share of the proceeds from filing jointly. He gets $200 and you both come out ahead.

## Claiming dependents

If you and your ex-partner have very different incomes, the higher wage earner could claim the child for a bigger tax benefit and share the overage with the other. For example, if you would get $50 for your child and your ex-partner would get $100, you could let him claim your child and the two of you would split the $50 "profit." You would both win financially.

## Head of household

The size of your tax break depends on the category under which you file your taxes. If you can, file as head of household. It means you are the main financial support in a family that includes at least one dependent. A child is your dependent if you provide more than half of the care for that child, or if the divorce decree states that the child is your dependent.

## Earned Income Credit

If your income is low and you have one or more children living with you, you may be eligible for the earned income credit—an income tax refund of up to $874—even if you are not otherwise due a refund. Child support is not taxable annual income, so if your child support puts you over the mark, you may still be eligible. To qualify for Earned Income Credit you must file as head of household (explained above) or qualifying widow (if your spouse died within the last two years). Complete qualifications are in the instructions that come with your tax form 1040A or 1040 long form.

## Tax forms

Federal tax forms are available at most post offices, banks, U.S. courthouses, and public libraries. To know which form you need, call the Internal Revenue Service and ask them to send you the primer called "Your Federal Individual Income Tax." It explains which forms you need and helps you know what questions to ask the IRS or your tax preparer. State tax forms are available from the Revenue Department of your state government. After the first time you file taxes in your own name, the IRS and your state will mail tax forms to your home. If you move, you must request the forms again.

If your employer withholds tax from your paycheck, then you file taxes only once a year. If taxes are not withheld, you must file both federal and state taxes quarterly.

Though child support and property settlements are not taxable income, alimony is. If you are facing divorce, get tax advice from a CPA or tax lawyer before you finalize the settlement of property. A family law attorney may not consult a financial expert; make sure it happens. The structure of your divorce decree determines how much you'll be taxed.

You may be able to receive child-care credits on your taxes. These are not deductions; they are based on a percentage of your adjusted gross income (AGI). The guidelines for the child-care credit change regularly, so always ask your tax preparer how you can get the most benefit.

## Tax helpers

The IRS will help you fill out your personal tax forms at their local office. You can just walk in and ask, or you may be able to make an appointment. The assistance is free. Call ahead for the office hours and to make sure you can get help when you need it.

Volunteer Income Tax Assistance (VITA) is a national program to help medium- to low-income people file personal taxes. The volunteers are trained in basic tax law by the IRS. They can prepare simple tax returns, basic forms, and attached schedules such as those for itemized deduction or capital gains. They have joined forces with IRS e-file to file tax returns electronically for free for those who, at the time of this printing, make $34,000 or less in a year. They also can file through the mail. If you qualify and want this help, search the internet for "Volunteer Income Tax Assistance" or call the IRS at 1-800-829-1040.

If you want to hire a professional to help you, you have several options:

■ *H & R Block* is a service for filing tax forms only. These people are good historians; you bring them the information and they will fill out your form properly. They do not give advice.

■ *A public accountant* (PA) is a licensed service provider. He is also a historian and is also able to give elementary tax advice. PAs are more expensive than H & R Block. Look for someone who has a lot of experience.

■ *A certified public accountant* (CPA) is an expert at tax filing and advice. A CPA is more expensive than a PA. Unless you have a complex financial portfolio, you probably do not need a CPA.

■ *A tax attorney* is probably the most expensive service provider; she is paid by the hour. She gives tax advice and is also an advocate for her client when necessary, such as during a divorce. A tax attorney also can help you structure your finances to avoid taxes at various times of your life. A tax attorney is familiar with wills, trusts, insurance, and other matters that relate to preserving your resources during your life and in the event of your death.

## A home of your own

Many women think home ownership is an unattainable dream. Often the down payment, not to mention the cost of the house, seem prohibitive. But some houses are much cheaper than others; you might be surprised to hear that sometimes it is possible to buy a home for as little as $1,200 down.

If you have a fixed mortgage (which means the interest rate stays constant for the duration of the loan), then home ownership gives you a sense of security. Real estate agents will tell you that women are more likely than men to be emotionally tied to their homes, which provide stability, security, and a sense of family and belonging. Children also seem to settle down when they have their own room in their own home.

Consider Sam and Lulu, two young children whose mother had just bought their first home. They jumped out of the car and ran all over the yard and the house proclaiming, "And this is our tree! And this is our backyard! And these are our very own stairs! And this is my bedroom." Since leaving their father, they had lived in a succession of apartments and rental houses—all owned by someone else. Now, they felt, they had finally stopped wandering.

■ ■ ■ ■ ■ ■ ■

…home ownership gives you a sense of security.

As real estate professionals say, when you pay for housing, you're either buying your own home or someone else's. Mortgage interest is tax deductible. Within about five years, you usually start making money on your house because it appreciates in value. Owning a home can be an attractive part of a retirement plan.

After you've bought your first house, you can always sell it and buy another. But each time you move, your mortgage payment will probably go up. Staying in one place can save you money.

As a single wage earner, you may be able to get low-cost mortgage funding from your state. Check with local authorities to see if your state offers such a program. The interest rates for these mortgages are often several percentage points below standard.

There are less expensive homes with a lot of character and charm in older neighborhoods that often offer neighborhood associations, community centers, crime watch programs, and active parent groups at the schools. Quality of community life is more important than the average price of the houses in a neighborhood. A well-organized community is probably stable, neighborly, and safer.

A duplex is also a good possibility; you can live in one half and rent out the other to help pay your mortgage. Lease-purchase deals are also available, though they aren't always the best deals financially. Check with a real estate agent to see if this is the case in your community.

Once you have investigated low-cost loans, look for a real estate agent who has been selling houses in your desired area for at least five years. Ask for references from your friends. There are agents who specialize in moderately priced housing and enjoy working with low and moderate-income families. The seller pays your agent's commission; the services are free to the buyer. An agent should know about the quality of neighborhoods, help you secure mortgage money, and work with the mortgage company to see you through the deal.

An older house will cost less per square foot than a new one, but you should make sure to have it inspected. This can cost as little as $100 to $200. Do not trust your mortgage appraiser to do the job; some simply drive by the house and then price it based on the neighborhood average and the "curbside appeal." Ask your agent to recommend someone. The money will be well spent. Think of it as a kind of insurance against disaster.

Habitat for Humanity is a well-known international organization that builds houses for low-income families. Prospective buyers must submit an application; if approved, the applicant receives a no-interest mortgage and contributes a certain number of hours of labor, both on her own house and those of other Habitat homeowners. The mortgage is quite low.  Homes are usually in low-income neighborhoods where land is less expensive. For information, visit Habitat for Humanity International's website at www.habitatforhumanity.org or call the home office in Americus, Georgia, at 229-924-6935.

## The down payment

If you want to own your own house, you will probably need a down payment. This can seem insurmountable, but it doesn't have to be.

When saving for a down payment, put off buying a new car. A car payment may prevent you from buying a house; that money could go a long way toward your monthly mortgage payment. Do not take out any large, long-term loans; you could be denied a mortgage as a result. The buyer often has to pay closing costs on the purchase of a house, which can amount to $2,000 or more. Usually these are paid at the time of closing, but sometimes the cost can be added to the mortgage, to be paid off over time.

You cannot legally borrow money for a down payment. But you can get a large gift of money from your parents or other family members or friends. If you do not sign a contract, this "gift" can actually be a loan, interest-free or not. One woman's father gave her a large down payment for a condo; as a result, her monthly mortgage payment was only $500. He told her that no matter what happened to him, he wanted her to have a place to live that she could afford. Write a letter to the giver acknowledging the gift so that they can incorporate it into their tax records; keep a copy for yourself. Whether you repay that gift at a later time is up to you and the giver. Some people have received down-payment money from employers, and church communities. It takes courage to ask for money, but it can get you into your own home.

If you work for a company that offers a 401K or other retirement plan, see if you can take money out of your account to use as a down payment on a house (see Making Your Money Grow, page 221).

One woman had a yard sale and netted over $400 toward her down payment. Another mother asked her two young sons, "Would you rather go to Florida or have bedrooms of your own in a house of our own?" It was no contest; the boys "jumped their jars," according to the real estate agent, and came up with $142, which they proudly carried to the bank to deposit in the family mortgage account.

## Shopping for mortgage money

For a nominal fee, you can pre-apply for a mortgage. Your credit must be good, though it needn't be extensive. The lender will approve you for a loan that she thinks you can manage, based on the information you provide. Then you'll know how much house you can afford to buy. You can also find a house first and then try to find a mortgage lender. You just have to hope that you have not chosen a house that is too expensive.

One caution about credit checks: If you, or those to whom you give permission, request too many checks of your credit, it will lower your credit rating. If you apply online and to a number of mortgage companies, this can happen. So investigate your options, but keep credit checks to a minimum.

Shop around on the Internet, in newspaper real estate sections, and with local banks and other lending institutions for mortgage money, just as you would for a car or other large purchase. Some lenders are more liberal in their underwriting policies than others. Some will give you a larger loan limit than others. Your real estate agent can also give you advice on where to look for money.

If you think you can afford a larger mortgage than a lender will allow you based on your income, ask an affluent relative or friend to co-sign the loan with you. You both will be legally responsible for keeping up the payments and the house would be in both your names, but you will pay the mortgage yourself. The co-signer can sign a quitclaim agreement, which will keep his name on the deed but prevents him from controlling it in any way. You can fill out the legal paperwork yourself. Check with your local court clerk's office for forms, filing fees, and other information.

■■■■ ■ ■■■

### SOME MORTGAGE TERMS YOU SHOULD KNOW INCLUDE:

■ *Adjustable rate loans* feature interest rates that fluctuate with changes in the economy. Should you select such a loan, make sure there is an interest rate ceiling of no more than 6 percent over the rate at the time you assumed the loan.

■ *Fixed-rate loans* keep the same interest rate for the duration of the loan.

■ *Federal Housing Administration* (FHA) loans were designed to let people with steady incomes, but not a lot of cash, into the housing market. They require a down payment of as little as five percent. The borrower has to meet credit and income guidelines, and the house must pass a stringent appraisal.

■ *Veterans Administration* (VA) loans are available to military veterans. No down payment is required. Credit, income, and appraisal standards are similar to FHA.

■ *Conventional loans* are available through banks and mortgage companies. The amount of down payment, the length of the loan, and other requirements are set by the lender and can fluctuate widely.

## Retirement

Even if you are only nineteen, plan for your retirement now, so that you can be financially comfortable later without a lot of financial sacrifice along the way. These days, people often work for only 50 percent of their lifespan. It's not unrealistic to expect that you might live thirty years beyond your retirement, and you want to have some financial flexibility during those years. Who looks forward to thirty years of poverty? More women than men are living below the poverty line, and this includes many senior citizens on fixed incomes.

Elsie N. wrote the following for her local newspaper:

> *I am 78 and live alone. My pitiful little "fixed income" is $243 a month. . . . In 1987 my check was increased by one dollar. In January of this year I would have gotten an increase of $10.90 but Medicare went up $6.90. So I got a $4 raise. That $4 won't buy a loaf of bread a week . . . try buying food, paying electric bills, heat bills and insurance on $243 a month, in addition to all the extra, unexpected bills like doctor bills, etc., and then you will know what "fixed income" and "growing old" means.*

The younger you are when you start saving, the more you will have at retirement.

## Making your money grow

Retirement planning is a three-legged stool:
1. Social Security benefits
2. retirement benefits accrued from work
3. personal savings and investments.

Personal savings and investments offers the most opportunity to create financial growth. Here are a few options to consider:

■ *A 401K plan* is funded by a pre-tax payroll deduction from your paycheck; the proceeds are invested in mutual funds of your choice. Your employer can match some or all of your contribution; the rates vary from company to company. This money remains in your account until you leave your job, at which point you may choose to withdraw the money. If you do, you must pay taxes on it or roll over the money to another retirement program. There are, however, three circumstances in which you can make a "hardship withdrawal" prior to retirement: major medical expenses, education for you and your dependents, and the purchase of a residence. A 401K plan usually offers an initial high rate of growth on your money, since your contributions may be matched by your employer. The money in your plan continues to grow over time, following the stock market. If you have access to a 401K plan, you should take advantage of it. Since the money is deducted from your paycheck, you won't miss it once you commit. And it adds up fast. If you put five dollars in each week and your employer matches your contribution, you get $40 per month, or $480 per year on an investment of $240.

▪ *Profit sharing plans* are offered by some employers. You receive a percentage of the company's profits, based on your salary as a percentage of the whole salary pool. The money is kept in an account for you by your employer. Long-term employment works to your advantage when profit sharing is available.

▪ *Securities*—bonds, stocks, certificates of deposit (CDs), and real estate funds—are among the products available as investments. Financial advisors suggest that you diversify your assets so that if one type hits a slump, the others will carry along your overall financial plan.

▪ *Bank savings accounts* will not earn much money for you. If you maintain a savings account, monitor the interest that your money earns and make sure that it approximates the inflation rate; otherwise, you are losing money. See also Ready-cash funds, page 226.

## Rich Mom, Poor Mom

If you are interested in learning how to make money beyond the income from your job, read *Rich Dad, Poor Dad: What the Rich Teach Their Kids About Money That the Poor and Middle Class Do Not*, by Robert T. Kiyosaki with Sharon L. Lechter, C.P.A. Check with your local bookstore or library for the latest edition of this popular, easy-to-read book.

The author suggests that you let money work for you instead of your working for money. While you are working at your day job to pay the bills, have your own business plan on the side to increase your assets. You have to define what you want your assets to be—they may be real estate, intellectual properties (such as royalties from writing, songs, and inventions), stocks and bonds, and others that the author lists. Once you get started, your assets pay you dividends. This business on the side is yours to manage.

Kiyosaki says that a second job earning an hourly rate is not the way to go. It is too slow and too time intensive. He says, don't work for other people; let other people work for you.

When you receive dividends from your assets, use them to purchase more assets. As your dividends increase and you put them back into your assets, your assets increase; this process continues until you have enough money to quit your day job.

Kiyosaki also recommends that you reward yourself from time to time with perks, such as a new car. He emphasizes that *your job is not your business*. Your job is for today. Your business is for today and for all your tomorrows, so that you may enjoy them and let your money work for you.

My own day job involves writing, design, and what I call planning and plotting. My employer is a nonprofit organization. I love my day job because I can do it well, it is interesting work, and our organization helps a lot of people improve their lives. However, I have a business on the side that involves real estate and writing. My writing brings in semi-annual royalties. My real estate includes rental properties that other people manage for me; and I have a new business of buying, renovating, and reselling houses to first-time buyers. I make the final decision on purchasing properties, my partner fixes them for resale, and an agent friend sells them at a profit for us all. My day job offers me no retirement benefits. My business offers me all that I need. It is fun, rewarding, secure (because I am my own boss), and profitable.

The hardest part is getting started. But the rewards are financial security and freedom.

## Financial advisors

When you have a small amount of money to save or invest (perhaps $1,000–$5,000) you may want to initiate a personal banking relationship with the manager of your branch or with another bank officer. Explain your personal and financial situation and ask for advice. "I need to be aware of my options. What can you offer me?" He should be happy to explain the range of investment programs that the bank offers, as well as other options. The advice is free, as are some of the investment options; no broker is needed. Banks also offer discount and full-range brokerage services for stocks, bonds, mutual funds, and certificates of deposit. Explore their services, and remember that the more you know about how money works, the better off you will be financially.

If and when you need a broker, consider looking for a woman. Female brokers have had to fight for every advance in a previously all-male club. There are more and more of them, and they understand what it's like to make it on your own. They may be more sensitive to single motherhood; some are single mothers themselves. But as always, get recommendations. Ask your banker. Check with women's networking organizations represented in your town. Even during the early stages, you will make more informed choices if you choose to educate yourself about your investment options.

## College funds

The amount of money you need to send your child to college may range from zero to $20,000 per year or more, depending on scholarships, loan resources, whether the school is public or private, and many other variables. Consider these important factors:

- How much are you *able* to offer?
- How much are you *willing* to offer?
- How much responsibility should your child assume for her own college education?
- How much has your ex-partner agreed to pay?
- How dependable are all of you?

Some of these questions have no right, wrong, or definite answers. College planning is influenced by values and goals for the whole family. Each family needs to draw up its own plan, and each family needs to understand that financial factors—and even people's commitment to a plan—can change. It's a good idea to build a positive business relationship with your ex-partner, devoid of animosity, so that you can keep him on your child's team when it is time to help pay for college tuition. (More than one man who was angry with his ex-wife has tried to punish her by refusing to pay college tuition for their child.)

There is a treasure trove of literature in bookstores and libraries that discusses allocating financial resources, selecting a college, and making the transition from home to college. These books provide information on college loans, scholarships, work opportunities, expectations, and more.

Some colleges and universities offer tuition discounts to the children of employees who have worked there a certain period of time. This can be an employee benefit equal to thousands of dollars. One woman who worked for a university received $17,000 tax-free each academic year for her children to go to the college of their choice. One year, both were in college, one a senior and one a freshman. That year, her employee tuition benefit totaled $34,000 in pre-tax dollars. That was more than her annual net income. Because her ex-husband picked up most of the remainder of the college bills, she actually saved money—on food, utilities, car expenses, and other expenses—when her children went away to college. Her children graduated with small student loans, and her ex-husband was grateful that she was able to provide this, assistance, even though her salary was less than a third of his.

Some states use lottery funds to provide qualifying college students with scholarships. If yours does, investigate the application requirements and apply early. Some states have lock-in tuition plans and pre-paid options for parents who want to send their children to public colleges. Many families open mutual fund accounts, or other interest-generating accounts, for their children.

When one single mother's children were five and eight, she joked, "Well, he'll play ball and she'll be damn smart, and they'll get scholarships." The funny thing is, they did.

The responsibility your child assumes in paying for college is not only financial. It begins by doing the hard work so that she will be eligible for grants and scholarships. High SAT scores are often the result of the desire for knowledge and many hours of work, beginning early in life.

> ▪ ▪ ▪ ▪ ▪ ▪ ▪
>
> Make sure your child knows early on that higher education is an option for her.

You can help by checking your child's homework assignments, attending her school functions, and otherwise emphasizing the importance of education to her. Make sure your child knows early on that higher education is an option for her.

## Ready-cash funds

Ideally, you maintain a small savings account so that you have cash on hand in case you need to fly to a funeral, buy a new washing machine, or pay a car repair bill. You could save for a vacation or other major expenditure. But you may choose, instead, to deal with these situations, good and bad, by using credit.

It is far more important, however, that you have savings equal to three months' salary. You never know when you may lose your job, through no fault of your own—or even quit in disgust, though this is not recommended.

Jan was fired. Six months later, her unemployment insurance ran out, and she found a similar job that paid slightly less. Three weeks after she was hired, her new employer was purchased by another company and Jan was let go. She was able to pay her bills only because her parents supported her and her children. This is not an unusual story. Bankruptcy court is full of people who've had similar experiences.

Stash away at least three months' salary as your insurance against disaster. But make your money work for you. Choose a cash equivalent, interest-bearing account. See your banker for advice.

### If it's hard for you to save

Barbara Gilder Quint, former stockbroker, author, and lecturer, suggests these ways to save money:

▪ *Pay yourself first.* When you deposit your paycheck, deposit something into savings, no matter how small. Or take advantage of an automatic deduction plan offered by your employer or bank.

▪ *Fool yourself.* If you get a raise, continue to live on your old salary and put the extra money in savings. Or split your raise and put half in savings and half in checking.

▪ *Save windfall money.* This includes part or all of birthday money and other gifts, tax refunds, and other such money that you didn't expect to receive.

▪ *Drive your car another three months.* If you are going to trade in your car, wait three months and save the money you would have allocated for new car payments.

▪ *Pay bills you don't owe.* Whenever you pay off a long-term credit card or a medical bill, keep paying that monthly amount—but now to your savings account instead of to your creditor.

▪ *Save your change.* Pay cash at the grocery store, gas station, and other businesses, and put the change in a separate place. At the end of the week, deposit your change into your savings account.

■ *Do not make long distance telephone calls.* Write letters, e-mails, and cards.

■ *Cut one routine expense for a limited time.* Skip renting movies or going out to lunch or happy hour for a week or two and put that money into savings.

■ *Go cold turkey.* Cut every optional purchase to the bone (see pages 203–205). Put the leftover money into savings.

## Wills

Everyone needs one. If you don't design your own will, the state will do it for you—and your family might not like the results. The state will give your entire estate to your child, if you are not married. The court then appoints a guardian for your child, if she is a minor, and appoints a conservator of your estate. In no time at all your assets are disappearing in legal fees, leaving your child with less.

There are books that tell you how to write your own will. There are also online will services that are basically interactive self-help law books. Nolo makes software called Quicken Will-Maker Plus; it will allow you to set up trusts, but it will also flag certain procedures and sometimes recommend that you see a lawyer. All of these options allow you to bypass a lawyer, and it can be cost effective to do so. (It can cost $500 to $1500 or more for an attorney to write your will and other related documents.) The advantage of going to a lawyer is that she can handle complex affairs, answer your questions, and offer advice that may significantly improve the outcome of your estate for your child.

Should you die, you will probably want a trust fund set up for your child while she is young and in case she contracts a long-term illness. You can name the trustee in your will and she can act as you would if you were alive. When setting up trusts, many people follow the "thirds" rule:

■ one-third of the inheritance at age twenty-five (This allows for one "bad" marriage after which the ex-spouse could get half of your child's property.)

■ one-third at age thirty (This allows for one generic mistake.)

■ one-third at age thirty-five (Your child receives the balance once she has "settled down.")

Distributing your property in a will is basic. Setting up a trust is more complex and, if you use a lawyer, will probably cost you a little more.

Shop around for a good lawyer. Talk to friends and relatives. Ask, "Who do you know that is honest? Who has experience? Who is a specialist? Who do you like in this business?" Call recommended lawyers and ask if they will charge you to interview them. If you see a lawyer who doesn't work out, ask her for a referral. Insurance agents will know good lawyers, since they deal with them regularly.

■ ■ ■ ■ ■ ■ ■

If you feel lucky
or fortunate,
do you feel rich?

Make sure that your will provides for custody of your minor child, in case her father is unable or unwilling to take her. You may want to name a friend or relative. If you don't specify custody, your child could become a ward of the court and go to a foster home. When you specify custody, you have some control.

Read your will once a year to make sure it still reflects your financial situation. A single mother who had remarried stumbled on her will one day and found she had given her two children everything, including the kitchen sink, in a house she no longer owned. Go back to your software, your book, or your lawyer when you need an update.

## Feeling rich

You can feel rich when you pay off a credit card bill. You can feel rich when you find a five-dollar bill in your coat pocket. You can feel rich when you see a credit on your water bill because you overpaid last month. Part of feeling rich is feeling lucky, feeling fortunate.

If you feel lucky or fortunate, do you feel rich? If you can answer yes to that question, then you have many opportunities in your life to feel rich: On Friday, when you look ahead to a long, sunny weekend. When you gather the first spring flowers in a bouquet and put it on your dining room table. When you see your child returning from his father's house, reaching up to give you a hug.

If you can take the focus off of acquiring things and put it on developing relationships and celebrating creation, then money takes a back seat, and you can feel rich right now.

# CHAPTER 12

■ ■ ■ ■ ■ ■ ■ ■ ■

# Personal and Home Security

*"Now you know why*
*I read so long into the night, Mommy.*
*It's because I think of all kinds of things—*
*the house might burn down,*
*a robber might come,*
*the tree might fall on our roof—*
*and I keep thinking of them*
*and they won't go away*
*in the night*
*in the bed,*
*so I read, and then*
*I don't think of them.*

*"At Daddy's house I'm not afraid*
*because Daddy works until two in the morning*
*and he could smell a fire*
*and wake us up,*
*and Grandma and Granddad watch TV*
*until really late at night.*
*So I'm not afraid.*

*"But here there's just you.*
*So I read."*

—Laura, age 7

## When is it reasonable to be afraid?

As single mothers, we need to recognize the difference between paranoia and justifiable fear within ourselves, and then use our heads to make our environments safe for our families.

## Night fears

Many women fear sleeping alone. That makes a lot of sense in the twenty-first-century world of drug addicts and rapists and psychotics. Women and children have a right to live without fear and without being violated, yet by 1992, at least 12.1 million women had been victims of rape at some point in their lives, according to a Department of Justice study. Rape is only one of many violent crimes committed against women. For an enlightening look into crime statistics in these United States, go to www.ojp.gov:80/ovc/ncvrw/2002/pdftxt/statisticaloverview.txt. Even though most people are probably good neighbors and many others have the decency to leave us alone, there is a violent minority of our population that is armed and on the prowl.

Noises in the middle of the night can drive you crazy. An eighty-year-old widow panicked after the death of her husband. Her adult children had left town after the burial, and she was alone. She could not sleep. She found a neighbor who was willing to spend nights with her until she could get used to the idea of staying by herself in the home she loved. She never adjusted. Within a month of her husband's death, she left town and spent the rest of her healthy years living with her children. She considered leaving her home a less than ideal arrangement, but she could sleep again at night.

Fortunately, many single mothers are young and may be better able to adapt to new circumstances. One woman got herself a hamster, and when she heard noises in the middle of the night, she said to herself, "Oh, that's just Harry" and went back to sleep. Another woman rented a second-story apartment in an old house above a family she got to know well and who, she felt, would come to her rescue in an emergency. A third woman worries about entering her empty house at night; when she leaves the home of friends, she tells them, "I will be home in ten minutes, and I'll call you. If I don't call in fifteen minutes, you call me. If I don't answer, call the police." This makes her feel safe.

Identify what you fear as a result of living alone, and then find a solution to alleviate that fear. If you have to use sleeping pills or alcohol more than once every two weeks for that purpose, then you need to find a healthier solution to your fear.

> ■ ■ ■ ■ ■ ■ ■
> Feeling secure is a state of mind. **Being** secure is a matter of preparation.

You can expect your child to have her own fears. One ten-year-old boy is afraid to sleep in a room by himself at his mother's house. His father's house has an electronic alarm system, which makes the boy feel safe. His mother's house does not, so she allows him to sleep in the room with whomever he chooses, using a foam mattress for his bed.

Children often fear the night. Your child may feel less secure with you than she would if her dad was also in the house. Night lights, white noise machines, teddy bears, baseball bats by their beds, a certain kind of window covering—whatever makes your child feel safe will help her sleep better and wake up refreshed.

## Analyzing your environment

Feeling secure is a state of mind. *Being* secure is a matter of preparation. Recently I went to my own neighborhood hardware store and asked to see home security devices. The clerk said, "Oh, you want a dog and a gun," and laughed. Then he took me on an amazing tour of home security hardware, all reasonably inexpensive. And when I asked for things he didn't have, he said I could look in his catalogs and order anything I wanted. That's the good news.

The bad news is, a professional burglar can get into any home he wants to. However, he would rather open a door lock quickly and quietly than blow out a hole in the wall with dynamite. The harder you make it for a burglar to get in, the sooner he will look to other homes for an easier job, and the safer you will be.

A typical burglar wants to get into your home in about ten seconds. You want to delay him for at least twenty seconds and ideally forever.

You may be able to arrange for a police officer to come to your home and evaluate its security. She can tell you how effective your current security system is. She'll look at your hardware, ask you about living habits, and suggest improvements. Police suggestions often include both state-of-the-art security equipment and inexpensive alternatives, so you can tailor your efforts to suit your taste and budget. If an officer cannot do a site evaluation, describe your doors, windows, and visibility over the phone and see if you can get some good advice.

## Don't appear vulnerable

Here are some things you can do to feel safer:

▪ Keep some mail in a man's name coming to your house.

▪ List your first and middle initial instead of your first name in the phone directory, or get an unlisted number.

▪ If you have an answering machine, do not mention your name in the message. Say only "*We're* not able to answer the phone right now." This suggests that a man lives with you, or at least that *someone* does. You can also have a male friend or relative record your message.

▪ If possible, do not put your name on your mailbox. If you must, use your last name only and put it on a computer-generated label in a plain font (An elaborate font may suggest that a woman lives there).

▪ Close your blinds and curtains at night. Do not dress in a room with open blinds, which encourages Peeping Toms and rapists.

▪ Refer to yourself as Mrs. _____ when you call to arrange for household repairs. When strangers come to your door or into your home, try not to divulge your marital status. Don't chat about your personal life with the plumber, the carpet cleaner, or the man who comes to repair your washer. One of them might come back uninvited. One single mother leaves articles of menswear in plain view—an old jacket in a dry cleaner's bag, men's socks, underwear, and shaving gear in the bathroom. Her favorite: size thirteen work boots, muddy and left outside her front door.

## Doors

Unlocked doors and windows are an open invitation to a burglar.

When you move into an apartment, have all the locks changed by a locksmith. Make sure you have permission to do this before you sign a contract. Also make sure repairs to your apartment will take place only when you are there. Avoid a large complex where a maintenance person has a key to your apartment; sometimes these people, as well as security guards, serve as "inside" contacts in burglary rings.

Exterior doors and interior doors that lead to basements or garages should have double-cylinder, dead-bolt locks that require a key on both the inside and outside. Other kinds of locks are less secure; they can be opened easily with a credit card, a strip of plastic, or a screwdriver. Keep a key somewhere inside near the door, in case you have to escape a fire. You may want to leave a key with a neighbor, but do not hide one under the doormat or in the mailbox or anywhere else. Burglars will find them.

A woman moved into a walk-up apartment that came with four locks. She was delighted. A week after she moved in, someone broke in while she was at work and took all her electronic equipment. She added a lock and replaced the equipment. Two weeks later, another break in. She added a sixth lock and then a seventh lock to no avail. In despair she called a locksmith who asked her, "Do you lock all your locks faithfully?" "Oh, yes," she sobbed, "Well, next time, only lock four of them." She did as he suggested. The burglar could not tell which locks he was unlocking and which he was locking, and the woman was never bothered again.

Put a peephole in your door at eye level so that you can see anyone at the door. Old-fashioned peephole glass is only about one-quarter-inch in diameter, and while it magnifies the view, it is inferior to more modern models that are as big as three inches in diameter. Get a larger model and don't open the door to anyone you don't know. Intruders often pose as salesmen, repairmen, or people looking for lost dogs. Direct them to the police department, or just say, "I'm sorry, you can't come in." Walk away, and *don't feel guilty* for saying "no." Then call a friend, explain what happened, and describe the person. Teach your child how to use the peephole and when not to open the door.

Some exterior doors are hollow core instead of solid wood; they are intended for interior use and can be easily kicked in. Watch out for these in inexpensive apartment complexes and wherever construction materials seem minimal, even cheap. You can tell if a door is hollow by knocking hard with your knuckles at its edge (where it will sound solid) and then at its center (where it may sound hollow).

Doors with large windows should have metal bars over the glass area on the inside so that the screws cannot be removed from the outside.

Security doors cost $500 and more, but they do discourage burglars.

## Windows

You can install iron bars on the outside of your windows, especially on ground-level windows. They can be an attractive design feature, but they are expensive and can trap you inside in case of a fire.

Sash windows should have metal locks. You can buy one that locks with a key, which is safer than the usual swivel-latch kind. If your sash windows are wooden, you can nail your windows closed where the upper and lower window wood overlaps in the right corner. Leave the nail heads sticking out just enough so that you can pull them out when you want to. If you prefer open windows in the spring and summer, remove the nails, open the windows no more than six inches, and nail them in that position. This is cheap and effective.

Storm windows further discourage a burglar; those with solar screens also reduce your heating and cooling bills.

A sliding glass door or window can be locked with a wooden dowel or broomstick handle. Cut one to the proper length and lay in the groove of the sill. Install key locks on the metal frame itself if you want to be more secure.

If you have a skylight that opens, it needs a lock too.

When you return home at night, go on a quick tour of your house to see that all the windows and doors are secure. Your child—or someone else—may be unlocking them. One rapist would go to a house during the day, pry open a window lock, close the window and leave, then return at night through that window. Checking your locks takes only a minute and should be part of your routine, just like checking the mail.

Sometimes people do not lock their bathroom windows, thinking they are too small for a burglar to enter through them. Wrong. Lock yours.

## Lighting

I recommend that you install outside lighting and leave it on all night. If your apartment entrance is not well lit, ask the manager to change that. If your house is not well lit by a streetlight, install outside lights under the eaves. You can buy an inexpensive timer or a photocell (about $15 to $30) that will automatically turn lights on at dusk and off at dawn. Motion sensitive lights turn on only when an object moves in front of their sensor and can be triggered by people, vehicles, and animals. They stay on for several minutes, and then shut off until another motion is detected.

Inside, you can plug a small timer into your electrical socket and then plug a lamp, radio, or TV into the timer. Set the timer to turn the light on and off automatically at certain times. That way, if you are away from your home when dusk falls, your timers will turn your lights on and make it appear that someone is at home. They cost about $15 and are easy to use; a hardware store clerk can show you how in thirty seconds. Consider a variable timer, which alters the on-and-off time slightly each day; it may confuse a burglar who might be casing your home while you are on vacation.

## Electronic alarm systems

You can pay thousands of dollars to a security company to provide, install, and maintain your system. You can go to a store like Radio Shack and get a less expensive but effective system. Or you can forget alarm systems and still have a reasonably safe environment using the guidelines described above.

Electronic alarm systems have a few disadvantages. They are usually expensive and can malfunction, going off without cause. Like the boy who cried wolf, an alarm that goes off by mistake loses its power to signal danger; neighbors learn to accept its noise as an occasional nuisance in the neighborhood.

A properly working alarm can deter burglars and give you peace of mind. A sticker on your window announcing that you have an alarm system can also help. A red electronic signal moving across your door when the alarm is on is more effective. Some systems employ silent alarms when activated and others a loud noise. Noise should strike terror into a burglar's heart and alert neighbors to danger, so that they can call the police. Silent systems, and some noise systems, also trigger alarms in private security company offices; they send out their own armed security guards to check out the alarm.

You can buy an alarm that responds to noise, movement, pressure, or breakage of some mechanism. One tip about alarms: A loud outside alarm will alert the neighbors and the police. A screeching inside alarm will scare the pillowcase from a typical burglar's hands and make him beat a hastier exit.

To investigate what's available in your area, look in the Yellow Pages under "Security," or call your local hardware store and ask where you can buy a low-cost system.

As a point of comparison, in my area, a one-room motion sensor, the least expensive electronic device at Radio Shack, sells for less than $100. A whole-house system starts at about $200, depending on the size of the house. You must be able to install the system yourself or pay someone to do it for you.

Once you begin looking into electronic security, you can become overwhelmed by the many options. Remember that a burglar is looking for an easy job and that, even with the most sophisticated equipment, no house is guaranteed to be safe against burglary. Shop around before you buy. You might call up the police department again and go over your choice with the officer to whom you have talked previously.

## While you are on vacation

Have neighbors pick up your mail and newspapers and put some garbage in your can before each trash pickup. Leave a key with the neighbors in case of an emergency, and have them check to make sure no notes or flyers are left on your front door. (You can repay your neighbors with the same service when they go on vacation.)

Have someone cut your grass or shovel your snow. Turn down the ring on your telephone or have it temporarily disconnected, a free service now offered in some cities. Leave a bathroom or hall light burning and some draperies partly open. Put a timer on a living room lamp and on a radio that you turn up loud.

## "Join Hands with the Badge" programs

These programs, under a variety of names, are offered to neighborhoods by most police departments. Usually a police officer comes out and talks to a group of neighbors about crime prevention, including understanding personal security, watching out for each other, and advertising the neighborhood's anti-crime program. It works best where there is a feeling of community and stability among the neighbors.

Apartment complexes can present a problem. Sometimes it seems that the closer people live to each other, the less they interact—possibly because privacy is at a premium. There is often a high turnover in apartment tenants, and people think, "Why waste time getting to know these strangers?" That mentality breeds burglars, some of whom live in complexes and break into their neighbors' units. They watch and wait.

An old woman who lived in an apartment complex saw a burglar breaking into her car. She had a gun, so she leaned out her second story window and shot him in the heel. Police came and asked a crowd that had surrounded the burglar, "Who shot this man?" The old woman said, "We don't know." The apartment complex manager later called the police to come and talk to residents about security, and at that meeting the woman acknowledged her deed, to the laughter (because of her age) and cheers of the residents. The gun question aside, this incident brought residents together to take community action to reduce crime.

## Apartment complexes

Every city has apartment complexes made up of five, ten, or twenty large buildings set at odd angles and identified as A through K, or by some other scheme. If the police receive a call about a break-in, they can find the complex but may have difficulty finding the particular apartment. That gives a burglar a little more time to get in and get out.

If you decide to live in a complex, avoid ground-floor units, which are the most vulnerable. Make an effort to get to know your neighbors. Make sure your landlord will allow you to add deadbolt locks, if they are not already there. If you want an alarm system, make sure the lease allows it before you sign.

## Miscellaneous tips

■ Don't leave your back door open, thinking no one will notice.

■ While burglars prefer to enter on the first story, if they see a ladder in the garage, or if a tree snuggles up to your house, they may climb.

■ If you return home to find a busted doorframe or other sign of entry, do not go in. Go to a friend's house and call the police.

■ Keep a phone by your bedside—either a cell phone or a phone whose jack is in your room. Install a lock on your bedroom door and use that room as a place to retreat if you or your child need to.

■ Burglars don't like dogs. If you do, consider getting one to alert you to possible intruders.

■ Keep the shrubbery around your house or at the entrance to your apartment trimmed low to discourage burglars. Alternatively, plant very thorny shrubs beneath windows.

■ Privacy fences provide good screens for burglars.

■ Have emergency numbers marked on the outside of each telephone.

■ Go over the 911 emergency call number with your child, and have him roll-play making an emergency call.

## Telephone contacts

People will call you up wanting all kinds of information about your personal life. Many of these people are harmless. However, some burglars use the telephone to identify potential victims. A typical opening is, "Ms. _____, my name is Joe Smith, and I would like to ask you just a few questions about your television viewing habits." You agree. "What program are you watching now?" This line of questioning moves on to " How many people live in your house over the age of eighteen? What is your occupation?" By the time you finish answering these questions, a burglar will know that you are a single mother absent from home until 5:00 P.M. Monday through Friday, and you make enough money to have a TV and other valuables in your house.

Avoid answering any personal questions asked by strangers on the phone for any reason. Memorize a standard answer with which you are comfortable. Some suggestions are:

*"We are not interested."*

*"I have a policy that I do not buy anything or answer questions over the telephone."*

*"I need to get off the phone."*

These are all "no" statements. Do not give the caller a reason why you don't want a product or can't talk with him; just keep saying no. Some of these people are very sophisticated and have been trained to come back at you in response to anything except "No." Do not feel sorry for the caller. You do not need to take responsibility for his feelings. You have a right to privacy, and your needs come first.

To get rid of most telephone solicitors, contact the nationwide do-not-call registry and list your telephone numbers with them. It only takes a minute. You can call 1-888-382-1222, but you must be calling from the telephone that you want to register. You can register online at www.donotcall.gov.

## What a burglar does in your home

He does not carry a toolbox, ladders, or ropes, just a small screwdriver and a credit card; with these he breaks into your house. He heads for the bedroom; on his way he figures out all the exits. He grabs a pillowcase off the bed and fills it with jewelry, money, guns, and silver. He checks in shoe bags and between mattresses in the bedroom, between frozen meat in the freezer, and in other common hiding places. He does this in a matter of minutes. Then he goes for the heavy electronic equipment: DVD players, VCRs, TVs, stereos, radios, and computers. The entire operation should take him no more than ten to twenty minutes. If he has an accomplice, he gains entry first, and then signals the driver to pull up the van (which probably looks like it belongs to a legitimate business). They load up your stuff and drive away. If his operation was successful and he got some good stuff, he may hit your neighbor in a few days. He may even come back and try to rob you again. The profile of the most common kind of burglar is someone who is on drugs. He's supporting his habit; it's business.

### Game plans

When you are in a crisis situation, you will take whatever action you have previously mentally rehearsed. For example, a seventy-year-old woman returned from church one day to see two young men standing on her lawn. Without a word, she walked by them and onto her porch. They followed, grabbed her, and began to rip off her clothes right on the porch. The next thing she remembers is seeing them fleeing from her yard. She heard a whistle and looked down to see herself holding one. It was her whistle, hung around her neck—she had received and practiced using it at a senior-citizen safety meeting a month before.

Many of us go through "what if" situations in our minds. It is a good idea to do the same thing with your child in a matter-of-fact way, asking questions like, "What would you do if a strange man sitting in a car called you over to his open window, asked for directions, and exposed his penis to you?" This happened to an eleven-year-old girl walking across a college campus to her mother's office. Sometimes children will think these questions are funny; at other times they may say, "That's creepy," or some other response. You can put aside her fears by saying, "Well, this probably

> ■ ■ ■ ■ ■ ■ ■
>
> When you are in a crisis situation, you will take whatever action you have previously mentally rehearsed.

will never happen to you, but what would you do if it did? How could you get yourself out of it?" See if she can provide more than one solution.

If she comes up with the game plan, she is more likely to be able to use it instinctively if, God forbid, she needs to. Then you can make additional suggestions like, "Well, what about running to Mickie's house?" Teach your child how to avoid trouble, what her escape options are, which friends to contact in emergencies, and what telephone numbers she can call. Help her form her own game plans.

## Fires

Here are a few guidelines for preventing fires in your home:

▪ Install smoke detectors. Some are set off by kitchen smoke, so people take them down when they cook and forget to put them back up. Make sure your detectors stay activated. One man bought a family Christmas present of a smoke detector with a battery, wrapped it, and put it under the tree. Before Christmas, the family awakened during the night to an alarm in their living room. It was the smoke detector going off inside the package. The family and the house were saved.

▪ Do not allow anyone to smoke in bed in your house.

▪ Repair or replace electrical cords that have exposed wires.

▪ Have gas appliances checked once a year by your gas company repairperson. This is a free service.

▪ Do not store kerosene, gasoline, or propane in enclosed or hot spaces. Avoid storing them at all, if you can.

▪ Space heaters are fire hazards, and some homeowners insurance companies will increase your premium if you declare you own one.

▪ Discuss fire prevention, including safe handling of stoves, irons, candles, fireplaces, and matches, with your child.

■ Rehearse fire safety rules and exit routes with your child once a year.

■ Purchase fire escape ladders for upper stories. Make sure your child knows where the ladders are and can access them easily.

## Guns

I do not recommend guns. They are dangerous to adults and children alike. Accidents with guns happen at home to the very people you intend to protect. More homicides are committed by family members with guns than by any other combination of people and weapons.

Here is what a convicted rapist had to say about guns: "The gun is in her bag. She don't know when she's gonna get jumped. She might even not have time to get to the bag. There's a lot of rapes been happening lately. I see guns as causing problems. She doesn't know when she's going to get raped. Carrying it in her purse: no problem. Put it in the drawer: no problem. No big deal. Only thing they're doing is, if he [the rapist] gets by with it, he's got a gun that he can sell and cause some other crime or somebody else to get killed."

However, the decision about whether or not to have a gun is a personal one. If you want a gun, call your police department and find out where to buy one, how to register it, and how to keep your child from having access to it. Learn how to operate it as safely as possible at a local gun range.

## Rape

Rape is a violent crime of power and anger. Nothing is more destructive to a woman than the violation of her body. Rape is every woman's fear.

It takes two elements for a crime to be committed:

■ *Idea or intent* in the mind of the criminal, and
■ *Opportunity* to commit the crime.

Only you can remove the opportunity. Be aware of your surroundings at all times and be prepared. It will cut down the odds of your being raped.

When traveling alone in your car, keep plenty of gas in the tank. Travel on well-lit, well-traveled streets. Keep your doors locked. Keep your windows rolled up while stopped in traffic. If you need air, use the air conditioner or roll down your windows no more than two inches. If someone tries to run your car off the road, try to overtake or stay close behind another car. If someone bumps your car on a deserted street, do not stop; continue driving until you reach a gas station or other public place. Do not stop your car to assist strangers. Call the police for them instead.

If your car breaks down, park on the shoulder of the road, raise the hood, get back into your car, lock the doors, shut the windows, put on your emergency flashers, and call 911 on your cell phone. If someone stops to help, lower your windows no more than two inches and ask them to call the police. Politely refuse all other help. These precautions are increasingly important, particularly in deserted areas, from dusk until dawn, and out in the country. But they are sound procedure at any time.

If someone tries to force his way into your car, turn on the headlights and flash them repeatedly. Sound the horn repeatedly to attract attention. If he should break the window, do not let him reach the door latch. Jab at his hand. Do not ever get out of your car unless your attacker gets into it.

True story: A woman was pumping gas and, as always, she left her car doors open. She used a credit card at the pump to pay for the gas. Meanwhile, a man surreptitiously entered the back seat of her car on the side opposite the pumps. A clerk inside noticed the man get in. He announced to the woman over the outdoor loudspeaker, "Please come inside. There is a problem with your credit card." She wasn't aware of a problem, but finally did go inside. The clerk told her about the man inside her car; he escaped as they were talking. After that, the woman decided to lock her doors whenever she exited her car, even for a short while.

Rape is such an important topic that every woman owes it to herself to be informed. Call your police department first. The police should have useful booklets on rape, the contact information of local agencies, and information on rape prevention and self-protection workshops in your town.

Many women learn and enjoy self-protection skills, such as martial arts. Rape prevention workshops usually illustrate simple physical moves you can use to throw your attacker off balance and allow you time to escape. Investigating these resources now may help prevent a tragedy later.

Do not hesitate to pass on rape prevention information to your daughters and sons as well. It is in their best interests for you to prepare them as you prepare yourself.

# CHAPTER 13

# Fixing Things Around the House

It's so nice to have
   a man around
   the house

Basic tools

A gold mine:
   your local
   hardware store

Hiring a professional

Trading skills

## It's so nice to have a man around the house

Marguerite's ex-husband was a little clumsy with a hammer and saw, but he still did most of the basic fix-it work around their house—carpentry, electricity, plumbing, and painting. They called in professionals for difficult jobs.

After she and her husband separated, Marguerite and her two children moved into an old house with friends. Her upstairs bathroom showerhead did not deliver the water massage she was used to in her former home. She was frustrated; she knew what needed to be fixed, but her fix-it man was gone. With some hesitation, she went to her local hardware store, bought a massage showerhead, asked the clerk how to install it, borrowed a wrench from a friend, and did the work herself. The actual job took her about thirty minutes. She felt a tremendous sense of accomplishment and power.

When your fix-it man is gone, your choices are to live with the problem, learn how to do the job yourself, or get someone else to do it for you.

## Basic tools

Depending on who you are and where you live, basic tools can vary from a telephone (to call for help) to a toolbox the size of a refrigerator. The wonderful thing about living in an apartment or condo is that the management does much of the building maintenance. However, management may be slow to move on your job or may be unwilling to fix anything. You may own your own home—which means that you are the management. But even in a well-maintained apartment complex, you still need to hang pictures, tighten screws, connect electronic equipment, and do other basic work to maintain your own equipment and space. For these small jobs, it's nice to have a

- hammer
- flathead screwdriver
- wrench
- phillips head screwdriver
- pliers
- pair of heavy rubber gloves
- flashlight

## A gold mine: your local hardware store

Barbara was at a friend's house down the street when her two sons called her and said, "Mom, come home quick! You know that outside faucet thing that you put the hose on? Well, it was bent over and we tried to straighten it, and now ... well... there's water spraying up all over the place."

It was Saturday. Barbara ran home, thinking fast all the way. How do you get a plumber on Saturday? Look in the Yellow Pages? She saw the little river of water already trickling down the gutter as she ran. When she approached the house, she saw that the boys had put a trash can lid over the broken spigot to keep the water off the house, Barbara calmed the boys, went into the house, sat down by the phone, and said, "What am I going to do?" Her Uncle George, a real handyman, lived sixty miles away—this was an emergency. Who do you call in an emergency? Who knows how to fix things? The hardware store. They would know what to do. She called. The clerk said she needed to shut off the water at the main valve by the street. She could try it with a wrench, or they had a tool for six dollars that was made for that purpose. She bought the tool, shut off the water, and called Uncle George, who came out and fixed the spigot later in the day. She watched him do it and got a brief lesson in plumbing.

■ ■ ■ ■ ■ ■ ■

Your local hardware store can become as valuable to you as your family physician....

Later, the staff at the hardware store taught Barbara how to replace leaky washers, install a timer switch on the light in her living room, fix her leaky toilet, and many other things.

If you need a fan or a set of picture hangers, you can buy them cheaply at a discount store. But your local hardware store, though it can be more expensive, employs clerks who often have home repair experience. It is the place to go (or to call) when:

▪ You have an emergency and don't know where to turn for help.

▪ You need advice about a fix-it problem or a type of product.

▪ You want to buy and install something that you've never done before.

Your local hardware store can become as valuable to you as your family physician, especially if you own your own home. Inexpensive how-to books on home repairs are also available at hardware stores; if you can follow a recipe in a cookbook, you can follow most fix-it directions. If a job is clearly beyond you, a book will help you know the right questions to ask the professionals.

Some hardware stores have free how-to classes on practical skills, such as installing a ceiling fan, replacing a leaky washer, laying bricks, and so on.

## Hiring a professional

Helga's hair was always perfect. One day I asked her how she kept it that way. "The secret," she said, "is my hairdresser. She always cuts my hair just right. Maintaining it is easy once you have a good cut." I asked her how she found her hairdresser. "I saw a woman whose hair I really liked. I walked up to her and asked her

---

### KNOW THYSELF. IT MAKES SENSE TO GET HELP IF:

▪ You are not good with your hands.

▪ You don't have the time to spend half a day or more on a job.

▪ You don't like getting up to your elbows in tools and dust and goo.

▪ You are frustrated by fix-it work and you are facing a big job.

who her hairdresser was. She told me, and I've been going to that hairdresser ever since."

You can do the same with professional fix-it people. Find a friend or neighbor whose home you admire, and ask that person to recommend a painter, for example. People who set high standards for their homes—especially professional people who have more money than time—often keep lengthy lists of reliable fix-it people. Ask people at work. Ask relatives. Ask your local hardware store; they often post the business cards of customers with whose work they are familiar. Ask a real estate agent; they often purchase property to rent or resell. People are usually flattered to be asked for advice. Try to get at least three names to call, so that you can compare prices and other aspects of the job.

> ■ ■ ■ ■ ■ ■ ■
> If the person you interview does not have experience and references, continue your search.

Hire experience. If the person you interview does not have experience and references, continue your search.

*Caution:* Check out a prospective worker thoroughly. Home repair and remodeling errors by contractors occur frequently, and errors are costly to correct—if they can be corrected. If you get the name of a carpenter from a friend, call up the carpenter and ask for the names and phone numbers of two other people for whom he has worked. When you check references, ask:

■ Did she listen to you?
■ Did he implement the job as you asked?
■ Was she pleasant to work with? Flexible?
■ Was the quality of the job excellent?
■ Did he work in a timely fashion?
■ Did she damage any of your property?

- Did he clean up his mess after each work session?
- Did she charge the price that was quoted or were there cost increases?
- Would you hire her again?

Do not hesitate to call perfect strangers to ask these questions. Introduce yourself on the phone. "Mr. Jones, you don't know me, but Mr. Smith gave me your number. I need a carpenter to help me with kitchen cabinets. Do you have time to tell me a little about Mr. Smith? Did he do a good job for you?" Then go through your questions and ask if you may see his work.

Beth had once worked with a man who also painted houses. Beth called up her former boss and asked her if she thought the man would do a good job painting three rooms in Beth's house. The boss gave him a glowing recommendation. Beth hired him. He and his fellow worker set up their equipment, and Beth and the children left the house to spend the day with a friend. When they returned, Beth found paint splattered all over her furniture, rugs, and hardwood floors; the painters had not used drop cloths properly. Some of the trim was painted cleanly; other parts were not. Paint had slopped over onto windows, floors, and walls. Beth learned that an assistant was responsible for the badly painted trim. The lead painter had said he would sand and wash surfaces where necessary before painting, but he had not. With one room finished and two rooms partially painted, Beth dismissed the painters. There were bad feelings on both sides. Beth called her former boss, who felt responsible for the situation. She had given the painter a good recommendation based only on what he had told her; he had never actually done any work for her. Three months later, Beth was still removing paint spots from odds and ends. She painted the unfinished rooms herself.

When you contract with a person to do a repair or remodel job for you, get a bid, not an estimate, and get it all in writing. A bid should include:

▪ A "punch list" of exactly what will be done. A punch list for painting a room might include:

- Remove all hardware from room.
- Strip all wallpaper, fill holes, and sand surfaces till smooth.
- Prime walls with latex interior primer.
- Paint walls twice with [name of paint brand and color] latex satin interior paint.
- Paint ceiling once with [paint brand and color] latex ceiling paint.
- Paint trim once with [paint brand and color] latex satin interior paint.
- Use brush on trim.
- Replace all hardware.
- Remove paint, if any, from window glass.
- Use drop clothes, and clean up any splatters on floor.
- Clean up debris and dust at the end of each workday.
- Dispose of empty paint cans off site.

▪ The time limit for the job and financial penalties (reduced final payment) for each day the job goes beyond the date of scheduled completion. Home repair workers are famous for starting a job, then moving on to other jobs before they finish yours. They entice you by telling you they can get started right away, but don't tell you they'll be stopping during your project to work on other jobs. Overlapping jobs provides workers with some security—there's always more work to be done and more money to be earned. Meanwhile, your room that needs to be painted is a jumble for over a week instead of two days.

▪ A guarantee in writing for one year, or whatever time-frame you agree to, after completion of the job.

▪ A payment schedule. Pay no more than one-third of the total fee up front. Then pay the remainder in increments as the work is done. Never make a final payment until after you have done a final inspection of the job and you are ready for the worker to walk out of the house and never return.

Get not one bid on the job, but three. Make sure each is bidding on the same job; they should all bid on your punch list, which should be thorough enough to ensure comparable bids. The lowest bid is not necessarily the best bid. Paying more for quality work is worthwhile in the long run. Personal interaction is also important; if your worker is difficult to get along with, he can make the whole experience unpleasant and the end product not quite what you had wanted. Remember: references, references, references.

## Trading skills

If you can't afford to hire someone and don't want to do a job yourself, you can ask someone else to do it for you. Relatives, friends, neighbors, work associates—anyone is a possibility.

Make them an offer they can't refuse. Find out what their needs and pleasures are, and see if you can supply something of value to them. Like food. Send Uncle Doug home with a hug and a loaf of cranberry bread. Promise to babysit the children of your handyman neighbor for a certain number of hours for free, so that he and his wife can go out on the town. Cook a dinner, sew a tablecloth, do a little decorating, mow the lawn, or wash and wax the car. Do their taxes or write a resume. If you know a lot about music, offer to put together a ninety-minute party tape. Everyone has something they would like help with. Ask them and see if you can provide it in exchange for their help.

When you approach someone to set up a barter deal for the first time, start small—a job that takes no more than two hours, for example. If both of you are satisfied with the arrangement, you can continue to work together in this way, increasing the size of the barter deals as necessary and convenient.

Be aware that when you contract to exchange services with another person, you are accepting whatever quality the other person provides, just as if you were paying money for the service.

Check out her work ahead of time. Say, point blank, "Will you do a good job for me?" and smile, smile, smile. Ask to see a sample of her work. Many bartering arrangements are between friends or acquaintances; state up front, "We both need to realize that this is strictly business. Right? And, oh, by the way, can we still be friends?" A little humor never hurts. Because friendship is an element in the deal, you have an added incentive to prevent disaster. Starting small provides some insurance for both the work and the friendship; in case of unfortunate results, you can forgive and forget and get on with the friendship. There is a risk.

And there is a plus. Working with someone you like can further cement your friendship. It's nice to be able to trust the person who is working on your property, and she will probably have a personal incentive to do a nice job for you.

Some neighborhood associations form talent pools. People sign up to barter their skills with other neighbors. There are tool pools as well. The more people you know, the greater your resources for bartering talents, tools, and time. In this way, you can save money while you meet your fix-it needs.

# CHAPTER 14

# Managing
# Space and Time

Letting go of perfection

Getting your child
   to help

Managing the mess

Getting rid of things

Managing time

Cooking

Fast food

"To do" lists

Learn to say "No"

Simplify your life

Slow down

*We were goin' down some street—*
*three of us in the car,*
*me knowin' we were late ... again.*
*And we'd probably slip behind all day,*
*all overflowing Saturday.*

*With my foot layin' heavy on the gas*
*and my eye jerking between road and speedometer*
*I was tryin' to whiz through the city*
*but escape a ticket.*
*Jonathan said, "I'm glad I've got my seat belt on.*
*Do you have yours on, Mommy?*
*We might get into an accident."*
*I said, "I've got mine on, too.*
*But don't worry, we're not goin' to get into an accident*
     *today, honey."*
*"How do you know?" said Laura.*
*" 'Cause I don't have time to get into an accident today,*
     *honey."*
*Laura giggled.*
 *"Oh, Mommy, you're so funny," she said.*

## Letting go of perfection

Rachel's four children went to her ex-husband's house for a holiday. She spent her first day alone cleaning up her house. "My house is always a wreck," she said. "Max [the youngest, age five] is the worst. And it's so frustrating. I can never get ahead. I keep my laundry down in the basement, and some of it never comes back up. The kids go downstairs to find clean clothes for school. I've heard of other mothers who live out of their laundry rooms. And I don't know where I'd put the clothes if I brought them all up. We don't have enough room in our apartment. There is one closet upstairs and one downstairs. That's it. The children don't know where to put things because there isn't enough storage space. I have to be very creative in finding little niches for things. Does it ever get better?"

▪ ▪ ▪ ▪ ▪ ▪ ▪

Does it ever get better?

The answer is, yes. Her son Sam, age thirteen, had already started doing his own laundry. Her daughter Kate, age eleven, had done a load once or twice. The older your child gets, the more responsible he can be for his own things and the more helpful he can be in many ways.

Long ago, Rachel had given up on trying to keep a perfect house, but she thought that other single mothers probably did. Actually, most single mothers consistently bemoan their constant battle against "stuff" littering the floors, tables, countertops—wherever there is a horizontal surface in the home, in the car, and in the yard. Rachel's problem was compounded by the fact that she and her four children lived in a one-bedroom apartment. With two children in the only bedroom, two in bunk beds in the dining room and Rachel on the couch in the living room, they were crowded.

Whenever there are children in a home, there will be stuff to clean up; your home is their home too. They never seem to mind that littered, lived-in look, at least not enough to do something about it. But most mothers prefer a neat, clean environment, and children do too.

Everybody has to compromise. Your child needs to help clean up, even though that may not be on his agenda. And you need to lower your standards to a certain extent, in order to keep from constantly yelling, "Clean it up!" Somewhere between total chaos and total perfection lies a place of peaceful compromise where all the parties can agree, "Well, this will do for now." The mother usually sets the standard to work toward, and her children usually test it from time to time—at which point the mother has to reaffirm the standard.

> ■ ■ ■ ■ ■ ■ ■
>
> Whenever there are children in a home, there will be stuff to clean up....

## Getting your child to help

From the time they are toddlers, children can help around the house. A toddler can put a toy on a shelf. A five-year-old can take the dishes out of the dishwasher and put them on the countertop for you to put away. An eight-year-old can wash the dishes. A fourteen-year-old can do just about anything that you can do.

No thinking mother wants to overburden her children with housework and adult responsibilities. On the other hand, American children may do less to assist their families than the children of any other country. As mothers, we often err in requiring too little of our children. Regular chores are a good way to learn responsibility. What a disservice it would be for a mother to settle her grown son in his first apartment without his knowing how to cook, clean, shop for supplies, and otherwise manage household affairs in the new apartment. Childhood is a time in which we gradually shoulder increasing responsibilities as preparation for competent adulthood.

The difficult part is that a single mother has to marshal the troops to do their work without any reinforcement from a partner. In the short run, it is often easier just to do the job yourself. You'll get no complaint from your child if you do. But in the long run, assigning your child responsibilities and making sure she follows through with them will make her feel good about herself. It will keep the house neater and will free you to use your time in other valuable ways.

Try these techniques to get your child to help around the house:

- Make a simple request: "Please take out the garbage."
- Appeal to his sense of family: "You are a part of this family; you enjoy the benefits of family life, and you are expected to contribute to the maintenance of our home."
- Bribe her: "If you wash the dishes for me, I'll rub your back." The problem with this technique is that your child may ask you the next time, "If I do this for you, what will you do for me?" (Answer: "Feed and clothe you.") Use this sparingly.
- Use a kitchen timer to help him work on delayed tasks. For example, if you go to the store for a loaf of bread, set the timer for five minutes, at which time you want him to turn off the TV.
- Make sure she knows what is expected. If you say, "Clean up the living room," does that include putting things away, vacuuming, and dusting, or just putting things away?
- Set up an inspection: "Let me know when you finish so that I can inspect your job." When you inspect, point out improvements you think he needs to make, if any, and set up a final inspection.
- Establish consequences: if she fails to do her job, ask her a second time and give her an additional job to do.

■ Praise his work: "You did a great job on the car. It means a lot to us all. Thanks."

Use any technique that works—short of arguing, screaming, or slapping.

## Managing the mess

Here are some ideas that mothers have used successfully to try to maintain order and civility in their homes while their children are young.

■ When the whole house is a mess, clean up one room. The bathroom is a good choice, since it is small. Continue room by room through the house if you have the time and energy. But just one clean room can lift your spirits.

■ Keep your own room neat and pretty. Use it as a refuge from the madding crowd.

■ Alternatively, let your own room be a mess, the one place in your life where you don't have to conform to order. If your room is a mess, keep the door closed.

■ Enlist your child to help you clean up the communal rooms in the house after dinner and before he settles down to do homework, watch TV, read, or do other quiet activities. That way, when he goes to bed, the house will be fairly neat for the night.

■ Loudly announce, "OK, everybody clean up the living room and dining room. Go!" One mother used this approach whenever she felt overwhelmed with the mess. Everyone in earshot would get up and pitch in to straighten up the rooms. It only took five minutes with everyone working, it was generally fun, and it promoted a feeling of family.

■ As soon as your child learns to read, make her a to-do list. After breakfast (or cartoons, or whatever), she must immediately go to work on her list. She scratches off the chores one by one until they are done. Then she can play.

## A FEW WORDS FROM THE CHILDREN

Child:  *"But Joey (a friend) doesn't have to fold clothes."*

Mother: *"Joey doesn't live in this house. He has his rules, you have yours."*

Child:  *"Dad never asks me to fold clothes."*

Mother: *"Dad has his rules, I have mine. We are both trying to help you grow up to be a responsible adult."*

Child:  *"I'll do it later; my favorite TV program is coming on."*

Mother: *"Do it now, please."* Or, *"OK, we'll make a contract. What time can you have it done by?"*

Once your child commits to a specific time, hold her to it. If the task doesn't get done, assign a work consequence. Contracting with your child puts more responsibility on you to monitor the job, but it allows your child some flexibility and provides some experience in learning to manage her own time.

Child:  *"I don't know how to mop the floor."*

Mother: *"Let me teach you right now."*

Child:  *"You always ask me to do more work than Sherry. How come she gets to go play?"*

Mother: *"I love you, and I'm not going to ask you to do anything unreasonable. I am trying to be fair about workload, but you must remember that in the end, I am the judge."*

The lists allow you to avoid assigning jobs verbally and getting verbal complaints back. Your child can complain to the list!

■ Assign routine daily chores—cleaning up the kitchen, feeding the dog—to family members on a rotating basis. For example, Sam washes the dishes on Monday, Wednesday, and Friday. Jill washes them on Tuesday, Thursday, and Saturday. Mom washes them on Sunday. Everyone must begin washing before 7:00 P.M. If your children are older than ten and they forget, warn them once. The next time, assign a work consequence. Once you train them to be responsible for managing their own time on their day with that chore, you will *not* have to say, "Sam, isn't this your day to do the dishes? It's almost seven o'clock!" It makes your job easier, and it makes your child more responsible.

■ When your child is doing housework, let him crank up the radio or otherwise work to the beat of his favorite music. The faster the beat, the better for your young worker; it's energizing and uplifting. If you can work *with* your child and find some fast music that you all enjoy, it can be a lot of fun.

## Getting rid of things

Encourage neatness by providing ample storage space in convenient locations for everything you own. If you need a chest of drawers in your living room to keep board games, magazines, or other clutter, then put one there. Do whatever works.

Space limitations spawn problems for which single mothers have found interesting solutions. Faith keeps her exercise bicycle in her living room, since there is a bare corner where it just fits. Her children and their friends use it frequently, and adult guests often climb on the seat to take it for a spin. The bicycle has turned out to be a conversation piece.

Not everything in Faith's house gets as much attention as the bicycle, however. There are over fifteen grocery sacks full of papers that she has moved from one house to another at least twice before, papers she has not looked at in years because she hasn't had time. Recently she went through about ten boxes full of household goods, many old toys, and children's clothes, and much of that she gave away. She now faces the fifteen sacks and intends to reduce her inventory to a fraction of that. Soon she will have gained more room and less clutter—a big improvement in a small house.

Getting rid of clutter—by selling, recycling, or throwing it away—automatically gives your house a neater appearance. Since your child will probably strew his belongings around the house in the normal course of his activities, every effort toward an uncluttered look is its own reward.

> ▪ ▪ ▪ ▪ ▪ ▪ ▪
> Getting rid of clutter— by selling, recycling, or throwing it away— automatically gives your house a neater appearance.

## Managing time

"Time ain't on my side" just may be the single mother's theme song. There are some management techniques that can help, but in the end, you need to recognize that:

- You are finite.
- You are doing the best you can.
- It is OK to look up to the sky and yell, "Give me a break" and...
- It is OK to take that break.

## Cooking

By all means, let your child help you prepare meals. He can set the table and help with small tasks. Starting at about age four, children can do "Get me" work, as in "Get me the milk and butter from the refrigerator," or "Get me a big pan from the cabinet."

Even small children enjoy breaking eggs, stirring together ingredients, forming dough into balls, and other cooking activities. They can shuck corn, snap beans, and tear lettuce.

Small tasks done are a big help. If you and your child are in the kitchen together, it gives you an opportunity to talk about your day. In order to make this pleasurable, sibling fights, rambunctious children, and loud noises must stay out of the kitchen.

Teenagers can cook an occasional meal for the family, perhaps once a week. If you let your teen choose the meal, he will probably come up with pizza, nachos, hamburgers, or some other fast food delight. That's fine; just ask him to add a green salad and milk. You can teach him a little bit about nutrition in an unstructured way by suggesting ways to flesh out the menu. Allow your teenager to ask for help from a younger brother or sister as long as you don't hear any complaints from the younger child. This will teach your older child management techniques that emphasize encouragement rather than bullying or nagging. Meanwhile, you can go into the living room, prop up your feet, and bask in a few minutes of freedom.

Children can and will eat all day long. To avoid dirty dishes in the sink and dirty plates, sticky wrappers, and open boxes all over the house, one single mother would declare "Kitchen is closed!" after she had washed the last load of dishes in the evening. After that, children could drink milk or water but could not eat anything. Another family lived by the "Use it or lose it if you don't wash it" rule—snacking privileges were discontinued unless everyone cleaned up all traces of food, dishes, and related garbage.

## Fast food

Mothers who work outside the home buy more prepared foods than work-at-home moms. Most single mothers work outside the home, and their daily fare is often easy foods—macaroni and cheese mixes, spaghetti sauce in a jar, fish sticks, prepared meat pies, frozen pizzas, hot dogs and pork 'n' beans, canned or frozen vegetables, a piece of toast—Voila! One more meal on the table.

Fresh vegetables and meals cooked from scratch may taste better than convenience foods, but you should not feel guilty about relying heavily on prepared foods. There was only one Julia Child, and she got paid for it. For the rest of us, whatever works is probably OK. After all, the problem most U.S. citizens have is overeating, not undereating.

There are a few simple guidelines for good nutrition to remember; they're the same ones your child learns in school and from his dentist:

■ The five food groups are vegetables; grains; fruit; meat, fish, and poultry; and dairy. Try to serve your child some of each over the course of the day.

■ Nutritionists recommend five—yes five—servings of vegetables and fruit each day.

■ Serve milk with meals. It builds strong teeth and bones.

■ It is recommended that you drink eight glasses of water each day. Few people do this, but encourage your child to try. It works well when she is watching TV or doing other quiet-time activities.

■ Go easy on the sweets and fried foods.

## "To do" lists

A number of time management experts recommend that you:

1. Write down all the things you need to do on a given day.

2. Prioritize them according to their importance to you.

3. Do them, one at a time, until your time runs out.

4. Move leftover tasks to the next day's list.

How you prioritize your tasks is important. Edwin C. Bliss, time management consultant and writer, suggests that action can be broken down into five categories:

1. **Important and Urgent:** changing a wet diaper—you can't really put this off to another day.

2. **Important but not Urgent:** an annual medical checkup—it's important, but you could postpone it forever, since no one is breathing down your neck about it.

3. *Urgent but not Important:* a lecture on financial planning you promised to attend with your sister.

4. *Busy Work:* reorganizing the bookshelves when you should be paying bills and balancing your checkbook.

5. *Wasted Time:* whenever you feel you would have been better off spending your time doing something else.

Bliss believes that people tend to allocate too much time to things in categories three and four, and not enough time to things in category two. He suggests setting priorities according to *importance,* not urgency.

Don't expect to get more than about six things on your list done in a day. If you do more, that's great, but concentrate on those most important first six tasks.

■ ■ ■ ■ ■ ■ ■

…your time seems so short, but you are doing valuable things and making a contribution to the world.

At the end of the day, reflect back on the day and pick out five things you did that you are proud of. They don't have to be on your list. A victory at work, a kindness to a stranger, a quiet time of sharing with one of the children—anything counts. Remember: your time seems so short, but you are doing valuable things and making a contribution to the world.

## Learn to say "No"

If someone asks you to assist with a Brownie troop, canvass your block for the Heart Fund, sign up for two hours to register voters for the next election—think seriously about saying no, even though these are all worthy causes. If you say yes because you believe strongly in the cause and are eager to use your time to promote it, that is fine. But if you feel a twinge of pain when the request comes, if you ask yourself the automatically, "How will I find the time?"—then say no. One good rule to follow is, "When in doubt, say no."

Granted, if everyone took that attitude, worthy causes and volunteer systems would die. But people go through phases in their lives; as the phases change, the demands on our time change. A single mother frequently has little time to do anything but attend to her job, her children, and herself. When they become teenagers, she will have more free time, and when they leave home, even more. Then she can devote time to discretionary work for causes and family and friends without overburdening her or causing her to default on her primary responsibilities.

## Simplify your life

Find ways to cut down on the number of errands you run, bills you pay, loads of laundry you do, trips you make to the grocery store, personal phone calls you make, or day-care centers you take your children to each day. Wherever you can save yourself time and extra steps during the day, you will also save energy. "Less is more" means that cutting down on material consumption and simplifying our overly complex lives allows us to live more satisfying lives.

## Slow down

Take five- to fifteen-minute breaks during the day. If you've been sitting, get up and walk. If you've been working physically, sit down and prop up your feet. Change your pace and your activity. Stare out the window, read a magazine, close your eyes and feel. Breathe deeply, drink water, do whatever relaxes and refreshes you. It will give you greater energy to keep going through the end of your day. Think, "relax." You can go to the store in a frenzy, or you can go to the store in a more leisurely way; it will take the same amount of time either way. Your mental attitude can help you approach life in a calmer, more peaceful manner.

Relaxing is a learned skill. These days, there is a lot of pressure to accomplish big things at work and at home. We are pressured to be superworkers. For what? Life is short. Childhood is even shorter, so enjoy your kid. "Waste" a little time with them. Look around you. Enjoy the air, the sky, the glint of sun on a building, the refreshing drizzle of rain.

Schedule some leisure time into your week, with or without your child. Because it is important but not urgent, scheduling it helps you to carry it out. Plan something low-key, like listening to music or taking a walk. Look forward to that time. Think about it during your busy times, when you feel stretched taut. And when the time comes, put on your most comfortable clothes and shoes—or go barefoot!—and enjoy.

# CHAPTER 15

# Updating Your Social Life

Everyone's gone
  to the moon

The importance
  of connecting
  with friends

So where do you
  find friends?

Men as friends only

"While I'm out
  on the town,
  what about
  the kids?"

Socializing with
  the children

The art of celebration

*The newness terrified me.*
*Still I floated on, rejoicing*
*by myself*

*and with others.*
*My children came riding on me weightlessly*
*laughing and gathering up my edges.*
*And the firm broad faces of friends*
*(seeking re-election) on billboards*
*hung on stars in the sky by night.*
*I gathered them to me.*
*They animated and we danced*
*like popcorn blossoming*

### Everyone's gone to the moon

It's Saturday night. You are all alone. Well, the kids are there, but it sure would be nice to have a friend to talk to. Chances are the friends you and your partner had as a couple are not around anymore. After the separation they may fall away from you for one of five reasons:

■ People who related to your ex-partner more than to you will probably feel like they need to take his side and will not make an effort to see you.

■ Many couples have difficulty making the transition. They feel you and your ex-partner have failed, and they're afraid that marital failure may be catching. Their own fear, together with the sadness and sorrow they may feel for you, makes them uncomfortable.

■ Other couples may see you as a direct threat to the stability of their own relationship. Especially to some women, you have become a "radioactive" single, someone on the loose looking for a partner, and they don't want that partner to be theirs.

■ In a social situation with couples, as a single, you may be the odd one out.

■ You may not care to continue the relationship.

In addition, you may change the places you frequent after you separate from your partner. Because you are making all the decisions for your own life now, you may decide to go to a different gas station, grocery store, or place of worship. You may move. You may change jobs. You may drop the old health club and join a new one. And all these changes about where you spend your time and money mean you see different people in the course of a week.

For all these reasons, some or most of your friends will surely change. And that can be good.

## The importance of connecting with friends

The need to be with friends is universal. James S. House, sociologist at the University of Michigan, concluded in a study called "Social Relationships and Health" that loneliness can kill you. "The data indicates that social isolation is as significant to mortality rates as smoking, high blood pressure, high cholesterol, obesity and lack of physical exercise," according to House.

A good social network of friends takes the pressure off you to find a man. When you are lonely, it is too easy to establish a quick romantic relationship with someone who does not really meet your needs. Nutrition experts caution us never to shop for food when we are hungry. Likewise, we should never shop for a romantic partner when we are starved for friendship. A man is not necessary to living a full and satisfying social life. The first step in seeking new relationships is to establish some solid friendships with people who are not romantic possibilities. They are just friends, men and women with whom you can let your hair down and not feel judged. They just like to be with you.

■ ■ ■ ■ ■ ■ ■

> A good social network
> of friends takes
> the pressure off you
> to find a man.

Like finding a new job, making new friends requires effort. And with the frantic pace that you probably sustain as you juggle job, children, housework, and other arrangements, you may not have much energy for establishing new relationships. But one of the most important insurance plans you can secure is a strong network of friends to stay with you through thick and thin. One friend may call up when you are sick and offer to go to the grocery store for you, a second one may take care of your child in an emergency situation, a third may be someone you can call on when you feel depressed or angry. You'll want several friends with whom to share good news and to celebrate, to have fun, to share your child. A strong network of friends can act as your main support in lieu of a romantic partner.

## So where do you find friends?

They are all around you. Single mothers, like their former partners, find themselves reaching out to people, sometimes those they didn't have time for before they separated. Since you are not investing your emotional energy in building a relationship with your ex-partner, you can invest it in people you encounter every day.

Your co-workers may become more important to you; you may find yourself saying, "Let's go out for lunch today" more often. Lunch is OK, but beware of going out regularly with co-workers in the evenings and on weekends. It is often wise to build a network of friends with people away from your workplace. That way, you have friends to whom you can complain about work when you need to. Within your network of friends you'll be sharing intimate disclosures, and you never know when a co-worker might use such information against you. Most people will not turn on you, but are you willing to take that chance? Also, getting away from co-workers means you are getting away from work concerns. Sometimes after-hours shoptalk can be tedious, so give yourself a break. When you associate socially with people who work in other places and in other occupations, you get a little variety and a rest from the constant presence of your work scene.

As you pursue your own interests, you will find people with whom you have much in common. Find new friends at clubs and organizations. Read your local newspaper, which carries information on special events, clubs, volunteer activities, and classes. If you like to cook, ask at a kitchen shop if there's a gourmet club in your town. If you like athletics, check at the local YMCA to find out about sports teams and running clubs. If you like to read, ask about book clubs at the public library. If you are interested in politics, call up your political party or organization and offer to volunteer. If you want to find out about computer clubs, check with a local dealer.

Business and Professional Women (BPW) and other professional organizations can be located by calling the YWCA or the Chamber of Commerce. If you ask around enough, you will find some appealing groups to join.

Hundreds of volunteer organizations are waiting for you to get involved: the United Way, the American Red Cross, the American Cancer Society and other health organizations, the League of Women Voters, your child's parent-teacher organization, your neighborhood homeowner's association or your apartment complex's tenants association. Check with the mayor's office or the public library for service options, or look in the Yellow Pages under "Social Service Organizations" or "Human Services Organizations."

If you have the money for tuition, consider taking a class in an adult education program or college. Art classes are available at many community centers and museums. Music, drama, sewing, professional development courses—look around, and you will surely come up with interesting options. Remember that there are online courses that you can do from home at night and on the weekends. Many, such as those through the University of Phoenix, are structured so that the whole class, including the professor, is online simultaneously and able to participate in lively class discussion.

Singles groups established for social purposes usually include elements of both friendship and romance as a part of their operation.

### Men as friends only

A male prisoner who had been locked up for two years on a drug charge was released for his first eight-hour furlough. His fiancée drove him to her house. He said later, "I walked in the door and I felt the carpet under my feet, I saw soft little pillows here and there, and it was . . . it was . . . it just *smelled* like Woman." You can get starved for the opposite sex like that, even if you don't want to be romantically linked.

For a lot of reasons, it is nice to have a man as just a friend. Men tend to be rough, direct, and assertive if not aggressive, and they are often risk-takers. They look different and yes, they do smell different. You may long simply to be around a man and yet not want a romantic relationship. A friendship with a man can satisfy that need to connect with the other half of humanity.

Some married men form friendships with women other than their wives; they talk with this "other woman" about finances, sex, job difficulties, problems with their wives—things that they can't or don't share with their wives because they feel they have too much emotion and are too much at risk. These men find other women to talk with. That's one kind of friendship, a sort of talking friendship. But if the wife knows about the relationship, she may feel wary of it. She may easily become jealous and feel threatened.

Be on guard with the husbands of your friends. Once your separation is public knowledge, perfectly docile men with whom you and your partner related socially can come on to you sexually. You just have to make your limits clear. Use humor when possible to deflect the advance, help the man avoid embarrassment, and save the friendship. It can be easier to be friends with an unmarried man, with whom you can pal around in the sunshine, when you want a date to a function, when you want to go on an outing, or when you want an adult companion for a night of movies and popcorn at home with the kids—someone in the "brother" category.

When you find a man whose company you enjoy, be very honest with him and say, "Look, I like you. How about going out to dinner (or lunch, which is less threatening) as friends? You pay for yours, I'll pay for mine." Your offer to pay your own way is one indication that you do not have romance in mind. A straightforward approach is refreshing. What if he says no? You smile and say, "OK. Maybe some other time. The ball is in your court." And let it go. If he says yes, then you take that first step.

One woman approached a newly divorced man with just such an up-front suggestion: "I want to be your friend. I'm not interested in a romantic relationship with you at all, but I like you, and you will probably need a lot of support right now. I would welcome a new friend, but remember it has to be just that: friendship." And she meant it. They took walks together, ate lunches together, talked over their lives, and it remained a good friendship even after each remarried.

### "While I'm out on the town, what about the kids?"

Even if you have an infant in diapers, you need a social life all your own; everyone does. It is a mistake to sacrifice it completely because you have a child to care for. When your child is older and looking back on things, she will probably say, "Gosh, Mom, I wish you had been able to go out more when we were kids." Children should not be an excuse to hide in the house and avoid a social life.

In fact, it is to your child's advantage that you socialize; if you do not, you can become resentful of being tied down at home, which can create tension. Be glad to go, have fun, and be glad to come back refreshed. Your child can help you decide what to wear and will love seeing you dress up.

See also Babysitters, pages 126–127.

### Socializing with the children

In some parts of our society—such as bars, most workplaces, adults-only parties, clubs, and meetings, adult education class-rooms—children are taboo. But in people's homes and in many public settings—parks, museums, restaurants, and movie the-aters—children are welcome. If you find another single mother whose children are about the same age as your child, then the chil-dren can romp around together while you and the other mother share an adult conversation. Any adult whom you consider a friend could be integrated into your family life.

Here are some ideas for socializing as a family with friends:

■ Have a potluck dinner at your house.

■ Host a TV party on special occasions—like Super Bowl Sunday, election night, or the Academy Awards. Serve pop-corn and soft drinks.

- Have an invite-a-friend event, either in your home or not, to which each family member can invite one special friend. This could even be a sleepover followed by a lazy breakfast. (In this case, your friend should be female.)

- Select an inexpensive but good all-in-one-pot food, like vegetable stew or chili, and target one day a month—the first Saturday, for example—to invite a new person or a small group over to your house for a meal and conversation.

Much entertaining in our society involves food. If you keep the food simple and let everyone serve themselves, you'll be freer to concentrate on the conversation and other details of the evening. Also, serving a simple meal that you prepare regularly reduces your stress level. Keep everything as casual as you like. If you enjoy candles and cloth napkins, great; paper plates and napkins are equally satisfactory. Do whatever makes you comfortable and allows you to enjoy the evening. Your guests will pick up those vibrations.

Everyone appreciates an invitation to a meal, and you get to share another adult's world view, cares, concerns, and humor for a short while. If you target one day of the month to entertain, you can make it a regular part of your life.

On special family occasions like Thanksgiving, especially if you are unable to be with members of your own family, invite people to share the occasion with you. Create your own extended family.

Foreign students love invitations from American families on traditional occasions, and they are often wonderful with children, in part because they miss their own brothers and sisters. If you can't go to a foreign country, let the country come to you! Colleges often have lists of undergraduate and graduate students who would like to participate, and you can choose the nationality and gender of your guest. The first time you try this, invite a foreign student and an American friend or family member.

Explore the great outdoors with friends and their children: a walk around a lake, a trip to a park, or an afternoon hike. Even if your house is a mess, the great outdoors is always ready to receive and enrich visitors.

It's not just you who benefits from social contact with other adults—your child will as well. She will be exposed to new ideas, new jokes, new ways of doing things, and new people who pay attention to her. Building a social life with your child bonds you together as a family. You are sharing the same friends, having common experiences, and creating common memories. One day, your child will say, "Hey, Mom, remember that lady who spilled her hot coffee all over the table and it fell through the crack onto the cat, and the cat screeched and took off into. . ."

■ ■ ■ ■ ■ ■ ■

Building a social life with your child bonds you together as a family.

A word about other adults and your child: those who see her good qualities get repeat invitations. You should keep those who are obviously uncomfortable or unaffirming away from her. Children quickly pick up on how people feel about them, and who wants to feel like a nuisance? Fortunately, there are many people who will appreciate your child for the beautiful and interesting person she is.

## The art of celebration

Some people are particularly good at this. They light candles with dinner. They always find fresh flowers or greens to decorate their homes. They consider a phone call from you to be a gift. They delight in your child's accomplishments—a good report card, membership on a sports team, a clever comment, a helpful gesture. These celebrators consider making it through a week of work to be reason enough to get together for laughs on Friday night. They understand that simply doing your job conscientiously is a tremendous accomplishment, one to be proud of. If you can find someone like this—or, even better, more than one person—recognize that this person is remarkable and take lessons. Make every effort to develop your own ability to celebrate life. Step back from your problems enough to point out the good things happening in your life and in the lives of your friends, and then celebrate them. Life is good, and for that we can be thankful and celebrate. Even in the darkest pit, you can light a candle.

# CHAPTER 16

Romance

"Will I ever trust
a man again?"

Dating can be a drag

Sex and the
single mother

Date rape

Looking for love in all
the wrong places

Married men

Singles groups

Meeting new men
through the
personals

Online and print ads

Chat rooms

Online clubs

Dating companies

Quality relationships

Co-dependent
relationships

Levels of commitment

Making excuses for
having children

Revealing a
sexual relationship
to your child

Your man and
your child

Living together

Kids' reactions

Blended family blues

Prenuptial agreements

*I am a mountain.*

*I waited for you.*

*You have climbed me.*

*You have put your flag in me.*

*I wear your colors, your smell.*

*My rock will not fail you.*

*My soil will flower for you in spring.*

*Your body is so warm on me*

*where you stand there is no snow.*

### "Will I ever trust a man again?"

Jeanna's husband had several affairs while he and Jeanna were married. One day he left for work and said he would not be coming home that night. He left Jeanna for another woman whom he eventually married. Jeanna was stunned.

So was Louise, when her husband left her for another woman. Louise was attractive, intelligent, educated, and sociable. When her husband walked out, her self-esteem took a dive. She began wondering what was wrong with her, and she stopped trusting men. She was so hurt by her husband that for over a year she couldn't face another relationship with a man. At the same time, however, she was looking at the men around her, judging them against her idea of the ideal man, even though she didn't want even an ideal man anywhere near her.

You feel vulnerable and whipped when you're newly single. Around men, you feel like a pimply-faced adolescent on review at a school party, wondering, "Will anyone ask me to dance?" Your confidence as a woman is damaged. Even if you left your ex-partner, the pain that relationship caused hurt you badly enough for you to need to heal before approaching a man again.

### Dating can be a drag

June had been separated from her ex-husband for seven months. One evening, the phone rang. "Hi," the voice said, "I'm Lionel. I met you at the [organization] meeting a couple of months ago."

"Right. I remember who you are. How are you doing?" said June.

"Fine. Listen, I just wanted to call and ask you to dinner next Saturday night."

Plunk.

Thoughts whizzed through June's head like lightning: *But I'm married. Well, no, I'm not married anymore. I guess there's no reason why I couldn't go out. Is this a date? There's no reason why I should say no that I can think of, I mean, I guess it's OK for me to go out to dinner with another man.* And what June said to Lionel was, "OK, I guess that would be all right."

It wasn't exactly a warm or sophisticated response, but June was caught off-guard. Though she had been looking at men everywhere for months, she never thought one would ask her out. Her self-image was still that of a thirty-five-year-old wife and mother. Now she was faced with a situation that challenged the leftover image of herself as wife. But she wasn't a wife anymore—she was a date.

June's first date was hardly a misty-eyed romantic whirl. She met Lionel at an Italian restaurant. He ordered in Italian. They ate a meal that Lionel pronounced "excellent" and June thought was good spaghetti. Afterward, they both drove to June's house. Lionel asked himself in. (June's children were gone.) They sat on the sofa for a while, and June found it an effort to make conversation with him. He told her a little about his wife's leaving him and how devastated he was. Then, out of the blue, he grabbed her and began to French kiss her. It was awful. They were both embarrassed, and she walked Lionel to the door. That was their first and last date.

June brushed her teeth.

It was sad, in a way (in spite of the good spaghetti), but that evening did change June's perception of herself and restore some of her confidence. Part of your continuing job as a single mother is to let go of old definitions and see yourself with new eyes—the reality, the possibilities, the strengths of the new you.

June never did date again. Instead, a friendship with another man developed into a serious relationship, and in two more years she made the transition from single mother to wife in a blended family.

## Sex and the single mother

Everyone likes to be touched. It can be both comforting and exciting to have someone hold you, stroke you, and moan and groan because you turn him on. Meanwhile, you are doing the same thing. Sex is powerful. It can be either ecstasy or shattering, depending on how you feel about it. For now we will talk about sex that is healthy, satisfying, and fun.

What do you do when your romantic partner is gone? You can

- Satisfy yourself.
- Find a sexual replacement.
- Do without.

Some women enjoy masturbation a great deal and for them, self-stimulation is a perfectly acceptable sexual experience. Other women prefer not to practice sexual stimulation in any form, and the choice not to have sex is perfectly acceptable.

> ▪ ▪ ▪ ▪ ▪ ▪ ▪
>
> If you feel good about yourself and the way in which you choose to use your body, then you don't need anyone else's approval.

The most important and reasonable sexual right of every woman is to control her own body. Whatever she chooses to do with it—as long as it doesn't hurt anyone else—is OK.

There are lots of single mothers who choose to be sexually active. The focus of societal pressure on single women (whether mothers or not) has changed; where once sex was strongly discouraged and those who indulged were punished socially, now our culture actively pressures women to be sexually active. In former days it was more difficult for a woman to say yes; now, it is more difficult to say no. Many men believe that if a man pays for a date, the woman is obliged to have sex. One thirty-five-year-old single woman was approached by a man at a bar. She said no. He said, "You better take it while you can get it, baby. I may be your last chance."

Unfortunately, some women need sex and men in their lives; they can fall for that—or any—line. But who's to judge? If you feel good about yourself and the way in which you choose to use your body, then you don't need anyone else's approval. If you don't feel good about it, if you feel frustrated or out of control or inadequate or "dirty" or any other negative feeling, you should stop to reflect on what you are doing and why it is causing these negative feelings. If you can't improve the situation by yourself or with the counsel of friends, seek professional counseling for either emotional guidance or sexual therapy. Both are absolutely confidential.

A word about safe sex: protect yourself from AIDS for the sake of your child and others who love and depend on you (see pages 167–168).

## Date rape

One unfortunate fact of contemporary dating is the prevalence of date rape. Date rape is sexual assault against a woman by some-one she knows. Let's say a woman is out on a date with a friend of her brother. They both enjoy the evening. He brings her home and comes in for a drink. He begins to rub her shoulders, then he kiss-es her and it moves on from there. At some point, she says no, but he does not stop. She resists him physically. He comes on stronger, pulls her down, penetrates her, climaxes, and, soon after, leaves. She is stunned.

Later, she says, "I told him no, but he didn't stop." He says, "She said no, but she didn't mean it. She had been coming on to me all evening." The truth is that it was not her fault; she was raped. That she knew him does not make it any less of a crime.

If you've been date raped, you should go to a friend's house or call a rape crisis center. Do not shower or change clothes, no matter how much you want to. Go to a hospital to be examined for evidence of rape and for treatment of any injuries, then seek coun-seling, preferably from a rape crisis center, to help you decide whether to press criminal charges and to deal with the long-term emotional injuries from the experience.

If you mean no when you say it, and a man continues to esca-late the sexual experience, reinforce your no with a statement like, "Date rape and other physical violence against me is a crime pun-ishable by time in prison. Neither of us wants to go through that.

Good night." You can bet he will be angry, but he may stop. Remember that your body is your own to give or not, to stand up for or not, as you choose.

## Looking for love in all the wrong places

A bar is not necessarily the wrong place to look for a man, but there are risks in meeting people in such places. You need to be careful you do not end up with a substance abuser or a habitual cruiser. You need to know how to say no firmly and to accept that, because it is a bar, some men will size you up as a piece of meat instead of a person.

## Married men

Married men are bad news. Once you give your heart to a married man, you lose. He may leave you and go back to his wife, or to another woman—after all, he's already demonstrated that he's a cheater. That could be the best scenario. He might maintain the relationship with you for years, with or without promising to leave his wife; while you long to have him all to yourself, it is his wife who attends public functions with him and who gets all the legal privileges—which she should, since she has to put up with him. On holidays he's with his family. As long as you stay with him, he can easily believe that there's no reason to change the situation. The harder you push, the uglier things get; he may brush you off like dandruff, keeping his wife and their life. What are you left with?

He may leave his wife for you, in which case you will have played your part in dissolving a family. If he does, some of his financial resources and his time will be siphoned off to his former wife and children.

It is poor form and a poor risk to get involved with a married man. But it can happen so easily. A friendship with a married man can turn into something more, or you can become involved with a man without knowing he's married. If you are being hotly courted by a married man, you can say, "Look, I am not interested in you.

Whatever problems you have with your wife, well, you need to settle them with her. Good luck to both of you." If his marriage does end, then you can begin a relationship with him in good conscience—a relationship you both can be proud of.

## Singles groups

Singles groups exist in many towns. Some are sponsored by churches or synagogues; of those, some have a religious emphasis and some do not. Other singles groups are independent of any affiliation. To find what is available in your area, you can check with your Chamber of Commerce, a marriage counselor, other single people, and your local newspaper. (They do stories on singles from time to time and keep files on them.)

Each singles group has its own personality, just as any organization does. Once you've identified a group, track down a member by phone or e-mail and inquire about the group. Ask when and where it meets, what the typical ages of the participants are, if children are involved, and what a typical meeting is like. If it seems right for you, take a deep breath, go to a meeting, and check it out yourself.

The Vanderbilt University Single Mother's Group investigated singles groups in Nashville. Three women volunteered to attend meetings of three different organizations. Two of the women returned with positive reports; the third woman didn't get a good feeling about the group from her initial phone conversation. Later, at the meeting, she found a "sleazy" atmosphere. One man picked up her two-year-old daughter and held onto her in a way that alarmed her. She snatched her daughter away from the man (who offered to come fix up her house. Where did she live? Maybe she could do a little sewing for him...) and she left the meeting early. It was not a group she could recommend.

## Meeting new men through the personals

The history of classified personal ads in this country began when Colonial American men placed ads for wives in newspapers in England.

Reading today's personal ads can be entertaining. Some people are looking for relationships; others are looking for sex without complications—no relationships, no commitment.

Any form of date hunting that involves strangers is a major risk. The blind date pales by comparison. At least a blind date comes with a recommendation from someone you know. Dating strangers leaves you open to everything from identity theft to rape—and worse.

On the other hand, most people know someone who met a date through the personals and married him. I know two men who found their wives that way; they appear to be good husbands and fathers.

So if you feel inclined to foray into the dating jungle that is filled with the good, the bad, and the ugly, just use your brain before you lose your heart.

## Online and print ads

You can either answer someone else's ad or place your own. Remember, though, that there are crazy people out there reading the ads too. Nancy Evins, a hypnotherapist-counselor who has much experience working the classifieds, says you want to avoid having some man stand outside your window screaming, "I'm going to kill you! I'm going to kill you!"—which actually happened to her once as the result of an ad.

The larger risk, by far, is in answering an ad. Because you have to give your phone number or other contact information, you cannot easily control the access of anyone who responds.

The safest way to place an ad is to list a post office box or a new, free e-mail address (separate from your regular one) for responses. Communicate with anyone who responds from the separate e-mail address. This way you can maintain your anonymity, read the responses at your leisure, and choose the ones you want to respond to.

When you write an ad, mention the age, height, and general professional background of the person you would like to meet.

Include whatever information best communicates your values and interests. Religion sometimes puts men off, but words like "spiritual" and "spirituality" can be safer. Humor and originality often get good responses.

When a man responds to your ad, check him out. If he mentions a phone number, call him from a phone other than your home or your cell number, in case he has caller ID. Do not give out your personal phone numbers immediately. If you write to him, continue to use your P.O. box for a while. If he still sounds interesting after a few interactions, meet him at a very public, neutral place for lunch or some other safe, preferably daytime, encounter. Arrive and leave separately. Proceed slowly—don't reveal your home address or workplace to him until you feel safe and comfortable.

Do not trust men to tell you the truth. One woman met a man who said he was divorced. She checked with the city clerk's office for a record of the divorce; there was none. Soon after, his wife called her and said, "How did you like the dozen roses my husband gave you and charged to my account?" When a man is reluctant to give you his home phone number or is otherwise evasive, be very suspicious. As always, check it out. Call his home; what do you have to lose?

Another woman was dating a man she met through an ad. She grew bored and placed another ad, to which he also responded. Keep in mind: either party can play games—and both can.

You can safely work the classifieds if you check out stories to see who is and is not married and who is and is not as he presents himself. Check out his relatives; they are a good indication of the man and, if a relationship develops, they are the people you will be getting along with him. Good and lasting matches have been made in this way. But be wise: if you take risks, protect yourself.

## Chat rooms

When using chat rooms, follow the same safety precautions as for online and print ads. Use a free e-mail account, like those available from yahoo or hotmail; then you can easily abandon the address if your chat experience turns out to be unsatisfactory. Say goodbye on line. If he continues to contact you, say goodbye to the e-mail address and open up another.

## Online clubs

There are groups for book lovers, classical music fans, and people with many other interests. If you pursue potential dates this way, you may be able to find a person with whom you have something in common. Friendship is the basis of a lasting relationship; the more you have in common, the easier it is to develop a deeper relationship.

## Dating companies

These companies may or may not make an effort to screen their applicants. Many of the same rules for personal ads, chat rooms, and online groups apply to matchmaking companies. Try to protect your anonymity until you get to know your date and have time to check him out yourself.

Computer matchmaking companies can charge less than $100 or much more. If the price is high, it's likely that the men who are listed have money—they had to pay the same fee!

However, as one woman says about income, "So what? Their income is hardly the issue; they could be relatively affluent weirdoes, rapists, or axe murderers." Some of the nicest men I have met—men who love children—are hard workers but hardly wealthy. You have to take risks and expose your own vulnerability in order to form relationships. Most men are pretty normal. But three important words to keep in mind are caution, caution, caution.

## Quality relationships

One dear old lady from a wealthy Boston family was well loved and well educated, but she had never married. Apparently she was very beautiful and had several serious suitors, but she refused them all. She said, "The right man just never came around." She has lived a long, interesting, and satisfying life with many friends.

Then there is Zsa Zsa Gabor, who has married eight times so far.

Most of us settle for less than perfection, but compromise puts a strain on all relationships. Each person has to decide for herself, "Is this enough for me?"

Many mothers offer the same wisdom about men: "If you miss one bus, another will come along soon." After you or he ends the relationship, you'll meet other men who will be just as interesting, charming, or funny. You don't know if the next man will come along in a month or in three years.

Some people say, "A bird in the hand is worth two in the bush." If you've got a man in your life, perhaps he's better than none—but maybe he's not. If it were always true that any man is better than none at all, then relationships would not end. We all need and want quality relationships in our lives. Our children do too. Be patient, give it time, accept false starts philosophically, and keep your standards high. People stay in our lives longer that way.

▪ ▪ ▪ ▪ ▪ ▪ ▪

If you miss one bus, another will come along soon.

## Co-dependent relationships

Co-dependency became a buzzword late in the last century. A surprising number of single mothers say, "That's me!"

Normally, we complete developing our own identities in late adolescence; gradually we pull away from parents and other authorities and become autonomous. Co-dependent people, both men and women, have not completed this process. A co-dependent woman's view of who she is comes from others rather than from herself. She is dependent on others' view of herself, and feels a sense of personal worth only when others tell her she is worthy.

Co-dependent people often come from families that have problems with alcoholism or other chemical dependency, families where there has been physical or sexual abuse, families that are religiously fundamentalist, or families with psychological problems—unhealthy families.

Characteristics of a co-dependent person include:

- the need to control
- an inability to trust others
- an inability to identify and understand his own feelings
- being over- or under-responsible
- thinking in extremes, in terms of all or nothing
- a high tolerance of inappropriate behavior from loved ones and of pain and suffering in herself
- low self-esteem
- ungrieved losses (deaths of relationships, unfulfilled dreams)
- fear of abandonment
- difficulty in resolving conflict
- difficulty in giving and receiving love
- unrealistic expectations of always being strong, good, and happy
- being dishonest about his feelings, saying he feels one thing when he really feels something else.

In his book *Lost in the Shuffle*, Robert Subby wrote that in a co-dependent person, "The need for love, acceptance, approval, and recognition becomes the transcendent value."

If you are co-dependent, you may feel you need to repress your feelings and needs. You may find yourself sacrificing too much of yourself to maintain a working relationship with your parents, husband, lover, boss, or other problematic person.

When you look at the list of core issues above, you can see that many—perhaps half—of those issues appear naturally in the early stages of single motherhood, including low self-esteem and ungrieved losses. Even though you may have achieved autonomy in late adolescence, the process of becoming a single mother may cause you to temporarily lose that solid foundation. Now you need to re-establish your autonomy, without your ex-partner, as a process of pulling away from him and your former life.

If you have co-dependent tendencies, you need to be careful about the romantic relationships you develop. Be sure that they allow you to grow stronger in your own sense of self and your ability to stand up for yourself and to set limits on the behavior and demands of others when these conflict with your own needs. Many cities have support groups for co-dependent people. Ask a mental health agency or counselor for a referral.

## Levels of commitment

Angel had two children, ages ten and seven, when she met Charlie, who was ten years older than she. He was a lot of fun. They soon became involved sexually, and they found that they enjoyed each other's company. He helped her, she helped him. They became good friends. Charlie was good with Angel's children, and they loved him. They began to ask Angel when Charlie would become their stepdad. When Angel said, "I love you," Charlie responded, "Oh, I'm just an old guy." Sometimes he would tell Angel she could do better, since he was such a stay-at home type; he said that he felt he was standing in her way. When she protested, Charlie would become upset and leave the house.

For a while, Angel couldn't figure out what was going on. Then she realized that he wanted to leave. Whenever things got too good between them, he would cut and run. When they finally talked about future plans, Charlie said that he had already raised his children (who were in their early twenties), and he didn't want to take responsibility for two more, even though he liked Angel's. Moreover, he felt he couldn't ask her to wait until her children grew up to consider marriage. What he did not say, but what Angel feels was implied by his behavior, was that he did not want to take her on as a financial responsibility.

It makes sense that Charlie felt nervous about spending a lot of time and money on three more people. Doing it on a day-by-day basis is different from committing your future to that responsibility. To Charlie's credit, he was able to understand his own reluctance and to deal pretty honestly with Angel about it. For a while, Angel hoped that Charlie would change his mind. A year later, he still hadn't. At that point, Angel decided to stay with Charlie until someone wonderful and willing came along. So far, no one has. They have a commitment of sorts, but it does not include "till death do us part."

While Charlie exercises his right to remain "free," he fixes things around Angel's condo and is generous with his time and money. That's the level of giving with which he is comfortable.

Almost anything can come between a man and a ring: his job, his ex-wife, his children. Anything he values more than a possible life-companion can cause him to put the brakes on a commitment. Probably the two biggest blocks are children and financial liability.

Lia and Mark lived together but were not married. Originally, they contracted to live together for one year and then assess their next move. At the end of that year, they decided to continue the arrangement for one more year. At the end of that year, Lia was ready for marriage, but Mark was not. Lia moved out; as she put it, "I've got to get on with my life, and I want someone I can count on to grow old with." Six weeks later, Mark came knocking on Lia's door, suggesting they live together again. Lia said, "You know my conditions." He nodded his head. He never could bring himself to say the "M" word. But at the marriage ceremony, it was Lia who burst out crying and had a hard time saying, "I do."

Every couple explores the limits of their abilities to commit. Either they find mutually agreeable boundaries, or they move on separately.

## Making excuses for having children

"It's like people see me as handicapped," Charlotte said. "The minute I tell a man I have a child, I can see in his eyes that he has lost interest. Some day, I hope, society will look at a single mother and her children as OK—because we are. It just makes me angry."

A single mother meeting new people is playing a baseball game of sorts, with two strikes against her. Strike one is when she says, "I'm divorced." The assumption is that she has failed, so she is a poor risk and used merchandise. Strike two comes when she says, "I have a child." The assumption is that her child is a liability—maybe not to her, but to a potential romantic partner. She's got one strike left. If she is independently wealthy, she hits a home run. Otherwise, she swings the bat and runs like hell.

*"My child is very independent."*
*"My child is a good kid. No problems from him."*
*"My child is bright and plays the flute beautifully,"*

Sometimes you may ask yourself, "Will anyone ever love my kid?" If people can't see your child as worthy of considerable time and attention, if your child doesn't like certain people you see socially, trust his instincts and don't continue to bring those people around. Find someone else or expect to suffer personally from an untenable relationship between your romantic partner and your child.

## Revealing a sexual relationship to your child

I don't know of any woman who sat her children down and said, "I must tell you that James and I are now sexually active." Teenagers would react in any number of ways, depending on how they felt about James, but all children would be at least slightly embarrassed. Younger children might wonder just exactly what you meant but might not want to ask for more information. Preschoolers might ask, "What's for dinner?"

But regardless of age, your child (unless she is still an infant) knows when you are getting close to a romantic partner in some way. It may be threatening to her. Many children cling to the hope that their biological parents will reunite; having another man on the scene, even if they like him, can make them feel insecure. Two children that I know run to the family photo albums and engross themselves in family history whenever they sense a shift in the family makeup.

One day your child may ask a question like, "Are you and James going to get married?" or say something like, "I wish James would stop taking you out every Saturday night. We used to have fun here, just the two of us." These are opportunities for you to clarify your relationship. Answer straightforwardly, such as, "We may marry some day, but we have no plans right now," or "I know I go out with him most Saturdays, but I want to be with him. Maybe we can talk about doing something together—the three of us."

The burning question in your child's mind is, "How is this relationship going to affect me?" That's the question you need to answer.

It is reassuring for a child to know that her life will remain stable. She needs to know that home, school, friends, parents—all these will remain as before, at least for now. If a change should occur, talk it over with your child before you make any decision.

If your child should press you for sexual information (which probably won't happen), you can say, "I like/love James. I like to touch him. He likes to touch me. That's part of being an adult. It all happens very naturally as a part of our close friendship with each other." That's all your child needs to know.

But everyone has his or her own style. One "James" I know left his house, telling his two pre-teen children, "I'm going over to Dede's house. I'll be back around ten o'clock." "What are you going to do over there?" his son asked. "We're going to make love," the father tossed over his shoulder. His daughter's eyes bugged out; she turned to her brother and grinned. The boy covered his mouth, scrunched his head into his shoulders, and giggled.

If you have exposed your child to good, age-appropriate sex education, she will know what you are talking about; knowing what's going on will ease her concern. The way in which you tell her what is going on in your relationship is personal and should be targeted to be comfortable for both you and your child.

## Your man and your child

You don't have to introduce your child to every man you go out with. Some women make a point of keeping the men they date casually from knowing their children; this protects the children and avoids potential hassles. At some point in the development of a relationship, however, you will bring your man and your child together.

You must feel your child is safe with any new man. He must not abuse him emotionally, physically, or sexually. You want the same response from him that you would want from a good father: he should enjoy your child's company, play with him, talk to and listen to him. But often, men are more interested in you than in your child. Still, you need to be able to trust the man not to harm your child. The number of "boyfriends," live-in partners, and step-fathers who abuse the children of their female partners is frightening. And the number of women who know about the abuse and let it happen is equally frightening.

If you start getting serious about a man, you must look closely at the quality of his relationship with your child. You want someone who likes your child, someone who interacts positively with him, and who considers him part of his relationship with you. A woman who has to keep her man and her child apart in order to keep peace is a woman in trouble. She constantly has to choose whom to pay attention to and whom to neglect. There's a great line in the movie *The Breakfast Club* when one teenage boy asks a teenage girl what her parents do to her that is so terrible. Her response: "They *ignore* me."

Does your man say hello to your child when he comes over and goodbye when he leaves? Does he ask her how her day is going or what's happening in her life? If you left them together in a room, would they have a conversation? If your child is little, can your man talk to her and help her play with a toy? Would he reach out to pick up and soothe a crying baby?

These are solid clues about how willing a man is to get involved with your child as a real person. How willing is he to invest in her a little? Keep your eyes wide open. If a man does not invest in your child in little ways, he will not invest in big ways later on. Time usually does not change this; it only intensifies the reality.

Try to avoid having a man stay overnight with you while your child is at home. Avoid hanging on each other or engaging in fore-play in front of your child. A casual kiss and a hug are OK, but more than that may make your child uncomfortable. A good rule to follow is, "If you can do it in front of your parents, you can do it in front of your child."

## Living together

Sandra and Ed went on a wonderful nine-day vacation together without children. When they returned, he went to his house, she to hers. He didn't call for a few days. When he did, it was just for a casual conversation; he closed with, "Well, I'll talk to you later. Bye."

"When?" thought Sandra. It was almost a week until the next phone call. Sandra was confused and very distressed. They had been so close, and now Ed seemed distant. Sandra told Ed she was upset. They met for lunch.

"I don't understand. What do you want?" asked Ed.

"I want to move in with you," she said. This was a surprise to her; she didn't expect to say it until the minute it came out of her mouth.

"I don't think I can do that," he said. "I have other [women] friends who wouldn't understand. They've been good to me. What would I tell them?"

"I don't care what you tell them. This is not a threat; it's just what I need for my sanity: Either I move in with you, or I need you out of my life. Don't call me again."

"Ever?"

"Ever."

Ed looked at his plate. His face turned red and seemed to swell. Finally he said, "Well, bring your kids over on Sunday, and let's talk about arrangements."

As it turned out, theirs was a live-in relationship that led to marriage, but it could have gone the opposite way, which Sandra would have accepted. She had gone too far in the relationship to be content with casual dating.

Living together has the advantage of being an arrangement for today, one you don't have to commit to for the rest of your life. Many couples think of it as a trial marriage. But there are big differences between living together and marriage. Your relatives will probably not accept your live-in partner as a member of the family; to them, he will remain your date. Further, depending on their religious or moral beliefs, they may not sanction the arrangement. At income tax time, you must file separately, since you do not qualify for the cheaper joint tax status of married couples. If he should die, you could not arrange his funeral, nor would you inherit any part of his estate, unless he has written you into his will.

Beyond family, legal, and financial concerns, there is a different feeling when you are married—a feeling of being yoked, of your belonging to someone and his belonging to you, a certain settledness. But as a married person, you don't make decisions as independently as you did before. Once you are married, you and your husband must jointly agree on most aspects of your lives together—including how to raise the children and how much money to spend on them. You give up some freedom for some security. And after you do, you may miss that autonomy and wonder if you acted too soon.

### Kids' reactions

Recent research by psychologist Marla Beth Isaacs and sociologist George Leon of the Philadelphia Child Guidance Clinic shows that children of divorce exhibit behavioral problems and manage social competence—their own friendships—in the following order. (All 87 subject mothers had custody.)

1. Children fared best when their mothers were not seriously romantically involved.

2. Children fared slightly worse when their mothers were seriously involved with a man.

3. Children fared worse than in examples 1 and 2 when their mothers remarried.

4. Children made the worst adjustment of all when their mothers lived with a man but was not married.

Isaacs and Leon suggest that a child whose mother lives with a man to whom she is not married feels insecure about his mother's and his own relationship with that man. His biological father may object to the relationship. And children, especially teens, may feel awkward about morals.

Isaacs and Leon do not feel that a mother should either move out or rush into marriage for the sake of her child. She needs to form her own life-partner relationship in her own time with the man of her choice, and if she moves too quickly in any direction because of the children, she may resent their "intrusion" in her relationship.

There are times when the needs of a mother and the needs of her child may conflict. These are times of hard choices. We are all searching for better lives both for ourselves and for our children.

## Blended family blues

It is a mistake to marry for social, legal, or financial reasons, or to recruit a father for your child. The quality of the relationship has to come first. If good quality is not there to begin with, how can you build it after marriage? If you've been married before, you know how wrenching divorce is; it's like death.

Above all else, you need realistic expectations about blending two pre-formed families into one through a second marriage. There are some myths about such marriages that need to be exposed:

- There will be instant family love, a cozy family feeling.
- It will be like a first (biological) family.
- As a stepmother, you will make up for the defects of the biological mother.

Each family has a separate history; each family experienced loss when the parents separated. Every member of the new family is faced with giving up a piece of her past. This does not mean that you erase it from your memory bank, but it does mean understanding that you can never go back to it. This is a particularly difficult process for a child who fervently wishes her biological family was back together. The process of creating a blended family includes a sense of loss of the biological family.

Your second husband is not going to be the same as your first husband, for better and for worse. Generally, you go into a first marriage planning to live forever with a man you love, heart and soul; you are young and full of dreams and romance. A second husband is, well, second; the newness is not there. A certain innocence and purity are missing, since you've already been married. You are older, more practical, more cautious, and less idealistic. And all that is OK; it's just different. I don't know any remarried woman who wouldn't have preferred to have found her prince charming the first time around, but there are no perfect princes.

And there are no perfect princesses.

Whether it is your first marriage, or your second, or your eighth, you need to know if your man is someone whose weaknesses you can accept and even smile about, and whose strengths are important to you? Are his values your own? Can you trust his behavior and motives? Can you talk with him easily? Does he like and accept you for who you are? Is he someone who feels like family, a supportive friend who will stick with you?

If you can answer such questions positively, consider yourself fortunate. A wise woman named Barbara Gupta says, "Whatever circumstances I find myself in, I learn to like them." That kind of positive attitude will help you through some very rough periods in trying to blend two families.

There are blended families who are very happy together. But not many are happy without a lot of hard, ceaseless work, especially in the early years. Some estimate that it takes five to seven years for a blended family to truly feel like a family. It takes a lot of time to build trust and loyalty among stepchildren and between stepchildren and stepparents. It takes time to build common family memories. It takes time for children to believe that a stepparent is not here today, gone tomorrow.

Children can resent the whole new arrangement. Ten-year-old Dorothy was alone in a room with her new stepmother while they decorated for Christmas. Dorothy said, "Well, you are here this Christmas. Miki was here last Christmas. I wonder who will be here next Christmas?" Was she expressing some insecurity about the temporary status of the women in her life? Was she jabbing at her new stepmother? Telling her to get lost? Implying she'd be discarded too? Maybe all of the above?

> ■ ■ ■ ■ ■ ■ ■
>
> "Whatever circumstances
> I find myself in,
> I learn to like them."

Children can be jealous of stepsiblings and stepparents; adults can be jealous too. Competition, one-upmanship, turf battles—all this can go on, day after day. There will be problems with children; you can count on it, even if the children are wildly enthusiastic about your marriage. After the honeymoon, problems set in. There is nothing that can make everyone believe that the new family is a sure thing. There are ties to biological parents and ex-partners that conflict with building a sense of family. Both adults and children resent the lack of freedom and space. And unconditional love is not there, perhaps for the first five years. After that, there is a chance.

One woman could not stand her stepdaughter. Something about the girl just irritated her. She decided she would look for qualities in her stepdaughter that she liked and try to focus on them. When she noticed that the girl always set the table with great care and precision, she praised her for it; she began to watch her stepdaughter more closely. Before long, she found something else that she liked about the girl; after a while, she was able to accept certain things that had irritated her before. At last, she welcomed the girl into her heart.

If parents do not agree on how to raise a child, it's a recipe for disaster. When a father takes the side of his child instead of presenting a united front with his wife, the stepparent loses control of that child. She will never again do anything her stepmother says unless her father tells her to. If a stepparent cannot control a child in his own home, there's no hope of a peaceful family life. Communication is essential. You need to become adept at conflict resolution. Expect strong feelings to be stronger in a blended family.

From a child's point of view, he doesn't belong anywhere. He was thrust into this new family, which may not have been his choice; even if it was, he still probably feels as if he is on the outside looking in. It takes a long time for the strangeness to go away. Begin your blending process by including children early on in the planning stages. Some couples plan a marriage ceremony to include their children. Some go on a honeymoon as a family and have another brief honeymoon for adults only. Some go house shopping as a family.

Blending two families is further complicated because nothing stands still. You can't count on your family structure remaining stable. Your husband's ex-wife may have custody, but his children might end up living with you anyway. Stepparents often have to make fast and unwelcome adjustments that they never anticipated, considered, or agreed to when they married. Even adult children can come home again. The potential for complications is staggering.

This may seem like a grim picture of blended families. It should, because they can become more tangled than day-old spaghetti. They can also work well and bring much happiness to family members; as long as children live in the home, however, a blended family is more challenging than a biological one.

The following elements encourage positive blending and promote a sense of family:

- a quality relationship between the parents
- a common understanding on how to raise the children
- 100 percent support of each other in front of the children
- a basic liking of all the children
- an expectation that there will be difficult times
- a commitment to making the family work.

Parents in a blended family should look to a variety of resources, including:

- counselors
- family meetings
- conscious practice of good parenting skills
- time spent together as a family
- time out or privacy for both children and adults as necessary
- family vacations
- books and articles on blended families or other family concerns.

## Prenuptial agreements

Before marrying for a second time, consider asking a tax lawyer to draft a prenuptial agreement for property settlement. It is natural and logical for you to want your assets to revert to you should another divorce occur. At the same time, you can draft a will that arranges your estate for the benefit of your child after your death. Marriage brings with it certain legal rights for your spouse. You may love and trust your new husband-to-be, but you should know the law and your options before making such an important move. No one gets married expecting to divorce. Every marriage is a risk, and you want to cover all your bases.

The best we can aim for in this world is to establish for ourselves a supportive community of people to contribute to and to draw from as we maneuver through life. The children, family, friends, and men in our community may come and go. We will need to let go of individuals from time to time. We will need to add on individuals from time to time. But it is our job to make sure that we never let go of the concept or the reality of our community, whatever form it takes. To be alone is to be less than human. To live in community is to risk experiencing pain, but also to be able to connect with the depth and power of all humanity and experience true wholeness.

■ ■ ■ ■ ■ ■ ■

To live
in community
is to risk
experiencing
pain. . . .

# Starting Your Own Group

## Women's groups

Much of the information that follows is based on the structure of the Vanderbilt University Single Mothers Group that operated during 1986 and 1987. It was organized by the Margaret Cuninggim Women's Center and sponsored jointly with the Vanderbilt Child Care Center. Its genesis, its structure, its purposes, and its activities were tailored for one group of women in one city. However, it proved the point that women within two years of divorce (pre- or post-divorce) can benefit from getting together to discuss their challenges relating to the subjects discussed in this book.

## Divorce adjustment groups

Many towns offer periodic courses, groups, seminars, and lectures on the theme of adjusting to divorce. Some of these offerings are structured to include children of divorce. Almost all are available to both men and women. And while quality and content vary, almost all can provide single mothers with:

■ information about local resources

■ guidelines for what to expect from divorce as a life circumstance

■ contact with other people in the same boat with whom to share experiences.

You can find out about groups in your area by calling your local mental health association, the YWCA, a counselor, social service organizations, or a clergy member. Announcements of such events are often made in newspapers and posted on library bulletin boards.

If you can't find something that suits your needs in your town, you can suggest to the resources above that they create a way to address divorce adjustment.

Just as a variety of foods gives the body optimum nutrition, so a variety of relational experiences gives a single mother optimum overall health of body, mind, and spirit during divorce—a tumultuous time of change. Frankly, a group of single mothers meeting to discuss the challenges of single motherhood can be arranged informally and easily in the homes of participants or in a church willing to sponsor such a group by providing meeting space. The difficult factor is child care, but that can be worked out creatively.

A group open to single mothers only is different from a group that includes men in the following ways:

▪ The structure automatically puts women in control of the group, promoting a feeling of empowerment and increased self-esteem.

▪ There is no male-female sex interest, allowing women a time out from feeling pressure to dress, make up, or behave in response to the presence of men.

▪ There is no male-female sex interest to upset a woman who needs time out from involvement with all men. She is healing her wounds and can count on an all-female support group to be a place of refuge.

▪ Women feel freer to say *anything* in an all-female group, to talk about sexual subjects as well as personal intense anger and deep pain associated with their ex-partner. It is safe for very negative feelings to surface in the group, often as an expression of humor to relieve personal tension.

## Starting your own group

Your town may already have a single mothers group. Unfortunately, there is no national clearinghouse for single mothers groups. They are far less common than male-female divorce adjustment groups. Family counseling centers sometimes structure all-male or all-female support groups under the guidance of a counselor, but you have to pay an hourly fee to participate. This can vary from approximately $60 to $200 per hour.

After you have checked out what kind of groups are available in your town, starting with a counseling center or the YWCA, you can decide if any of the existing groups will meet your needs. If they do not, you may want to help structure your own group.

### Finding a sponsor

Rather than starting a group meeting in your own home, think seriously about finding a sponsor for the group, for the following reasons:

▪ *The facility*: You don't have to clean it for meetings, it has restrooms, and it has parking (you hope).

▪ *The facilitator*: She is responsible for preparations for each meeting. You may want to skip a meeting from time to time, but the facilitator will keep things going on schedule.

▪ *Continuity*: At some point, you may decide to drop out of the group (this usually happens when a woman feels she has her feet on solid ground), and the sponsor will be responsible for maintaining the group for the benefit of other single mothers.

A sponsor provides stability and assumes all responsibility for meetings. All you have to do is attend.

To find a sponsor, contact the resources listed above and talk with people until someone listens to you. You may locate a sponsor who is willing to organize and publicize your group and provide a facilitator, but who does not have an adequate meeting facility. Then someone will have to find a facility in which to meet. Or you may begin with the facility first, and then try to locate a sponsor.

### The facility

You need a meeting room that will hold ten to twenty women. You need access to a restroom. Parking nearby is ideal, especially if the group meets at night. And have a room for the children, if possible.

## Child care

The Vanderbilt University Single Mothers Group was started by a woman with four children who came into the Women's Center and asked if the center knew of such a group in town. We said we would find out if one existed, and if not, we would start one of our own. This woman had four young children and worked at a part-time job. She didn't have the money to pay for a babysitter for four children in her home on a regular basis. So the Women's Center decided to arrange for on-site child care. For each two-hour meeting, the charges were

- 1 child: $1.00
- 2 or more children: $1.50.

Such low fees allowed the women to bring their children with them to the meeting, knowing the children would receive care from a competent caregiver for a price they could afford. The children got to know each other and looked forward to going with their mothers. Every Tuesday, one four-year-old would ask her mother, "Is this club night?" The mothers and children felt that the support group event was one in which they all participated. Group members got to know each other's children, and the atmosphere of the group became one of family.

We held our meetings at the Vanderbilt Day Care Center, so that the children could use one of the classrooms. They met at one end of the building while the mothers met in a room at the other end.

The caregiver was a regular staff person at the Day Care Center during the day. She picked up some extra money with the Single Mothers Group, receiving $7.00 per hour for her work. If the child-care fees paid by the mothers did not add up to $14.00—the cost of two hours of her time—the sponsor paid the difference.

There was a well-lit parking lot right outside the facility.

## Cost

There was no charge for participating in the group. Women frequently commented that they could not easily afford to come if a fee was charged.

## Meeting schedule

We met the first and third Tuesday of each month, from 6:45 to 8:45 P.M.

## Facilitator

We considered using a graduate student in psychology at the university, but in the end, a staff person from the Women's Center and a community volunteer with counseling experience co-facilitated the group. This probably worked out better than the graduate student, since the staff person and the community volunteer made a long-term commitment to the group, and consistency in the facilitator is important in building group cohesiveness.

The role of the facilitators was not to do all the talking, but to encourage the participants to talk, to explore their own issues, to ask their own questions, and to solve problems solve with the support of the group and community resources. The facilitators opened the building at night, coordinated communication among participants with a group telephone directory, and arranged for guest speakers.

## Advertising and group size

Announcements of the first meeting of the group were posted in area day-care centers, mailed to appropriate family counseling services, and published in a local newspaper. In response, single women called to find out more about the group. Later, the facilitators did radio and TV interviews to advertise the group and to discuss single mothers' issues.

The three women who showed up for the first meeting formed the core of the group. As other women joined, attendance averaged about eight to ten women per session. We felt that number, rather than twenty to thirty women sitting in a circle, enabled the group to maintain an intimate atmosphere where everyone felt comfortable talking. Due to scheduling conflicts, not everyone could attend each meeting, so the population was somewhat different each night, drawing from a total population of about fifteen regular attendees.

## Newsletter outreach

There were many women in the community who were unable to attend any meetings, though they wanted to. Work, child care or transportation problems, or exhaustion prevented them from doing so. When they called to find out more about the group, their names were put on a mailing list for the once-a-month newsletter.

This newsletter was a one- or two-page typed letter telling about group news (who got a job, whose mother was in town, etc.), dates of upcoming meetings and activities, news articles about single mothers or current research of interest. There was usually a cartoon or some other attempt at humor. When the group came up with good ideas for children's activities, they were included.

Between meetings, the newsletter served as an important connecting link for group members, and it made the women who could not attend meetings feel they were not isolated, odd, or abnormal but part of a group of women with whom they shared common concerns.

## Group activities

There were two meetings per month. One meeting was a "dump session," in which we all sat in a circle and talked about what had been going on in our lives since the last meeting. Members talked about jobs, ex-partners, children, finances, dating—all the good and bad news in their lives. The facilitators, including the one who was not a single mother, participated in this process. Much problem solving was done in these sessions as the group responded to the individual with ideas, options, resources, and encouragement.

The second meeting in each month was a time for getting information. A professional, such as a lawyer specializing in family law, might speak to the group, or we might discuss a certain subject, like the night we developed the list of free and cheap fun for mothers and children (see pages 93–94).

After a while, mothers started bringing in snacks and juice to have at the meetings. We appreciated the opportunity to eat together. Then someone suggested we get together socially outside of the group, so once a month we decided on an outdoor activity that mothers and children would enjoy, such as going for a walk or playing in a park. We also enjoyed having a potluck at someone's house, although we usually tried to keep social activities away from people's homes since we were all pressed for time and it was a chore to prepare for and clean up after this group. These social activities were optional, but people always participated.

Outdoor activities worked best. On one occasion, the group went to a nearby state park to camp out overnight. Some of the women had never been camping before, and we were all learning together how to set up borrowed tents and build a campfire. We went for hikes, went swimming, walked children back and forth to the restrooms, roasted marshmallows, sang songs around the campfire, and drifted off to sleep. This was a highly successful, very inexpensive trip that both mothers and children enjoyed—and will never forget.

## The Big Hug—and beyond

We closed each group meeting with The Big Hug. All the mothers stood in one large circle, with their arms around each other, and someone would call out, "Here we go: One, two, three!" On "three," we all took one step toward the center of the circle. The resulting group squeeze was The Big Hug. Every member and all of the children enjoyed this tradition. It was a great way to end the meeting, feeling bonded to a group of sisters and empowered to face the world.

# BusyMom

*A Story About How Everything Turned Out Just Fine*

Once upon a time there was a woman named Jane Wifeof-man, but everyone called her Jane. She lived with her two children and a Husband. On the Saturday before Mother's Day, the Husband would go out and buy Jane a gift to show her what a good job she was doing with the children. Then on Sunday he would take the family out to dinner.

But all was not well with Jane and the Husband. They divorced. Jane got custody of the children and changed her name to BusyMom Notimeforherself, but everyone called her BusyMom. She washed clothes, packed lunches, worked in an office, made doctor appointments, wiped away tears, worked in the office, met with teachers, figured her own taxes, worked in the office, grabbed a movie when she could, cleaned the house when she could, and sometimes collapsed at night when the last munchkin was tucked into bed.

Everyone worried about her after the divorce, marveled at how well she was coping, and then sort of dropped out of sight, except for family and a close friend or two.

And, of course, the children. They were always there—twenty-four hours a day. Well, not in person, but *in her mind*. "They're at the day-care center now." "They're going to school now on the minivan." "It's about lunch time for the kids." "Oh, my gosh, I've got to race to the day-care center to pick them up before 5:30!" On a separate freeway in her mind she was thinking, "The piles on my desk seem to grow larger . . . this was the day I was going to make some progress. I'm losing it . . . my supervisor told me I looked tired and should get some more rest. The Coke machine broke… no caffeine…I hope no one saw me dozing at 2:30. What a hell of a day I've had."

"Hi, Mommy!" said one of her kids one afternoon.

"Hi, sweetheart. How was your day?" said BusyMom. And those little arms reaching around her neck healed her for a moment.

Along came the second Sunday in May. Mother's Day. No Husband to say Happy Mother's Day. No gift. Just another day. BusyMom said to her two children who were passing through the kitchen, "It's Mother's Day." Three-year-old Stevie said, "Tie my shoe." Five-year-old Rhea said, "I'm hungry." And BusyMom thought to herself, "Yes, it certainly is Mother's Day."

This is the way things went for a few years. One day when Rhea was eleven, she grinned and whispered in her mother's ear, "We have a surprise for you for Mother's Day. I hope you like it." It was the first time the children had planned something like this. Maybe it finally clicked with Rhea that this was an important day for them all, an opportunity to tell Mom just how much they appreciated her care and love through all the days stretching from before Rhea was born until this day, that there was something that they could do, resources that they had to initiate a happening. Thus, "We have a surprise for you for Mother's Day." What? A kiss? A hug? An offer to do the dishes? A pink plastic mirror? A drawing? It didn't matter. BusyMom knew this was a big step. After all these years, two important people were remembering her in a special way on Mother's Day: *her children*, on their own and because they really did love her.

BusyMom sat down and cried. Secretly she pondered. She couldn't decide whether she wanted hugs and kisses or the free dish washing! It was so nice to wait on her children, to trust in her children who had learned a new way to give.

## THINGS TO THINK ABOUT FOR MOTHER'S DAY:

▪ If you want to know if your child loves you, ask her.

▪ If you want your young child to recognize you in a special way on this day, hope for help from his day-care center or his schoolteachers. Otherwise, wait a few years and your child will do it on his own. Formal recognition requires maturity; that doesn't mean he doesn't love you now.

▪ Let an older child know that Mother's Day is coming and give her some choices, like, "I'd like you to make me a card, fix me breakfast in bed, bring me some flowers from the yard, paint my toenails or whatever you might want to do. Mostly I'd like a little recognition on my day." Discussing Mother's Day possibilities can be great fun.

▪ Think about another single mother you know who would appreciate being remembered on this occasion. Make her a card, call her on the phone, or otherwise let her know you appreciate her contribution as a mother.

▪ If you want to go out to dinner on Mother's Day, do it. Take your kid and go to a restaurant or on a picnic in a park. Enjoy!

# RESOURCES

###

## Divorce

Davidson, Mary L., *The Everything Divorce Book*. Adams Media Corporation, 2003.

## Finances

Kiyosaki, Robert T. & Sharon L. Lechter. *Rich Dad, Poor Dad: What the Rich Teach Their Kids About Money That the Poor and Middle Class Do Not!* Warner Books, 2000. Read this book, apply the principles, and watch your assets grow—for you and your children.

## Health and well-being

The Boston Women's Health Book Collective. *Our Bodies Ourselves for the New Century*. Touchstone Books, 1998.

Carnegie, Dale. *How to Win Friends and Influence People*. Carnegie Pocket Books, 1990.

Cushner, Harold. *When Bad Things Happen to Good People*. Avon, 1983.

Phelps, Stanlee, and Nancy Austin. *The Assertive Woman*. Impact Publishers, 2002.

Viorst, Judith. *Necessary Losses: The Loves, Illusions, Dependencies and Impossible Expectations That All of us Have to Give Up in Order to Grow*. Free Press, 1998.

Weight Watchers, a weight loss and management program. Their website, www.weightwatchers.com, advertises, "Weight Watchers, the trusted name in weight loss for over 40 years, offers a safe and effective plan to help you reach your goals." Locations for over 20,000 U.S. groups are available through the website, or check your local telephone book for a number to call. Fees equal about one meal out per week.

## Parenting

Dinkmeyer, Don, et al. *Parenting Teenagers: Systematic Training for Effective Parenting of Teens (STEP)*. American Guidance Service, Inc., 1998.

Faber, Adele, and Elaine Mazlish. *How to Talk So Kids Will Listen and How To Listen So Kids Will Talk*. Avon, 1999.

Faber, Adele, and Elaine Mazlish. *Siblings Without Rivalry: How to Help Your Children Live Together So You Can Live Too*. Avon, 1998.

Roosevelt, Ruth, and Jeannette Lofas. *Living in Step: A Remarriage Manual for Parents and Children*. McGraw-Hill, 1976.

Thurber, Christopher A., and Jon C. Malinowski. *The Summer Camp Handbook: Everything You Need to Find, Choose, and Get Ready for Overnight Camp—and Skip the Home-sickness*. Perspective Publishing, 2000.

Wachtel, Ted, and Phyllis York. *Toughlove*. Bantam, 1985. A book about setting limits and avoiding being terrorized by an out-of-control child, most often a teenager.

## Other parenting resources

Parents Anonymous, Inc. (www.parentsanonymous.org), 675 West Foothill Blvd., Suite 220, Claremont, CA 91711 (909) 621-6184. From their website: "…The nation's oldest child abuse prevention and treatment organization, dedicated to strengthening families and building caring communities that support safe and nurturing homes for all children." This organization exists in part to prevent child abuse and neglect. They have a free newsletter and groups that meet in all states.

Parents Without Partners, Inc. (www.parentswithoutpartners. org), 1650 South Dixie Highway, Suite 510, Boca Raton, FL 33432 (561) 391-8833. Has groups in all 50 states for single parents and their children, as well as parenting materials.